A Sufi Message of Spiritual Liberty
Volume XIV

SUFI TEACHINGS
THE SMILING FOREHEAD

A SUFI MESSAGE
OF SPIRITUAL LIBERTY
VOLUME XIV

SUFI TEACHINGS
THE SMILING FOREHEAD

HAZRAT INAYAT KHAN

East-West Publications (UK) Ltd.
London
in association with
The International Headquarters of
the Sufi Movement, Geneva

First published by Barrie and Rockliff (Barrie Books Ltd.) 1963
Subsequent reprints by Uitgeverij Servire, Katwijk, Netherlands

This edition first published in Great Britain in 1996 by
East-West Publications (UK) Ltd.,
London
in association with
The International Headquarters of the Sufi Movement, Geneva.

Cover design by Max Fairbrother
Printed and bound in Great Britain by WBC.

British Library Cataloguing in Publication Data.
Inayat Khan, Hazrat 1882–1927
A Sufi Message of Spiritual Liberty – Rev. ed
Vol. 14, Sufi Teachings, the smiling forehead
I. Sufi life
I. Title
ISBN 0 85692 216 1

CONTENTS

PART II
THE DEEPER SIDE OF LIFE

PREFACE

THIS VOLUME, the fourteenth of what is to constitute the revised complete edition of Hazrat Inayat Khan's works on the philosophy, theory and practice of mysticism, is also the third appearing under the new serial heading of *A Sufi Message of Spiritual Liberty*. Adopting the title Hazrat Inayat Khan himself gave to his first publication, this series is intended gradually to replace the by now familiar one, published from 1960 as *The Sufi Message of Hazrat Inayat Khan*.

The editorial motives for continuing and revising the publication of the complete edition have been explained at length in the Preface to Volume VIII. Beyond recalling that the present series aims at the completion of the entire corpus of Inayat Khan's teachings, and intends to maintain its distinctive oral character, there is little reason to expound these motives anew. Suffice it to say that the new volumes VIII and XIV jointly represent a much expanded version of *Sufi Teachings*, the eighth volume in the earlier series.

However, a section of that earlier volume VIII, containing introductory chapters on the history, nature and aim of Sufism and the Sufis, is still retained for inclusion in a subsequent volume, just as some individual lectures on other subjects which in the opinion of the editors seem to be more at home elsewhere. Some subjects now appear under a different – mostly their original – title, while a very limited number of chapters had to be left out altogether, as they were compiled from two or more different sources, or derived from an uncertain origin.

Some of Inayat Khan's earlier sayings and expressions, conserved in the form of fragments, were compiled by his first disciples and with his consent reconstructed as articles. In later times – from 1921/22 onward – his lectures and talks were accurately and completely noted down and conserved. The present edition renders these in their entirety. Different items compiled in chapters of the first edition of *Sufi Teachings* are now – as far as they could be retraced to their origin – published separately as ideas, aphorisms and answers to questions. (See for instance the chapters "Love", "Justice and Forgiveness", "Conscience" and "Pairs of Opposites"). More detailed information on this subject is obtainable from the publisher or from the General Secretariat of the Sufi Movement: Anna Paulownastraat 78, 2518 BJ The Hague, Netherlands.

Like its predecessors, the present volume contains discourses and teachings given at different times and places, rather than a series of lectures on a single theme. However, in their choice of the published material the editors have endeavoured now to include lectures which throw a further light on a given subject, sometimes providing a more extensive explanation, sometimes treating the same topic from different points of view. The list of documents at the end of the book contains further relevant information.

Hazrat Inayat Khan considered a faithful rendition of his words essential in order to explain his teachings fully. Truth, according to him, is what cannot be put into words. No system could encompass the truth which to the Sufi is the same as God. Yet his whole work consists in giving this truth to the world, to be discovered in all its different aspects, as the various facets of a diamond.

In the chapters of these *Sufi Teachings* Hazrat Inayat Khan shows his constant desire to instruct and enlighten humanity, guiding it towards a better knowledge and understanding of the world's many problems and of life's endless difficulties.

PART I

THE SMILING FOREHEAD

CHAPTER I

The Smiling Forehead

BY FOREHEAD is meant man's expression. The smiling forehead is the pleasant expression; it depends solely upon man's attitude to life. Life is the same for the saint and for Satan, and if men are different it is because of their outlook on life. The same life is turned by the one into heaven and by the other into hell. There are two attitudes: to one all is wrong, to the other all is right. Our life in the world from morning to evening is full of experiences, good and bad, which can be distinguished according to their degree. And the more we study the mystery of good and bad the more we see that there really is no such thing as good and bad. It is because of our attitude and the conditions that things seem good or bad. It is easy for an ordinary person to say what is good or bad, just or unjust – it is very difficult for a wise man. Although everyone, according to his outlook on life, turns things from bad to good and from good to bad, everyone has his own grade of evolution and reasons accordingly.

Sometimes one thing is subtler than others and then it is difficult to judge. There was a time when Wagner's music was not understood, and another time when he was considered the greatest of musicians. Sometimes things are good, but our own evolution makes them less good for us. What we considered good a few years ago may not seem good at a later degree of evolution. At one time a child appreciates a doll most, later it will prefer the work of great sculptors. This proves that at every step and degree of evolution man's idea of good and bad changes. Therefore a thinker will understand that there is no such thing as right or wrong. If there is wrong, all is wrong; if there is right, all is right.

No doubt there is a phase when man is a slave of what he has himself made right or wrong, and there is another phase in which he is master. This mastery comes from his realization of the fact that right and wrong are made by his own attitude to life, and then right and wrong, good and bad, will be his slaves, because he knows that it is in his power to turn the one into the other. It is this attitude that the ancient Sufis called *mantiq**.

This opens the door to another mystery of life which shows that as there is duality in each thing so there is duality in every action: in everything that is just something unjust is hidden, in everything that is bad something good. Then one begins to see how the world takes all men's actions: one person sees only the good, another only the bad. In Sufi terms this particular attitude is called *hairat*, bewilderment. And just as to the average man moving pictures, theatres, bazars are interesting, so to the Sufi the whole of life is interesting, a constant vision of bewilderment. He cannot explain this to the world because there are no words to explain it.

Can one compare any joy to that of taking things quietly, patiently and easily? All other joys come from outward sources, but this happiness is one's own property. When a person arrives at this feeling it expresses itself not in words, but in the "smiling forehead".

There is another side to this subject: man is pleased to see the one he loves, admires and respects, and if he frowns at someone it is because it is someone he does not admire or respect. Love is the divine essence in man and is due to God alone. Love for man is a lesson, it is a first step forward to the love of God. In human love one begins to see the way to divine love, as the lesson of domestic life is learned by a little girl playing with her dolls. One learns this lesson by loving one person, a friend, a beloved, a father, mother, brother, sister, or teacher, but the use of love becomes wrong when that love is constantly developing for one only and not spreading. The water of a pond may turn bad, but the water of a river remains pure because it is progressing. By sincerely loving one person therefore one rears the plant of love and makes it grow and spread. Love has done its work when man has become all love – his atmosphere, his expression, every movement he makes. And how can such a man love one and refuse another? Such a countenance, such a presence becomes a blessing.

*i.e. logic

In the East, when we speak of saints or sages, it is not because of their miracles, it is because of their presence and their countenance which radiate vibrations of love. How does this love express itself? In tolerance, in forgiveness, in respect, in overlooking the faults of others. Their sympathy covers the defects of others as if they were their own; they forget their own interest in the interest of others. They do not mind what conditions they are in; be they high or humble, their foreheads are smiling. To their eyes everyone is the expression of the Beloved, whose name they repeat. They see the divine in all forms and in all beings.

Just as the religious person has a religious attitude in a temple, so the Sufi has that attitude before every being, for to him every being is the temple of the divine. Therefore the Sufi is always before his Lord. Whether a servant, a master, a friend, or a foe is before him, he is in the presence of God. For the one whose God is in the high heavens there is a vast gulf between him and God, but the one who has God always before him — he is always in God's presence, and there is no end to his happiness.

The idea of the Sufi is that however religious a person may be, without love he is nothing. It is the same with one who has studied thousands of books; without love he has learned nothing. Love is not in a claim of love; when love is born one hears its voice louder than the voice of man. Love needs no words; they are too inadequate to express it. In what little way love can express itself, it is in what the Persians call "the laughing forehead".

CHAPTER II

The Heart Quality

1

THERE ARE people who look at life through their brain, their head, and there are others who look at life through their heart. Between these two points of view there is a vast difference; so much difference that something that one person can see on the earth the other sees in heaven, something that one sees as small the other sees as great, of something that one sees as limited the other sees the unlimitedness. These two persons become opposite poles; it is as if one is looking at the sky, the other at the earth.

No one will admit that he looks at things with his head; everyone will say, "I look at life with my heart". If he knew what it is to look at life from the heart, the best person in the world would say, "I have not yet learned to look at life from the heart. I would like to know how to do it, I would like to learn it".

One might say that emotional and devotional people are flying in the clouds, while others with their reason and logic are standing on the earth. Yes, it is true. But angels ride on clouds; if the soul has the angelic quality the clouds are its sphere, not the earth. Now one may ask, "Where is the place for practicality in life?" Yes, but what one calls practical in everyday life and one is very careful about – what is it , how long does it last, what is it worth? No doubt it is true that man is born on earth to bear the weight of his physical body and with it its needs: a roof over his head and a piece of bread to sustain him. If that is all there is to think about, man makes a great mistake if he devotes all his life to what he calls practicality, practical life, and never thinks of the heavenly treasure that is hidden in the heart of man.

The heart of man can be likened to water. Either it is frozen and then it is snow, or it is water and then it is liquid. When it is frozen it has turned into a crystal; when it is liquid it is in running order, and it is natural for water to be running.

Then there are two principal kinds of water: salt water and sweet water. The sea which is quite contented in itself, indifferent to everything else, has salt water because it is independent of anything else. It gives health, happiness and pleasure to those who walk along it, because it represents perfection. It asks nothing from anyone, it rises and falls within itself, it is independent, it is immense. In that way it shows perfection. But with that independent perfection its water is not sweet, and the ascetic who has closed his heart, with the perfection of God and with the realization of truth is like the sea, independent, indifferent to all things. His presence heals people, his contact gives them joy, gives them peace, and yet his personality is uninteresting: the water of the sea is salt water.

When the sea is calm it is a pleasure to travel on it, and when the sea is rough there is no worse illness than seasickness. So is the powerful mind, the mind of a soul that has touched perfection: it is with tranquillity, calmness and peace that this mind gives everyone a way into it, as the sea lays itself with open heart before those who journey on it. Ships and boats pass through it, those who journey enjoy their travelling. But when the sea is disturbed by the wind, by storm, it is perfect in its annoyance, it can shake boats and steamers. And so the mind of the sage can have an effect upon all things in nature; it can cause volcanic eruptions, it can cause disasters, revolutions, all manner of things once its tranquillity is disturbed. Knowing this nature of the sage's heart and knowing the great powers that a man who has touched divine perfection possesses, people in the East regard closely the pleasure and displeasure of the sage. They think that to annoy a sage is like annoying the whole of nature, to disturb his tranquillity means to shake the whole universe. A storm in the sea is a very small thing, whereas the heart that has touched perfection, if once upset, can upset the whole universe.

The water of the river is sweet. It is sweet because it is attracted to the sea, it is longing to reach the sea. The river represents the loving quality, a quality that is seeking for the object it loves. A heart that loves God and His perfection is likened to the river that seeks the sea. It is therefore that the personality of the seeker is more pleasant than the personality of the one who is contented with what he knows. There is little danger in travelling on the river, there is great joy in swimming in the river, and there is a fine scenery along it to look at. So it is with the personality which is like the river: that running of the feeling of sympathy, that continual running, means a living sympathy. The river helps the trees and plants and the earth along it. So does the kind, sympathetic person whose feeling is liquid: everywhere he goes he takes with him that influence which nourishes, which helps souls to flourish and to progress.

Then one sometimes sees a little stream. It runs, it is not a river, it is a small little stream running, and it is even more beautiful to look at for it expresses modesty, it expresses fineness of character, it expresses purity. For always the water of a little stream is pure. It expresses the nature of an innocent heart, the heart that cannot be prevented from being sympathetic, from being loving, by any experience of the world which makes water turn bitter. The bitter experience has not touched it, and it is pure and clear. It inspires poets, it uplifts a composer, it quenches the thirst of the thirsty one, it is an ideal spot for a painter to paint. With its modesty it has purity and with its purity it has life.

There is also the water of a little pool. It is sometimes muddy, sometimes dirty. Why? Because of its narrowness, because it is small. In the same way the narrowness of the heart has always mud in it. Because it is narrow and because it is not deep enough, all the elements of the earth enter it and take away its purity.

Then there is the water of a large pool, where water-lilies grow, where little fishes swim, where the sun is reflected and the moonlight produces a beautiful vision, where one would like to sit and look at it because it expresses to everyone that sees it the liquid nature of the heart, the heart that is not frozen, the heart that is like water. It is still, it is calm, it can make one's heart tranquil to sit by its side. One can see one's reflection in it, for it is calm, it is tranquil.

The water of the spring is most healing and most inspiring because it comes from above and falls on to the earth; that is the character of the inspirational mind. The heart that, like a spring, pours out water in the form of inspiration – be it in poetry, be it in music, in whatever form – has beauty, it has a healing quality, it can take away all the worries, anxieties, difficulties and troubles of those who come to it. Like the water of the spring it not only inspires but it heals. Then there is a fountain that rises and falls in so many drops. It is man-made as the personality also is man-made. When man has made a personality, then the feeling that rises from the heart through that personality is like the fountain: each drop falling from it comes in the form of a virtue.

The water that rises from the sea towards the sky in the form of vapour represents the aspiration of the heart. The heart that aspires upward, that wishes to reach upward, that heart shows the quality of vapour. It is the heart of the devotee, of the seeker, the heart of the one who is always conscientiously seeking the higher ideal, touching the higher principles. In the form of clouds that heart of aspiration forms itself and pours down just like the rain, bringing celestial beauty in the form of art, poetry or music, or of anything that is good and beautiful.

There are hearts that have been impregnated with fire for a long, long time; there comes a sulphury water from them, purifying and healing. The heart has gone through fire, it has gone through suffering and therefore it can heal those who suffer.

There are hearts with many different qualities, like water may contain different chemical substances: those who have suffered, those who have gone through the test of patience, those who have contemplated. These hearts all represent one or the other kind of the water that heals and so do the personalities. Persons who have had deep experiences of any kind – of suffering, of agony, of love, of hate, of solitude, of association, of success, of failure – all have a particular quality, a quality which has a particular use for others.

Knowing this we will come to this conclusion: "Whatever has been my life's destiny, my heart through sorrow or pain, through joy or pleasure, has prepared a chemical substance that serves a certain purpose for humanity. And I can only give that chemical substance for the use of humanity if I can keep my heart awake and open". Once the heart is closed, once it is frozen, once it has turned from a warm heart into a stone, the person is no longer living. It does not matter what he has gone through, for even the worst poison can be of some use. There is no person therefore, however wicked, who is of no use, if only he knows that there is one condition for being useful to humanity, and that is to keep the heart open.

Now coming to spiritual attainment: this is something that we can never absorb through the head; it can only be received through the heart. Let two persons listen to the teachings of a teacher, one with his heart and the other with his head. The latter will think, "Is it so, or is it not so? And how is it, if it is so? How can it be, and if it is, why is it?" And there is never an end to the "why". The other person will listen with his heart; both logic and reason are at his disposal, but they do not trouble him. His heart is open, he listens to it and the quality of the heart is such that whatever falls upon an open heart becomes instantly revealed. When one says, "I cannot understand you", it is just like saying, "I have closed my heart to you"; there is no other reason for not understanding. And when one says, "I have understood it all", it means the heart was open; that is why one has understood.

Understanding, therefore, does not depend upon the head, it depends upon the heart. By the help of the head one can make things more clear, they become intelligible, one can express them better, but understanding must begin to come from the heart, not from the head. Besides, with his head a person says, "Yes, it must be so because I think so", but with his heart he says, "It is so because I believe it to be so". That is the difference: in one person there is doubt, in the other conviction.

In an Eastern language there is a word which is very difficult to translate: *iman*. It is not exactly faith or belief; the nearest word one can find for it is conviction, a conviction that cannot be changed by anything, a conviction that does not come from outside. One always seeks for conviction, one asks, "Will anybody convince me, will this thing convince me?" Nothing convinces, nobody convinces. Conviction is something that comes from one's own heart and it stands above faith and belief, for belief is the beginning of the same thing of which faith is the development and conviction the culmination.

What is spiritual attainment? Spiritual attainment is conviction. A man may think, "Perhaps it is so"; he may think about the best doctrine or about the highest idea that there is, and he will think, "It is so – perhaps". But there is "perhaps" attached to it. Then there is another person who cannot use the word "perhaps" because he does not think about it; he cannot say, "It may be so" when he knows that it is so. When a person arrives at the stage where the knowledge of reality becomes his conviction, then there is nothing in the world that will change it. If there is anything to attain to, it is that conviction which one can never find in the world outside; it must rise from the depth of one's own heart.

2

The scientists say that the body is formed around the heart; from the mystical point of view it is symbolical that the personality is formed around the heart. For a materialist the heart is a piece of flesh hidden in the breast; for the mystic the heart is the centre around which the personality is formed. Consciously or unconsciously man loves to hear the word "heart" and if we asked a poet to leave the word "heart" out of his poems he would never succeed to satisfy himself or others. Few people think about it and yet almost all poets who have appealed to humanity have used the word "heart" most. For what is man? Man is his heart. And what is heart? Heart is man: a dead heart – a dead man, a living heart – a living man.

People look for phenomena, for something wonderful, something surprising, something that amuses them. If only they knew that the greatest surprise and wonder can be found in their own heart. If there is anything that can tune man to a higher pitch or to a lower pitch, that can loosen the strings of his soul or tune them to the right note – it can only be done by the tuning of the heart. The one who has not reached his heart cannot reach God, and the one who has not reached the heart of his fellowman has not reached him. People may become friends, they may become acquaintances, relations, they may become connected through industry, political friendship, partnership in business or any collaboration, and yet they may be separated. Nearness in space does not bring the nearness of real friendship. There is only one way of coming near to one another and that is by way of the heart.

If there is anything most wonderful in heaven or on earth it is the heart. If there is anywhere a phenomenon, a miracle to be found it is in the heart. When God Himself is to be found in the heart what else is there that is not in it? As the Nizam of Hyderabad, the mystic poet,[1] said, "They speak of the largeness of the sea, the largeness of the ocean, the largeness of the land – if only they knew how large is the heart that accommodates them all!" The greatness of man, the smallness of man does not depend upon outer things. Be he rich or poor, whatever be his position in life, whatever his rank, if his heart is not great he cannot be great. And no matter what be his circumstances, if the heart is still great it remains great. It is the heart that makes man great or small.

One may see hearts of different qualities: there is a golden heart, a silver heart, a copper heart and there is an iron heart. The golden heart shows its colour and its beauty; it is precious and at the same time it is soft. The silver heart shows itself inferior compared to the golden heart; yet it is of silver that the current coins are made, so it is useful. There is the heart of copper of which pennies are made, and pennies are useful in everyday life; one has to use them more than gold and silver. Copper is hard and strong; it needs many hammerings to bend and shape it, to make something out of it. And then there is the iron heart which must be put into the fire before one can do anything with it. When in the glowing fire the iron has become hot then one can make something out of it. But how long does the heat of the fire last with it? A very short time! The blacksmith must be always ready; as soon as the fire begins to glow he must make something of it, for if he lets the moment go the iron will turn cold.

Besides these different aspects there is a heart of rock, and there is a heart of wax. The heart of rock must be broken, it must be cut in order to make something out of it; nothing reaches it, cold or heat, sun or water have little effect upon it.

The heart of wax melts as soon as it is heated. You can shape it without breaking it; it is soft, you can turn it any way you like. There is also the heart of paper you make a kite with. It flies and goes up; if the wind is in the north it goes to the north, if the wind is in the south it goes to the south. You can control it as long as the wind does not blow it out of your hands and as long as the wind is strong enough to hold it in the sky. But when there is no more wind it will drop down, and so you will try it again – like a kite.

Are these sufficient examples for the heart of man? There are numberless hearts, each different in quality, and once we begin to look at them and to distinguish their peculiarities and qualities we begin to see a living phenomenon, a miracle, every moment of our life. Is there anything we can compare the heart with? It is something that dies and then lives again, something that is torn and can be mended again, something that can be broken and be made whole again, something that can rise and something that can fall, and after falling can rise again, and after rising can fall instantly if it was to fall. There is a heart that can creep and a heart that can walk; there is a heart that can run and a heart that can fly. We cannot limit the various actions of the heart.

Imagine how the heart can be illuminated in a moment and how it can be darkened in a moment, how the heart becomes a maze for us to enter without ever being able to get out again, how it can become confusion and how it can become paradise. If one asked: Where is the soul? Where can we see the soul manifest to view? Where is paradise? Where is heaven? Where is joy and pleasure? If one asked: Where is love? Where is God? We can answer each of these questions by saying: it is in the heart.

Imagine how wonderful and at the same time how obscure to our view! If we call the heart the spark of fire then we can see its different aspects: as sympathy in the form of heat, as longing in the form of fire, as affection in the form of glow, as devotion in the form of flame, as passion in the form of smoke that blinds the eyes.

That which gives courage to stand firm in the battlefield, that which enables man to struggle throughout his life, that which gives him the strength to endure all that comes and strengthens him to have patience – what is it? It is the heart. If the heart fails, man falls, if the heart rises, man rises.

When the heart is directed towards one ideal, one object, one point, it develops, but when the heart goes from one point to another it is weakened, for then the fire element of the heart dies. For instance, a little spark can be brought to a blaze if one blows upon it, but the flame is put out by the wind. Why? Because blowing directs the air to one single spark, but the wind goes all around it and extinguishes the flame.

When man begins to say, "I love everybody", you can be sure he loves nobody. But when he says, "I love my mother, my father, my son, my daughter, my friend, or my beloved", then you can believe that he has taken his first step on the path of love. Can anyone in the world claim love and at the same time know love? The moment one knows what love is one loses the claim. One can only say, "I love", as long as one does not know what it is. Before saying, "I love", one must first show it by jumping into the fire. As Amir Minai, the great Hindustani poet, says, "Your first initiation in the order of lovers is to become nothing". And another poet says, "Oh love! You have taught me that lesson first which many others learn at the end".

When a person says, "If you will be good to me, I will be good to you; if you will be kind to me, I will be kind to you; if you will be nice to me, I will be nice to you; if you will respect me, I will honour you" – it is like saying, "If you will give me ninepence, I will give you a shilling"; it is business. When a person says, "I wish there was somebody who loved me, a friend, someone!", he is very mistaken. He will never be loved; he may wait for eternity. Love never asks love of someone else; love is more independent than anything else. It is love which makes one independent.

There is love that is like an infant. It must be taken in the arms, it cannot stand; if it is not taken in the arms it cries. It is not mature, it is not developed, it is not yet love. There is love which is like a wobbling child that has not yet learned to walk. It likes to walk but it likes to hold the cupboard, the chair, the table, someone else, in order to go so far. That love too is undeveloped. Then there is love that stands on its own feet and walks by itself. That is independent love, and you can depend upon it.

Love shows its quality by constancy. Where there is no constancy there is no love. People have wrongly understood the meaning of love; very often they do not know it. The real meaning of love is life itself, the feeling of life, the feeling: I live. That feeling itself is love. So what is love? Love is God. And what is God? God is love.

As long as one is involved in selfish thoughts and actions in life one does not understand the meaning of love. Love is sacrifice, love is service, love is regard for the pleasure and displeasure of the beloved. That love, once it is understood, can be seen in all the different aspects of life: love for those who depend upon one, for those with whom one comes in contact in one's everyday life, love for those of one's country, of one's race, for humanity. It can expand even to such an extent that there can be love for every little creature in the world, for the smallest insect. This expansion is like a drop of water expanding into an ocean. Man – limited as he is – the more he sympathizes the more he expands and the further he reaches heavenward: thus he can become as great as the Absolute.

Therefore, instead of teaching the lesson of indifference, as many mystics have done, the Sufis have learned the lesson of love, of devotion, of sympathy, and have called it the cultivation of the heart. It is known by the word *suluk*, which means the loving manner. What we call refined manner is only a manner behind which there is no life. When manner is directed by the heart quality then it becomes living manner, the manner that comes from love, and all such attributes as kindness, gentleness, tolerance, forgiveness, mercy and compassion – they all spring from this loving manner.

The great teachers and prophets, and the inspirers of humanity of all times have not become what they were by their miracles or wonder-workings; these belong to other people. The main thing that could be seen in them was their loving manner. Read the lives of the prophets. First of all see the way Jesus Christ had with all those who came to him. When sinners who were condemned and expelled by society were brought to the master, he received them with compassion. He was not on the side of those who accused them, he was on the side of the accused. That was loving manner. The fishermen* could never understand the master – even the most educated men would not have understood him, let alone the fishermen. Yet the master lived with them, moved with them and won their hearts in the end. That is loving manner.

Think of the Prophet whose beloved daughter was killed by an Arab, and when this man was brought before him and said, "Will you forgive me?" the Prophet forgave him. When his worst enemies were brought before him in rows, arrested, waiting his command, he was king, conqueror and judge, the one who could do anything he liked to them. When they asked, "What are you going to do with us, Prophet?" he said, "You are my brothers. God may forgive you. I pray for you".

The compassion of Buddha went to every living creature, to the smallest insect; this shows the expansion of his love. Remember therefore that for higher attainment on the spiritual path study is secondary; all knowledge of occult and psychic law, all magical powers, are secondary. The first and most important principle is the cultivation of the heart quality.

One may ask: How to cultivate the heart quality? There is only one way: to become selfless at each step one takes forward on this path, for what prevents one from cultivating the loving quality is the thought of self. The more we think of our self the less we think of others, and as we go further the self grows to become worse and worse. In the end the self meets us as a giant which we had always fought; and now at the end of the journey the giant is the stronger. But if from the first step we take on the path of perfection we struggled and fought and conquered this giant which is the self, it could be done only by the increasing power of love.

What do I mean by love? It is such a word that one cannot give one meaning. All attributes like kindness, gentleness, goodness, humbleness, mildness, fineness, are names of one and the same thing. Love therefore is that stream which

*the first disciples of Jesus Christ.

when it rises falls in the form of a fountain, and each stream coming down is a virtue. All virtues taught by books or by a religious person have no strength and life because they have been learned; a virtue that is learned has no power, no life. The virtue that naturally springs from the depth of the heart, the virtue that rises from the love-spring and then falls as many different attributes, that virtue is real. There is a Hindustani saying, "No matter how much wealth you have, if you do not have the treasure of virtue, it is of no use". The true riches is the ever increasing spring of love from which all virtues come.

CHAPTER III

The Heart – Aphorisms

THE LENGTH of his heart man shows by his tolerance.
The width of his heart man shows by his endurance.
The height of his heart man shows by his power of understanding.
The depth of his heart man shows by the capacity of assimilating all.

The heart of man is the shrine of God.
Take care when you touch it lest you may hurt the Unseen Dweller within.

Never hurt human feelings in thought, word or deed. The human heart is so delicate; it is like a fine tissue.
Once there is a tear in the tissue you can repair it – yet the tear remains.
And so it is with the human heart; once there is a tear in it, it can never be healed.

When God's divine love rises as a wave, it washes away the sins of the whole life in a moment, for law has no power to stand before love: the stream of love sweeps it away.

When we find faults and see no excuse, we are blind to the light which can free a person from his faults and give rise to that forgiveness which is the very essence of God – to be found in the human heart.

The very thought of the love of God fills the heart with joy and makes it light of its burden.

The heart in its depth is linked up with the divine Mind; so in the depth of the heart there is greater justice than on the surface.

The brain may be said to be the seat of the intelligence and the heart to be the throne of wisdom.

As the heart expands so the horizon becomes wider, and one finds greater and greater scope in which to build the kingdom of God.

Man's heart is like a piece of ground; you may sow anything in it and rear it.
When the fruit comes, then man knows whether it was a sweet fruit or a poison.

The heart, when it is not living and making its life a life of love, feels out of place, and all the discomfort of life comes from this.

My respondent heart be still – be still and listen to the consoling voice of God.

CHAPTER IV

The Path of Devotion

THERE ARE four paths by which man can attain to his highest goal. One is for the intellectual, the intelligent. By studying himself and the world, by understanding what he is, whence he has come and where he will ultimately go, man attains to perfection.

The second path is the way of abstinence. Those who follow this way detach themselves from all things in life; they renounce all the pleasures and comforts of life. They have no friendship, no attachment for anyone; they withstand all natural tendencies and inclinations. Those who have been in India may have seen some followers of this path, sometimes among the crowd, their body covered with ashes, sometimes in the solitude remote from all: by this their psychic power becomes very great.

The third way is that of those who live the life of the world and by their righteousness, by their piety become as a saint, a sage.

The fourth way is the path of love, of devotion. The whole universe has been made through love. The Intelligence itself in the next step towards evolution has become love. It is love that has directed the Intelligence; if not, the Intelligence would be spread all over, not directed in any direction in particular. All that is done in the world is done by love. One could not study the flower on the mantelpiece if love did not direct the intelligence towards the flower, to admire it and to know what it is. Therefore the mystics have understood that this power of love that has brought all into manifestation must be able to lead back from the seen world to the unseen.

Love is the sign of intelligence. Where there is no intelligence there is no love. Rocks have no intelligence and there is no love in them. Plants and trees have awakened to life and show some attachment. If we have a plant and care for it, it will respond to our care and flourish. Animals have more intelligence and show much affection and attachment. Pet animals in the house grow to have much affection and sympathy for their master; they are happy in his joy and become sad in his sorrow. Horses too show much affection. It is told that the horse of an Arab who had been wounded in battle stayed beside him for three days and nights, until his comrades came and rescued him. Man has the most intelligence, and he has the most love in his nature.

Someone may say, "But animals are cruel also". So is man. Is man not far more cruel than the animals?

There are three sorts of mystics: Yogis, Buddhists and Sufis,[2] and most of these have chosen the path of devotion, because it has beauty and gives a satisfaction that nothing else can give. Sufis may take the way of renunciation, the way of wisdom, but most of them have especially chosen this path of devotion.

Devotion is like fire, it has a magnetism, a warmth like fire. When the atmosphere is so cold that our body is chilled, we like to turn to the fire and draw near to it. In this cold world where nothing but cold and selfish hearts are all about us, each person caring only for himself, where there is a heart that has love in it, it has such a warmth, such a radiance that all are drawn to it, all want to be near it. He who works through the intellect may have a little intellectual attraction satisfying the desire of the mind for a little explanation of things. I have travelled for eight years all over India and have been in remote and inaccessible places where there was danger of robbers. I travelled to see the sages and mystics, and I have seen what charm had the atmosphere of those who were devotees, what fragrance had their presence.

We all know love to some small extent. There are many who have begun to love and then say, "I loved someone, but the one I loved did not prove to be my ideal". They are disappointed, they cast love aside and by doing so they cast aside the only thing that could lead them towards God, they break off the bridge that could unite them with God. Love is the only thing that takes away the selfishness which is the only barrier between man and God. Love alone illuminates the heart. The heart is in the centre of the being. When it is illumined the whole being becomes light; when it is dark the whole being is in darkness. The soul has its light, because the soul is light, but it cannot give its light to the external being if the heart that is between them is darkened, nor can the body give its experiences to the soul.

Then there are disappointed people who say, "There is nothing on earth worth loving". Of course it is true because the soul which is from God is perfect as He is perfect and seeks perfection. Man does not wish to prove himself perfect, but he seeks perfection in another. That perfection is only in God, the Unlimited, but man seeks it in the human being, in the limited being full of faults and imperfections.

Now you may ask, "How can we love God whom we do not see, whom we have never known?" You cannot love God only because it has been said in ancient times that there is a God and that we should love Him, or because it is written in a book. If someone says that you should love God because he is the Creator, you cannot praise Him as Creator; for we have always seen that the piano is created by the piano manufacturer and Pears' soap is created by Mr. Pears, and we know that the carpenter creates the chair and the table. A person once said to me, "I have a horror of the idea of God. When I think that God may suddenly seize me and call me to account for everything I have done, I have a horror. I have quite enough to interest me here. I do not want to think of God". I was rather amused and I could not blame him. The mistake is that the ideal of God is given before idealism is developed.

A child wishes to give its doll a piano, a chair, a table, all kinds of things, and so much ado is made about the doll. When the child has grown up it has perhaps forgotten the doll. If the child has accomplished anything by this, if it has achieved anything in life, it is that idealism has been learned. One should have the ideal of devotion which one admires, to which one aspires, which appeals to one's own degree of evolution. If a person wishes to raise himself, to be powerful in the world, he should think of President Wilson who has raised himself from the position of a doctor to be President of the United States. If he wishes to be great in politics he should think of the Prime Minister who has raised himself from his small position to be Prime Minister.

We cannot love God in heaven if we do not love man on earth. Christ taught first love of our fellow-man. Enemies apart, to love our fellow-man is the first thing necessary. Those who take this way have devotion and love for the Murshid, or they may love a teacher, or a hero, a saint, a prophet, and that love must be kept. If you say, "I have love for Buddha, but he did not believe in the soul and I do not like that – and he did this and that", such is not love or devotion. Keep the devotion for the ideal – with his disbelief in the soul and all! From this man rises to the degree of *fana-fi-rasul*, devotion for the unseen ideal, for the holiness, the goodness, the kindness of the being whom he has not seen. It is your idealization which produces in you the ideal. Buddha's body is lost in the earth long ago. You have made the Buddha.

But all this is idolatry as long as there is not the ideal of God. As long as there is devotion for the limited ideal there is idolatry and as long as man has not broken away from idolatry to the unlimited ideal, he has not reached his highest goal. The ideal has attracted, has drawn out your love by his holiness, his goodness, his saintliness, but then love itself springs forth and is for the Unlimited. Then a person will not say, "I have seen injustice in God, I have seen unkindness in God". He sees and loves Him with His kindness and unkindness, His power and justice and might, with all and everything and nothing.

When that is reached then this highest goal of attainment is reached; then man is perfect.

CHAPTER V

Love

Ideas – Stories – Answers to Questions – Aphorisms

TO AN angelic soul love means glorification
To a jinn soul love means admiration
To a human soul love means affection
To an animal soul love means passion.

One need not fall in love, one must rise through love.

Pour out floods of love, yet keeping your garment of detachment from being wet.

Question: Can love exceed wisdom or can wisdom exceed love? What happens in either case? Is love measured according to love, or is wisdom measured according to love? *Answer:* It is true that wise is loving and loving is truly wise, although in one person wisdom may be predominant and in another love. But both love and wisdom are needed. The cold-hearted man is never wise, and the really warm-hearted person is never foolish. Yet both these qualities, love and wisdom, are distinct and separate, and it is possible that a person may be loving but lacking wisdom, and it happens that a person who is wise may be lacking love to some extent. But no one can be wise if love is absent from his heart – call him clever. And no one will be truly loving if wisdom has not illuminated his heart, for love comes from wisdom and wisdom comes from love.

It is very difficult to say what love is and how one can love. Is it embracing people and running after them and saying sweet words to them? What could one show when one is loving? – for every person has a different way of expressing his love. One person perhaps has love hidden in his heart which does not manifest, and another person's love comes out in his words and actions. The love of one person rises like vapour and charges the whole atmosphere, and another person's love is like a spark hidden in a stone: outside the stone is cold, inside there is a spark.

Therefore to judge who has love and who has not is not in the power of every person, it is a very difficult thing. For instance love is a fire rising from a cracker calling out, "I am love!", but it burns out and is finished. There is also fire in the pebble which never manifests. If you hold the pebble it feels cold, yet at the same time the fire is there. Some day you can strike it and it is there, it is dependable, it lasts. As many people as there are, so many are the different qualities of their love, and one cannot judge.

Question: Is jealousy inseparable from human love?
Answer: It is like asking, "Is the shadow separable from the body?" Where there is form there is shadow; where there is human love there is jealousy.

Love can bring out what is worst and best in man.

Love can take many forms, even that of indifference. I remember I went once for a relative to the house of a physician, an Indian physician who had a very ancient method of writing his prescriptions. Each took him nearly ten minutes. I was shown into a small room where fifteen to twenty people were already waiting, and I sat down among them. He continued to write prescriptions for all wo came, and when he had finished with those who were before me he began to write prescriptions for those who had come after me. I had thought that the physician, as a friend of the family, would have seen me first, but he went on until he had seen everyone, and I was the last.

Finally he said to me, "Now tell me what you have to say". I told him, and he wrote out the prescription without any haste, and when I was leaving he said, "I hope you understand that I did not want to see you while all the other patients were still there. I wanted to see you at leisure". He was doing me a favour, and though he tried my patience it was still a majestic sort of favour. It gave me a good example of love in the form of indifference.

With indifference one still must have sympathy and love – be more and more sensitive as one evolves.

The Story of Hatim

The life of Hatim is written by the Persians and many stories are told about him. One of these stories is best known by the people in the East. It tells that a princess who was much renowned for her beauty and greatness had made as a condition for those who loved her and desired her hand that only the one who brought her a certain pearl which she longed to possess would marry her. There was one lover of the princess who really loved her, but did not find the way to obtain that pearl from anywhere.

The work of Hatim was to roam about from country to country and to do what he could for those who needed his services. He met this lover who, roaming about, was most unhappy because he could not find the pearl. Hatim consoled him and said, "Continue in your path of love, even if it be difficult, and remember that I shall not rest until I have brought relief to your heart by bringing you the pearl you are longing for". Hatim then went in pursuit of the pearl and the story tells what difficulties he had in obtaining it. When at last he got it he brought it to the palace, and the princess was won by that pearl. When she consented to accept Hatim as her lover, he then said that this promise should be granted to his friend, who was really her lover, while Hatim was the lover of those who were in need.

In this story the princess is God, and the pearl that she wanted is the knowledge of God. There was a lover of God, but he would not go and take the trouble one has to take to obtain this knowledge. Someone else was ready; his work was to take this trouble to go to the depth – even if it was not for himself but for another – to get the knowledge and to give it to the one who had the love to have it.

This story also explains us that there are two stages of workers. The first stage is that of the one who works for himself; the higher stage of working is to work for others. The one who rises above the stage of working for himself comes to the stage of working for others, bringing in their lives the blessing which is the need of their lives.

To what does the love of God lead? It leads to that peace and stillness which can be seen in the life of the tree which flowers and bears fruit for others and expects no return.

Peace will not come to the lover's heart so long as he will not become love itself.

Question: Why is it that with the growing of love difficulties arise from all sides? Is it not said by the ancients that God is a jealous God?
Answer: This is but a saying; God can never be jealous of His own manifestation. Only before love began one was unconsciously linked with the source alone, but once love has awakened on the physical plane, one is attached to someone on earth. It is like Adam and Eve being exiled from the garden of Eden. This naturally causes every influence to work against that love. Even the throne of God is shaken by love's outburst, because by a sincere link on earth which is power itself every other influence is automatically pulled and pushed, causing thereby a commotion in the world of hearts.

The soul of man is happiness; yet man is never happy since he is occupied with this world of woes. It is only love that can bring about that happiness of which is spoken in legends, which is beyond all pleasures of this mortal world. Those who consciously or unconsciously see or feel that happiness experienced by the lover and the beloved, naturally either knowingly or unknowingly react against it.

Spiritual love is nectar, but as soon as it is mixed with matter, it becomes a sweet wine mixed with a bitter poison.

If we give ourselves up to the absorbing love of any being, any thing, God becomes jealous and He takes that being from us. Therefore Abraham was called upon to sacrifice his son. This lesson was given: God does not allow another affection to be dearer than His love. If we love our children because they are ours and other children are neglected, God says to us, "These are the beings whom We have given you to love, to take care of them for Us, not to cherish them for yourselves". He takes from us whatever we love most forgetting Him, in order to show us that He is the Lord of the *Jalal, Jamal* and *Kamal*. The love of all beings lasts for a season, but it is His love that is always with us, in all forms and beings.

No creature that has ever been born has belonged in reality to any other. Every soul is the beloved of God. Does not God love as we human beings cannot?[3]

The Maharajah of Jaipur, Ram Singh, was a great lover of music. At his court were marvellous singers and dancers, they were like the *Apsaras* and *Ghandarvas**. From all India beautiful singers and dancers were called there; all the great musicians of India were there, also my grandfather Maula Bakhsh. The Maharajah did not know the secret of holding his wish. If he had known it he might have kept his happiness much longer. But he did not know it, and when everything was perfect he died.

That is why in the East there is a superstition that, if any thing or being belonging to us is much praised or admired, that thing or that person will soon be lost to us. Therefore if someone says, "Your child is very pretty", the parents will say, "No, he is not pretty, he is a plain child". And if the child is fair they make a black mark upon its face, so that it would not be perfectly fair.

Life provides you with a substitute for all you have lost.

Love is the fire that burns all infirmities.

Question: How do we see the love of God in the book of nature? We see all around us fruits and plants and animal life brought to fruition and then to destruction, and among men cruelty, misery, tragedies and enmities everywhere.

*In the Hindu Pantheon these are singers and dancers at the Court of Indra.

Answer: It is a difference of focus. If we focus our mind upon all that is good and beautiful we shall see – in spite of all the ugliness that exists in nature and especially more pronounced in human nature – that the ugliness will cover itself. We will spread a cover over it and see all that is beautiful, and to whatever lacks beauty we will be able to add, taking it from all that is beautiful in our heart where beauty has sufficiently been collected. But if we focus our mind upon all the ugliness that exists in nature – and in human nature – there will be much of it. It will take up all our attention and there will come a time when we shall not be able to see any good anywhere. We shall see all cruelty, ugliness, wickedness and unkindness everywhere.

Question: In focusing our mind on beauty alone, is there not a danger of shutting our eyes to the ugliness and suffering we might alleviate?

Answer: In order to help the poor we ought to be rich, and in order to take away the badness of a person we ought to be so much more good. That goodness must be earned, as money is earned. That earning of goodness is collecting goodness wherever we find it, and if we do not focus on goodness we will not be able to collect it sufficiently. What happens is that man becomes agitated by all the absence of goodness he sees. Being himself poor he cannot add to it, and unconsciously he develops in his own nature what he sees. He thinks, "Oh poor person! I should so much like you to be good", but that does not help that person. His looking at the badness, his agitation, only adds one more wicked person to the lot. When one has focused one's eyes on goodness one will add to beauty, but when a man's eyes are focused on what is bad he will collect enough wickedness for him to be added himself to the number of the wicked in the end, for he receives the same impression.

Besides, by criticising, by judging, by looking at wickedness with contempt, one does not help the wicked or the stupid person. The one who helps is he who is ready to overlook, who is ready to forgive, to tolerate, to take disadvantages he may have to meet with patiently. It is he who can help.

A person who is able to help others should not hide himself but do his best to come out into the world. "Raise up your light high", it is said. All that is in you should be brought out, and if the conditions hinder you, break through the conditions! That is the strength of life.

You are love – you come from love – you are made by love – you cannot cease to love.

Question: Is it a great lack in character when a person cannot give the love which friends require? When one receives love and is not able to return it, when one forgets one's friends being absorbed in one's work and occupation?
Answer: The question is: what work or occupation? There are works and occupations of a higher character which take one's whole attention, one's life. Such works may require renunciation and sacrifice. Then one does not become loveless; there is a duty of which one cannot be regardless. However if one can manage to give and take love at the same time, it is preferable.

Question: Will a person suffer one day through inability to love – merely giving a cold affection?
Answer: Love, whether hot or cold, is love.

Question: Is there cold love?
Answer: Since God is love the whole manifestation is love, the cold water and the hot fire.

Question: By which power does man attract his food and all he needs?
Answer: If there is any mighty power, it is the power of love. All that one desires comes from love. Even if one desires food, it is the love of food, and it is according to the power of his love that man will attract it. The question is only: what does he love most? Does he love something more than the ordinary things of life, then that must be his aim.

Hunger is an aspect of love. Love of the heart is what we call affection. Love of territory has caused many deaths. What man loves he must get. All words as seeking, wanting, requiring, searching, are words for loving. Love is the root of the whole phenomenon of life. Even if a poor man does not find his food, you will see that there is something else he loves more.

God is love and in Him I have my being – and I have no fear.

Let my intelligence shine out as love; let my limited self expand to Thy divine perfection.

CHAPTER VI

The Difference between Will, Wish and Desire

WILL IS the development of the wish. When one says, "It was the divine will", it means that it was a command, a wish that developed into action. When the wish becomes action it becomes will, it becomes a command. One may think it is only one's wish, but it is a wish as long as it is still. It is there, it has not sprung up, it is inactive, just like a seed in the ground: it is wish. But the moment the seed is coming out of the ground as a seedling and is in the process of becoming a plant, then it is a will. Therefore these two different names, wish and will, are names of one and the same thing: in its undeveloped state and in its process of development.

Desire is a weaker or primitive stage of the wish. When an idea, a thought, is not yet made clear in one's own mind and one's own mind has not taken a decision: "It must be so, I would like it to be so" – then it is a desire, it is a fancy. It comes and it goes, and one does not care. But when that desire is a little more developed then it is a wish. Then it stays there, it does not fade away like clouds, it is tangible, it is there. Yet it is not fulfilled, because for fulfilment it must develop.

There are some people in this world who say, "All my life I had bad luck. The bad luck was that never in my life my wish was granted". They can very easily imagine that a spirit was against them, or God was against them, or the stars, or that something was keeping back their wish. But it is not always so. In the first place God wishes the same that we wish; if God wished differently from our wish we could not worship that God who was always against us. It is not so! Besides, there is no benefit in opposing the wish of man; to God there is no advantage in doing so. No doubt there are planetary reasons, reasons of the universe at work, reasons of the cosmos that oppose the wish. As it is said, "Man proposes, God disposes". The name "God" is put in the place of the cosmic forces, but God with His mercy and compassion never has a desire to oppose anyone's wish. God apart, a good-hearted man would never like to oppose anybody's wish; he would do everything possible to make anybody's wish complete, to make a person's wish come true. A kindly person would do it.

But what mostly happens is that man proves to be the worst enemy of his own desire – for many reasons. One reason is that he is never sure what he desires. Out of a hundred persons you will find one who knows what he desires, but ninety-nine say, "Do I desire, or do I not desire – I don't know. I think I desire, but I do not know if it is so". Ninety-nine percent among men is in this condition; they really do not know if they desire. One day they say, "Yes, I do", another day they say, "No, I don't think I desire". Therefore their desire is decomposed in the unclearness of the mind.

Then there are others who analyse their desire, and they analyse it till they have broken it to pieces. There are many analytical people who have all through life destroyed their desires by analysing them.

There is a third kind of people: those who have adopted a passive attitude. They say it is a sin to desire. Yet they cannot be without desire, and in this passive attitude they say, "Well, I will not desire". They have crossed the desire that was there.

And there is a fourth kind of person who desires something, but by lack of concentration cannot turn his desire into a wish. Therefore the desire stays in its primitive stage all the time.

A fifth kind of person develops desire into a wish; he goes so far and no further. But the wish must be developed into will. So the desire is not carried through, so to speak, and never comes to its culmination.

Now this is a subject which is of the greatest importance in the life of every person in the world. No one can exist in the world without wishing for something, and if there is a person who has no wish he need not stay in the world. He must go somewhere out of the crowd; he cannot exist there. He must go out in the mountains and even there he should turn into a tree or into a rock in order to exist, because to be a living being without a wish is not possible.

The difference between persons – high and low – is according to the wish they have. One wishes for the earth, the other wishes for heaven. The desire of one takes him to the heights of spiritual progress, the desire of the other takes him to the depth of the earth. Man is great or small, man is wise or foolish, man is on the right road or on the wrong road according to the desire he has.

Now coming to the question of the opposing forces: according to the Sufis there are *Qadha* and *Qadr*. *Qadha* is the universal will, universal power; *Qadr* is the individual will and the individual power. No doubt the individual power in comparison with the universal power is like a drop compared with the sea. It cannot stand against the sweeping waves of the sea that come and destroy it. Nevertheless, the drop, being from the same source as the sea, has also a certain amount of strength, and the individual will also has a certain strength if it wills to hold against opposing forces.

If we want to make the individual will and the universal will more clear, it is in small things that we can do so. When a person is walking in the street and says, "I feel hungry, I should like to go to a restaurant and have a meal", that is individual will. Another person goes in the street and sees a poor man, and says, "Ah, this man – he seems to be poor, he must have something; can I not do something for him? I want to see him looking happier". As soon as he thinks of the good of another person, at once his will becomes the universal will. The reason is that the boundary that limits the will of an individual is the thought of the self. As soon as one has forgotten the thought of self, as soon as one thinks of another, that boundary breaks down and the will becomes stronger. The masters of humanity, those who have been able to do great things in the world, where did they get their will from? It was their own will which was extended by the breaking down of the boundaries of the thought of self. It does not mean that one should give up the thought of self, that one must never think of oneself, never think of one's lunch and dinner. The self is there, one has to think about it. But at the same time in order to expand, in order to let the will grow, the more one forgets oneself the more one is helped.

There are some who take the path of resignation, neither

doing good to themselves nor to another. It is a kind of attitude they have taken to say, "It will come from somewhere. Somebody will do it. If I am hungry somebody will come and feed me" – or, "If another person is in need, somebody will come and help him". Their wish is inactive, they do not let their wish become a will, they remain where they are, they are passive. No doubt, an intelligent passiveness and resignation can also bring about a wonderful result, but many of these people do it unintelligently. The quality of the saints is to be resigned to all that comes – but then they do not even form a wish. They take all that comes, flowers or thorns; everything that comes, they take it. They look into thorns and see that they are flowers. With praise and with blame they are contented. They are contented with rise and fall; they take all that comes, they take life as it is. That is the intelligent way of doing it. The unintelligent way is to say of anything that is difficult, "Somebody will come and do it". This is a kind of laziness. They may think it is passiveness, but it is laziness to think, if one has to do something, "Somebody will come who will do it".

In India it is told that a man was lying under a cherry tree and some ripe cherries were falling near him. But he was just lying there. A man came from a distance to whom he called out, "Please come here, will you please put this cherry in my mouth?" There are many to be found like this who out of a feeling of helplessness, of laziness, give in, who have no enthusiasm, no courage. In this way their willpower is broken down and in the end they are helpless. There is no comparison between the saintly spirit and the spirit of the helpless. Although both become resigned, the latter is not truly resigned: he would like to have the cherry in his mouth, but another person must give it to him. The saint does not care if he eats it or if he does not eat it; it is just the same to him. In that case it is allowable.

Then there are others who are over-anxious for their wish to come true; it destroys their wish because the strength, the pressure they put upon their wish is too great. It is just like guarding a plant against the sun and against water; if one guards the plant against the very things that should help it to grow, then it cannot grow. It is the same with the wish; if a person says, "This is my wish and it must come true, no one must think about it, no one must look at it", he is always afraid that perhaps this wish will not come true. He is eager, he is thinking with doubt, fear and suspicion and therefore he will destroy his own wish.

Again there is a person who is willing to sacrifice anything, or to persevere as much as it requires for even a small wish which he does not value very much when it comes to value. Yet he gives it every thought and he does everything in his power to make that wish come true. That person is taking the same path as the path of the masters. He must have success, and it is success which brings success. If once a person is successful, his success attracts success. Once a person fails then this failure attracts failure; for the same reason that, if a person is on the path of accomplishment, each accomplishment gives him a greater power to go forward, and when he is on the path that goes downward then every step leads him downward.

Now arises the question which desire and wish one must give up and which one must rear. One must have discrimination. If here is no discrimination one will take a wrong way; it may lead to success, but it will be a success in a wrong way. If one rears every desire and wish, and thinks, "This must be accomplished", then sometimes it may be right and sometimes wrong. Discrimination must first be developed in order to understand what leads one to happiness, a lasting happiness, a greater peace, a higher attainment. But once a person has discrimination and has chosen a wish, then he should not analyse it too much. Many have formed a habit of analysing everything every day. If a person holds a wish for ten years and every day analyses it in his mind he acts against it. Every day he looks at it from a new point of view, he tries to find the wrong points of his own wish and so he tries to crush it in every way possible. In ten years' time his wish would have come true, and instead it is broken to pieces. There are many intellectual people, many people who doubt, many analytical persons who are the greatest enemies of their wish.

And now comes the question whether it is wrong if a person expresses his wish in prayer, for many people say,

"God knows everything, so why should we tell God that such and such a thing should be done. God knows the secret of every heart. Besides, is it not selfish to bring our wish before God? If it is a good wish, it must come true of itself." The answer is that prayer is a reminder to God, prayer is a song sung before God who enjoys it, who hears it, who is reminded about something. But one thinks, "How can our prayer, our little voice reach God?" It reaches God through our ears. God is within us. If our soul can hear our voice, God can hear it too. Prayer is the best way, because the wish is beautifully expressed, which harmonizes us with God, which brings about a greater relationship between man and God.

Then one may ask whether it is good to think about the wish one has. One can never think too many times of the wish one has. Dream about it, think about it and imagine it, keep it in mind, retain it in mind and do everything possible towards its fulfilment – but with poise, with tranquillity, with patience, with confidence, with ease, and not by thinking hard about it. The one who thinks hard about his wish destroys it, for it is just like overheating, or giving too much water to a plant: the very thing that should help it, destroys it. If a person worries about his wish he certainly either has no patience, or he has some fear or some doubt; all these things destroy the wish. The wish must be cherished easily, with comfort, with hope, with confidence and with patience. Doubt is like rust, it eats into it; fear is still worse, it destroys it.

When a person has no discrimination and he is not sure whether it is a right wish or a wrong one, whether it should come true or not, one day he says, "I should so much like it to come true"; another day he says, "I do not care if it comes true"; after a week he says anew, "I so much wish it to come true", and after a month, "Oh, I do not care now". It is just like making a fire and then putting it out, then making the fire again and again putting it out. Every time he extinguishes the fire it is gone, he will have to make it anew. And so, if a person has formed a wish and cherished it for ten years, each time it is broken he has to make it anew.

And now comes the question what wish is the most

desirable. This depends upon one's own stage of evolution. A person who is only so much evolved that he can make no greater wish than for the need of his daily life, let him do it. He must not think, "Because it is only the need of daily life it is nothing, I must wish for something higher". He must not think that. If his heart is inclined to the need of daily life, he must think of it first. But if his heart thinks, "No, I cannot wish for this, I can think of something much higher", then he must take the consequences. The consequences will be that he will have to go through tests and trials – and if he does not mind this, so much the better.

There are many things in this world which we want and which we need, and yet we do not necessarily think about them. If they come it is all right, and if they do not come we feel uncomfortable for a time, but that feeling passes. We cannot put our mind and thought upon them if we are evolved, because then we think of something else, of something higher; our thought is involved in something much higher and greater than what we need in everyday life. We do not pay attention to what we need and that slips from our grasp. It is therefore that great poets, thinkers and sages were very often hard up for things that one could get in everyday life. With all their power they could command gold to come to their house – and the gold would come, they only had to command it. If they commanded that an army was to come into their power it would come – the army and anything they would command. Yet they could not give their mind to it, they could only wish for something which was equal to their particular evolution.

So each person can only wish for something equal to his evolution, he cannot properly wish for something which is beneath his evolution, even if he was told to do so. Very often in order to help a person in a certain situation I have said to him, "Now think of this particular object". But being much more evolved than that he thought with his brain, his heart was somewhere else, and so it never came true. One can give one's heart and mind and whole being to something which is equal to one's evolution. If it is not equal one cannot give one's whole being to it. Maybe a person gives his thought to it, but what is thought? Thought without feeling is no power.

If the soul and the spirit are not at the back of it, there is no power.

So this must be understood: that our wish must be different from what we need in everyday life. Never mix it! Always think that what we need in everyday life is one thing: something practical. Though if that be our wish, then it is all right. And then we are to cherish, to maintain our wish as something sacred, something given to us by God to cherish, to bring to fulfilment, for it is in the fulfilment of one's highest and best and deepest wish that lies the purpose of life.

Question: Is there any way of finding out beforehand if a wish will be good for us?
Answer: That is the most difficult thing to say. It can only be done by training oneself, and that training is: always to have a good thought for everyone, a kind thought for everybody, to develop a consciousness of justice within oneself, to have sympathy, to have goodwill for everyone in the world. If a person keeps this as a principle in his everyday life then every wish that will come to him will be productive of good results.

Question: Can we feel the accomplishment of a wish beforehand?
Answer: If one can feel the accomplishment of a wish beforehand it means that the wish is secure, that the wish is surely to be fulfilled. If with the wish you have got a feeling that this wish will come true, then it must come true. There is no doubt about it, because when you have that feeling it shows that you have no doubt, that there is nothing opposing it. Therefore that wish of yours is a promise at the same time.

Question: When Buddha said that we should have no desire, did he mean that we should have the attitude of a saint?
Answer: The Buddha never said that you should have no desire. The Buddha spoke of "the man who has no desire". It never was the principle of Buddha that you must not have a desire; Buddha was too wise to commit himself like this. What is meant is that we must develop so that one day we may reach to that stage where naturally we shall have no desires. But if we have a desire and say, "Because Buddha has

said that we must have no desire, therefore we must throw it away", it is working against ourselves. It is just like a man who, having heard that a saint had lived without food for a very, very long time and had experienced exaltation, would say, "Well, I shall give up my lunch every day if I can become spiritual by it". He may just as well have his lunch because he feels hungry. The one who went without food was not hungry, he had risen above it. We must have principles according to our stage of evolution, and never take principles higher than our stage of evolution, forcing ourselves to abide by them.

Question: Does it matter if one has several wishes at the same time?

Answer: Suppose one did salt and sweet and savoury and pepper all together in the mouth, how would the taste be? It would come to nothing. And so each wish destroys the other. You may have five best wishes at the same time, but one wish will destroy the other; therefore there is not one wish that you will enjoy. Besides, it is only to one wish that you can give your greatest power.

Question: The other day you said, "The one who turns his back to the world – the whole world runs after him". How is this to be understood?

Answer: This can be understood by seeing two persons bargaining. For instance a pedlar at the dock of Alexandria comes with an object, and you say, "How beautiful. I like it. How much will you take for it?" As soon as you have said this he wants you to give as high a price as he wishes to get from you. As soon as you turn your back and say, "I do not care for it", he comes after you and says, "Will you take it for half the price?". If you go still further and still turn your back, he will give it to you for the quarter of it. Exactly the same is the nature of this world; it is a greedy world. You follow it, it runs from you; you turn your back to it, it comes after you.

CHAPTER VII

Destiny and Free Will

THERE ARE two points of view: very often people either believe in destiny or in free will. Those who believe in destiny do not believe in free will; it is a question of temperament, and it also depends upon the experience they had in their lives. Some people have worked and had some success and recognized it as the outcome of their work. Then they think, "If there is anything it is free will. What we have done shows it: we have achieved results". And there are others who have worked but did not succeed. In that case they begin to see that something is keeping them back from getting results, and then they think, "There is something – destiny – which is holding us back". Many think, "It is a sort of laziness to be fatalist; after all it is a superstition". And others think, "Free will is just a name, a conception, an idea a person may have, but really it is all destiny".

Nevertheless, their idea of free will has its meaning and this belief has its peculiar benefit in life, while at the same time the idea of destiny is profound. Whether a person believes in it or does not believe in it, there is always an attraction about it. One who reads the future will always attract the believer in destiny as well as the unbeliever. The believer goes to him with faith, the unbeliever with smiles. Whether they believe that it is true or not, both are attracted to know about destiny because it is the greatest mystery there is. One's own life in which one is most interested always remains a secret, a mystery, and this mystery is greater than any other in the world. No one can say, "I have no interest in knowing about my life, in knowing why I have had that past, why I have this present and what future I shall have". To know about it is the greatest desire one has.

Concerning the idea of destiny one may ask whether a plan is laid out so that every occurrence in life must be according to that plan. And if it is laid out, on what ground? Who has laid it out? If it is God who laid it out, how far could it be just on the part of God to make one happy and another miserable, one great and another small, to let one enjoy and at the same time make another suffer – living under the same sun, walking on the same earth? If it is man's action, is it in the first place the action of the past or is it the action of the present and, if it is man's action, to what degree is he responsible for it? These questions take a person to the depths of life's mystery, and once they are solved a great philosophical problem has been solved.

Most often a person has a preconceived idea, and this idea he keeps as a wall before him; content with what he knows about it, he does not try to inquire any further.

There is no doubt that a man is born with a plan to be accomplished in life – not only with instincts, with merits or gifts, but with the whole plan of how his life is to be. There is a saying in the East that one can read the life of an infant from looking at its feet; even the little feet of the infant show the sign of the plan that it is to follow through life.

There is a story that explains a little more the relation between destiny and free will. A seer was working as a porter* in a rich man's house. Now there is a belief in the East that no sooner a child is born than angels come and write on its forehead the whole plan of destiny. But this seer-porter was a wonderful man. At the door, as soon as the angels came, he said, "Stop, where are you going? I am the porter here! You cannot go in unless you promise to tell me about the plan". The angels told him; he was a strong porter, he would not let them go without telling him. And so every time a child was born in that house he took down the notes of what was going to happen. Then the parents passed away. Theirs had been a rich house, but for some reason or other the money was lost. The children were left without shelter, and it fell upon the shoulders of the old porter to look after them with what little means he had.

As soon as they were old enough the children went to different countries with what little they had to spend. One day this servant of the house thought that it was his duty to go and see how they were getting on. Also for a seer it is most interesting to see the material phenomenon of the same thing he had seen inwardly as a vision. That comes as a satisfaction

---

*From the French portier, i.e. doorman.

to a seer; it is naturally amusing for him when he sees on the outer plane the same things he had felt inside himself. It gives him the greatest fun, the greatest amusement.

So the porter went and saw one child of the house working as a horse groom. He was very sorry to see the child of a house, where so many horses had been kept, in this situation. He went to the young man and told him, "It could not be avoided, it was meant that you should be so. Only, I want to give you one advice, because it makes me sad to think that you, in whose house were so many horses, now have to work as a horse groom. Here is a little money, take it and go to another city and try to work as a horse trainer. Horses of rich men may be given to you to train them, and I am sure you will be successful". The young man asked, "Can I do anything else?" "No, that is the only door out. Perhaps you would have been a horse groom all your life if I had not told you this. Anything else you cannot do; this is the only path for you. Do your work in a different way and you will have success". The young man did so and was successful.

The porter then went to the other son and asked, "What is your condition?" "My condition is that I wander about in the forest and bring back some birds. I sell them in the city and hardly get any money to live". In those days there was a fashion among kings to keep a certain bird as a pet; that bird was called Shahbaz, the king's bird. The porter said, "You must not look for game birds, look for this bird Shahbaz". The boy replied, "But if I cannot find it, should I then rather starve and die?"

"Do you know what your father was and what you are?"

"Yes, I had bad luck".

"You will have better luck if only you listen to me. You need not change your profession of catching birds, but catch Shahbaz. You can sell it for millions. That is the bird you ought to catch".

This story makes us realize what the seer does. A definite plan was made for those two young men; at the same time there was scope for free will to work – but within that plan. If one did not think of this scope one would go on in the lines of the plan and continue to live miserably. Seeing changes the scope. It is a great lesson and those who can understand this lesson can benefit immensely by it: seeing there is a plan and at the same time that there is scope to do better, and much better – yet within the plan.

Sa'di, the great poet of Persia, has said, "Every soul is born for a certain purpose and the light of that purpose is kindled in his soul".

Now the question arises if a person is born with what the Hindus call *karma*: some action of the past, or something he has brought with him on earth, a good influence or a bad influence, something that he has to pay. No doubt there is truth in it and we can see that truth very often: a person is placed in a situation where he has to give, where he has to serve, where he has to sympathize without any intention on his part, as if he has to pay a debt to someone. He may not have the slightest desire to do so – at the same time it falls on his shoulders, he cannot help it. It is as if a higher atonement has determined that it must be so. Whether the person does it willingly or unwillingly he must give his time, thought, sympathy and service to someone else.

Then one sees that a person receives money or comfort or love and sympathy from someone else. Whether he deserves it or does not deserve it is not the question to be thought about: one is in a certain situation and cannot help it. Whether people are willing or not willing, there is something that compels them, they cannot help it. This shows that one is born with that relation of give and take, one cannot help it. Among Hindus some people are accustomed to say that to them others are like children who have nothing to pay, just like parents will say, "We have nothing to get from our children".

This makes it clear that man is born with certain obligations which willingly or unwillingly he must fulfill. It also shows that, however powerful and however great a person may be, however good circumstances may seem, when there is to be a difficulty it cannot be helped; the difficulty will be there. And then at other times in life, in spite of all things lacking, a way is open; you have not to do much and it is all smooth. This also shows that there is a plan. It is not only qualification and cleverness that make successful, but a plan is to be accomplished. There are times when you are meant to have an easy life, success and all you wish, and other times when you cannot have these.

One may ask, "Is it so that something is born with a person, or is it the effect of a person's action on the earth?" The answer is, "Both". Suppose an artist first made in his mind a design of a certain picture and then, as he made that picture, so he was inspired by it. This suggested him to change the design and, as he went along making the picture, it changed to such an extent that it became quite different from the picture he had made before. He had thought of putting two horns on a particular figure and now he made two wings: instead of an animal it became a bird. Even to that extent life may be changed by action. A right action, a good action is productive of power; it is creative and can help much more than man can imagine.

Then arises the question to what extent man can help himself. The answer is that man has two aspects in him. One aspect is his mechanical being where he is but a machine controlled by conditions, by his impressions, by outer influences, by cosmic influences, by his actions. Everything working mechanically turns his life accordingly: he has no power over conditions, he is just a tool of influences. The more this aspect is pronounced in man, the less evolved he is. It is a sign of less evolution.

Another aspect in man is creative, in which he shows the sign of being representative of the Creator, in which he shows that he is not only linked with God but part of God: his innermost self is God. Be not surprised therefore if you hear those amazing stories of sages, masters, saints and prophets whose command worked in the cosmos and by whose will a generality, a collectivity moved as they wished it to move. It is nothing to be surprised at. Outwardly every man is almost of the same size; no man is as high as a camel, or as stout as an elephant. Outwardly men differ little, but inwardly there is no comparison in the size of the spirit, no comparison between the understanding, the power and insight of one man and that of another. One walks, one runs, one flies and one creeps; yet all walk on the same earth, live under the same sun – all called men. Nevertheless, there is no man who has not a spark of this power, who has not the possibility of changing conditions by his free will, if only he realized what he is. It is the absence of this realization which makes man a machine.

Now coming to the causes that change man's life, man's destiny: these are not only his own actions, but also the thoughts of another. For instance I have seen many cases where a loving mother was not pleased with her growing child who did not satisfy her. This must always make the child suffer in one way or another; it is never otherwise. He may become a qualified and capable man, but not having satisfied his mother is quite enough for him to quit luck.

A keen study will make us understand how these things work, but from childhood we have been so absorbed in our own life and interest that we do not think much about how the thought and feeling of those around us act upon us. A rich man, displeased with his porter or servant, may speak roughly to him or insult him, not realizing at the time that perhaps the feeling of the servant, who is dependent and bound to that particular place, who thinks that his situation keeps him in that position, is hurt. Then, when the rich man goes to his office, to his affairs, he gets that pinprick there; he does not know why. He thinks that he has given a pinprick to a servant who could not return it – but someone else returns it. He feels it but does not know that it is the answer of the same thing he has done.

The more we think about this the more we shall believe that God works through all beings – not only human beings but even through animals and birds. And when we are able to believe this we cannot help believing the words of Buddha, "The essence of all religion is harmlessness". Harmlessness does not mean refraining from killing: one can kill many without killing. In order to kill a person one does not need to murder him; a glance, a word, a thought can kill a person, and that is worse torture than death. It is this experience that will make us say, "My very feet, be conscientious lest you tread on the thorns lying on your path, lest they complain: You have crushed me".

There is no end to consideration once a person begins applying this principle. If there is any religion it is in having consideration for everyone: earnestly to consider what feeling can be touched by a moment's mistake. If there is any abode of God it is in the heart of man. If the heart is touched wrongly it has an effect upon destiny, and we do not know to what extent destiny can be changed by the feeling of another person: it can change it more than our own feeling could. One always wishes good for oneself; no one wishes to be unhappy.

Then there are planetary influences, and one may ask, "What are these planetary influences? What relation do they have with us?" The answer is that man also is a planet and, as one planet is related to another, so in the same way planets are related to mankind. Naturally the changing of the condition of a planet and what is produced by it, and what effect is produced by the planet, have an effect upon man's life.

One might ask, "Is man so small as to be under the influence of a planet?" Yes, outwardly. Outwardly man is so small as to be a drop in the ocean. If the planet is the ocean, then the individual is a drop. But inwardly the planet is a drop in the ocean of man's heart. Asif, the great philosopher says, "My ignorance, the day you will have vanished my heart will be open, and this whole universe will become a bubble in the ocean of my heart". Smallness and imperfection are the outcome of ignorance and relate the heart to limitation. The day when the heart is open the whole universe will be in it, and the source of destiny, its secret and its mystery will be in the hand of man.

What is the manner in which we should believe in destiny and free will? The best way of believing in destiny is to think that all disagreeable things we have gone through belong to destiny; they are past, we are free from them. The way how to look at free will is to think that all that is before us, all that is to come, is the outcome of free will, and to keep before us as a concentration the thought: nothing wrong will touch us, but all that is good for us, all that is best, lies before us. It is wrong to think that worse things are in store for us because destiny has kept our *karma* and intends that we must suffer, that we have to pay for our *karma*, for the one who is conscious of his *karma* will have to pay a high interest; the more he is conscious of it, the more interest he will have to pay.

In conclusion we come to understand that there are two aspects of will working through all things in life. One is the individual will, the other the divine will. When a person goes against the divine will, naturally his human will fails and he finds difficulties, because he is swimming against the tide. The moment a person works in consonance, in harmony with the divine will, things become smooth.

"But", one will say, "life has not been smooth for great personalities such as Christ. From childhood there were difficulties; his parents had to flee to the desert, and when the young Jesus was brought among the people there were still greater difficulties. The great saints and sages had great difficulties all through life; all was not smooth for them. Did they work against destiny, against the will of God?"

This question shows that to realize the will of God is difficult on the material plane. In the Bible we read, "Thy will be done on earth as in heaven". This makes us understand that it is not as easy for His will to be done on earth as it is in heaven. And this is a suggestion which teaches us a great lesson: there is a conscious will working and an unconsious will working. That unconscious working is abstract working, but the conscious working is divine working; it may be called divine will. It may have difficulties, but at the same time these difficulties have a meaning. In other words, success or failure of God, of godly power, means nothing: it is success in the end. And the success or failure of man also is nothing: it is failure in the end. If a man succeeds in collecting so much wealth or in attaining such a high position as he wants, what is the end of it? It will belong to someone else who will snatch it out of his hand. Therefore whether we have success or failure in life – if it is individual, in the end it is failure. But in the case of a godly purpose, whether it is failure or success, it is success in the end. It cannot be otherwise; it is only gain that is there.

Nanak says, "The grain that takes refuge near the centre of the grinding mill is saved". So is the man who keeps close to God and draws his power and inspiration from God. When his life is directed by that power and inspiration, whether he has difficulties or ease, his way is always smooth and the end is what it ought to be.

CHAPTER VIII

Free Will and Destiny

THE POWER an individual is acquainted with is the power of his free will – or he arrives to experience that his free will is clashing against the free will of another individual. Then he begins to see the clashing between the free will of two persons. If he happens to be powerful he gets the better of the situation; if the other happens to be more powerful then the other gets the better of it. And when they come to think about destiny the one who is slow in believing will say, "I do not know . . . .", but a man with some belief in things of the abstract will say that there is a destiny. He has every proof to convince himself of it.

There are many clever and qualified people in business, in professions, in politics, but their cleverness or qualification is not always the reason why they are successful. Very often we will find that a simple person, a person lacking cleverness or lacking qualification is successful. It is not always the rule but very often it is so: a most innocent person in a very high position, and a most clever person perhaps working as his waiter. People in high offices may have a secretary who knows more than they themselves – if not always, very often. And when we ask, "Why does that person stand here with all his cleverness while the other sits in the chair of honour? What is the reason?" – the answer is that destiny is working behind it all, fixing them and adjusting them in their places. There is a saying in the East: "The feet of the infant are to be seen from its cradle". In other words, what it is going to be you can see from the cradle; it shows signs which promise its future.

Then the question arises, "Is destiny the will of God?" And the answer is that in a sense the perfect will of God is that which the godly perceive in its fullness. If it were not so the hint in the Bible, "Thy will be done on earth as it is in heaven." would have no meaning. It does not say, "Thy will is being done on earth as it is in heaven". If this was so it would point to destiny, but it is the work of destiny and free will to come in connection in order to fulfill the will of God. It is free will and destiny, the two coming together, which bring about the will of God – but free will in its perfect state, in its fuller meaning.

A man arranges something in life — then conditions oppose it. In that case either the will, the will of God, is in that man, or the will is in the conditions. In the end, when one of these opposing forces will fail and one conquer, then the will of God is fulfilled; or when these two different aspects of will work harmoniously then the will of God is fulfilled. There is a Persian saying, "When two hearts become one they can remove mountains". In other words, when the will of one person and the free will of the other person become one, in other words harmonious, then they become a phenomenon; it works like magic. But when they do not work harmoniously then the will that is done is not the will of God, it is destiny.

I will give you a small example. A nice lady had a new maid. In order to entertain a friend who was coming to visit her, she asked the maid to go and buy a beautiful bouquet of flowers. When the maid went out and asked the price of the bouquet at the florist's, she thought, "How extraordinary on the part of my lady to spend all that money on this. I wish she would have asked me something else to do". Instead of doing what the lady had asked her she went and bought some cheese sandwiches, and was delighted in her heart thinking, "When I bring these to my lady she will be very pleased". When the lady saw what the maid had bought she was horrified. While she had expected that her friend would be entertained with flowers, there were cheese sandwiches!

This will make you understand more fully that hint in the Bible, "Thy will be done on earth as it is in heaven". What man always does out of his will is not always divine will. The divine will is done when man is in contact with the divine Spirit in himself; it is then that he begins to understand the meaning of the divine will.

Those who persevere in the path of power are persons of three kinds: the one whose way is uphill and the other whose way is downhill – both arriving at the same end, the first perhaps with greater, the other with less difficulty. The third has the most difficult way, for it is neither upwards nor downwards; it may be called the way of the cross.

The uphill way is the way where a person thinks, "I must have it, I must accomplish it". He spares no effort, no thought, no energy, nothing! He goes after it, in its pursuit till he has obtained it. This is the uphill way, because climbing to the heights of the mountain every step is very difficult and very tiresome. But if his patience helps him, if he continues to persevere, in the end no doubt he arrives at the top of the mountain. This may be seen in great or in small things. If a child tries to make a toy out of wax, and he cannot make it the first time and tries another time without accomplishing it, and the third time, after a week, makes the toy he wanted to make, he has really accomplished something. But if after having tried to make it twice he thinks, "Oh no, I cannot make it", he has failed. This path of course is a path of continual struggle.

I do not wish to bring into this the right and wrong of the motive, or the good and bad of the striving of a person, because that would take us to the subject of morals which we shall not touch just now. No matter what a person is striving for, if he perseveres continually without fail, he is coming closer and closer to the will of God.

Then there is the one who says, "Well, I will be resigned. What will be will be, what will come will come. I am ready to face it, I am ready to take it as it comes. If it happens that I should give I shall give, if it happens that I should take I shall take. Whether it is agreeable to me or not agreeable, whatever is coming, whatever conditions will offer – I will take all that life gives". This is the downhill way; it asks little effort, just like coming down from the top of a hill does not tire one so much.

Nevertheless, the one way is not more difficult than the other. It only depends on what temperament a person is born with. There is the persevering one who will go on striving against all difficulties; for him to go downhill is difficult, for him to renounce, to sacrifice is difficult. He is born with the spirit of attainment, he will go upwards in spite of all difficulties. If he lost his life it would not matter, he will go on in this path. And there is the other one who is born with renunciation. He will be content with all that comes, he is in harmony with conditions, he is in peace with people. Whether they treat him rightly or wrongly he will take it all peacefully, harmoniously, and in the end he will arrive at the same goal, in touch with the divine will.

The third way is the way of the cross: it is striving and being resigned at the same time. No doubt that is the most difficult way. The uphill way is the way of the master, the downhill the way of the saint, but the way of the cross is the prophetic way. The prophets, in all ages in whichever part of the world they have come, have striven continually and have been resigned continually to all that comes. On the one hand active, on the other hand passive they progress through life. Therefore their life is being pulled from both sides. When they walk one leg is pulled from the back, the other leg is pulled from the front; there are always two sides to their lives.

At the same time either of these qualities can be found in each person as a temperament, and the secret of one's life's success and the fulfilment of one's life's purpose lie in taking one's natural way. If it happens that a man is born with a quality of striving continually, his way is striving. He must not be passive, he must not be resigned, for if he does so he will fail and not accomplish his life's purpose. But if it happens to be his temperament that he is resigned, always resigned to all that comes, then he must take that way. There is nobility of spirit, of soul, in both these ways. But if unfortunately it happens that a person is born with these two qualities at the same time, his problem in life will be the most difficult, for he can neither do one thing nor the other. No doubt if he goes on in this way, in the end there is success – but success in the spiritual sense, not in a material sense.

Now the question arises whether destiny is working blindly, or whether it is working intelligently, consciously. Is it working with wisdom? The answer is that to some extent it is always working more or less consciously, but at the same time in its different ways of working its condition is different. For instance, a person has the habit of getting up at night while still asleep; he walks in the room and knocks against the door or the wall because his eyes are closed. That is one way of moving about in the room. There is another way: a person is thinking of his poetry, he does not know where he is going, whether to a corner of the room or to one or an other side; his mind is thinking of the poetry. He is walking but does not know towards what he is walking. His walking has a meaning, and has not a meaning. His walking at that time is a stimulus to his inspiration; it helps him, but it is not conscious walking. Yet he knows that he is walking. And there is a third condition: when a person intentionally goes into a certain corner of the room in order to fetch something; he has a purpose in going there. Destiny works in these ways; the nature of life, of the whole of life, can be understood by studying the nature of man.

Question: Is destiny working sometimes blindly, like the man walking in his sleep?

Answer: It is for a demonstration that I have tried to put something in words which cannot be put in words. If I were to say that there are only seven notes I would be wrong, and still I would be right too, because there are seven accepted notes. But the gap between each note can be filled, if we distinguish them clearly, by perhaps five, six notes – or more or less. So what we call "blindly" is according to our perception of blindness. When we see this according to the idea of the Absolute, as the one and whole Being, then we cannot say that it is working blindly or unconsciously. It is what it is; it may show its work in different stages of consciousness, but it cannot be blind, it is still conscious. There is still a wisdom behind it, but not that wisdom which we understand as wisdom.

For instance, a person walked in his sleep in his room while a thief was trying to take something out of his cupboard, and in his sleep he fell on the thief who then ran away, fearing that the man had got up. Here a purpose is fulfilled without intention. His walking in his sleep accomplished something, although the person did not walk in his sleep in order to fall upon the thief. So all things that happen, whether we understand the meaning or not, have their purpose and by that something is accomplished. Perhaps we know it at that moment, or perhaps we shall know it afterwards.

Question: What is the distinction between inertia and the disposition you have characterized as the second path?
Answer: Inertia could be understood as a kind of weakness, but this path is a kind of strength. It is a very strong person who can resign; a person who can sacrifice, tolerate and resign is not always a weak person. Yes, it is possible that a weak person out of weakness may tolerate, may sacrifice and may be resigned, but his feeling at doing so is different from that of the brave and courageous soul. The person whose character I described as saint shows the greatest bravery one could show. Is he not brave who patiently takes all things which trouble him, which hurt him, which torture his life, who suffers and endures all? A weak person will give an outlet to these things. For instance there is an artist whose art is not appreciated, who has no place in the world of art, and for some days he has to remain without a penny. If he busies himself in his studio, still working with no bread and butter in the house to eat and if he does not speak about it to anybody, is he not courageous? Is he not brave? Is he not noble? Is this weakness? No, the one who lacks these qualities would go out and say, "Look at me, in what condition I am!" That would be different. There is great strength in a person who can take all things with resignation.

Question: In the end, looking at the events when they have happened, must we not say that all is done according to the will of God?
Answer: Well, that is a Sufi way: begin with free will and finish with the will of God. The only consolation when a thing is not done is to interpret is as the will of God.

Question: Is the way of the cross the happy and satisfactory way?
Answer: If it is happy and satisfactory to you, it is. If it is not so, it is not.

CHAPTER IX

Kismet[4]

THE QUESTION is always brought up: Is there a power which rules the universe and controls all our actions, or are we free to do as we please; is our situation the result of our good or bad deeds, or are our actions and situation governed by the influence of the planets?

In answer to this I will first mention what contradicts each of these principles. If God makes us act then we are not responsible; then it is all God and we have no responsibility. If we are quite free then I will say that you are your own well-wisher, and no one will be his own ill-wisher. Then whatever you wish for – success, riches or whatever it is – you will have it. It seems however that it is not so. If happiness and good fortune were the result of good actions then everyone would be good, and no one would be bad. But we see that many very wicked people are very fortunate: every day a wicked deed and every day a good fortune – while many very good people are always unfortunate and in difficulties. Christ and all the prophets and saints suffered great adversities.

If everything is the outcome of the influence of the planets, then I will say that you should stay in your room when there is a planet that is unfavourable to you; you should do nothing. Also when there is a planet that is favourable you should do nothing, because the planet will bring you everything by itself.

Having told you the contradictions I will now tell you the truth of each principle. There are four great powers that govern the world: *Qadr* and *Qadha*, *Jalal* and *Jamal*.

Qadha is the power that governs the whole. For instance the king governs the whole country, but power is given to viceroys and to governors. The governor governs a whole province, but power is given to a commissioner. The commisioner governs his district; he knows more about its affairs than the governor knows and the governor does not interfere in his district. Each human being is given a power:

this is *Qadr*. In the same way a mother allows her child to go as far as the end of the room, but no farther: from here as far as the end of the room let it destroy as much as it pleases, but not more than that.

When we see a wicked person very happy we may think, "Has God forgotten him?" No, his jar is not yet full. When it is overfilled it will flow over and bring destruction to himself and those around him. Sometimes a very good person is very unhappy in life, but when the jar of his good actions is overfilled it flows over and brings happiness to him and those around him. We have some power, but our action is so limited; our power of seeing is so limited. We are very small.

The forces of *jalal* and *jamal* are the creative and the responsive forces. We are sometimes creative and sometimes we are responsive. *Jalal* is creative, *jamal* is responsive. The singer is creative, the one who hears and enjoys is responsive. All our troubles are owing to our lack of creative or responsive power. If we are in a situation which is difficult for us, which is hard, which we dislike, it is owing to our lack of creative power to make another situation for ourselves. When a situation, an opportunity would benefit us and help us and we are not benefited, it is owing to our lack of response. Everything in the world is creative or responsive. The benefactor is creative, he who is benefited is responsive.

But however interesting, however attractive these things are, the name of God is much greater; without the study of the name of God they are nothing. That is the only thing that is great, the only thing that is beautiful, the only thing of value, the only thing worthwhile.

Question: What gives the planets their influence?
Answer: The soul before its manifestation on earth passes through the sun, the moon and the planets. As there is only one sun and one moon each soul passes through sun and moon. There are many planets and each soul passes through one planet, not through all. This gives the soul an affinity with a certain planet, and through this affinity the planet has its influence upon the soul, upon the individual. There are of course in man's life many other circumstances and influences

beside those of the planet, and the outer influences, also man's will, may be stronger than the planet.

On its return journey the soul has also to pass through the planet, the sun and the moon.

CHAPTER X

Free Will–Aphorisms

IF GOD gave man free will and so refused to make his decisions for him, no other individual has a right to butt in and attempt to force a man's decisions.

So you can only help a person within the scope of his own character.

I mean that your capacity to help is limited by his ability to help himself.

And that must be the tragedy of God.

Every person has his own way in life, and that particular way is most suited for him.

Trouble not about the past, worry not over the future but concern yourself with the present,

for it is the present which is the picture of the past and the design for the future.

Looking at the past and finding one's errors is like cracking nuts and finding a shrivelled kernel.

Looking at the past and recognizing one's mistakes is like mounting the steps of a staircase.

Do not imagine what you do not wish to happen.
Do not say what you do not wish to be done.

The fatalist makes human beings as chairs and tables.
The mystic makes even chairs and tables living beings.

In spite of all his limitation a wonderful power is hidden in man's soul.

What makes man helpless is ignorance of his free will.

Free will is the basis of the whole life.

Free will is the mighty power, the God-power, hidden in man,

And it is ignorance which keeps man from his divine heritage.

When the rocks are asleep leaving Us to use them for whatever purpose We may,

when the trees are resigned to Our will to bear whatever fruit We may want them to bear,

when the animals are carried along with their passions and appetites,

We have made you partner in Our dominion and have given you a share in Our mercy, compassion, wisdom and righteousness,

that your heart may expand so that it may rise to Our perfection.

I erase the past out of my mind, brighten the present, and build a hope for the future.

CHAPTER XI

The Seer

1

WHY IS one person called a seer when we all have eyes and the power of sight? What else is needed to be a seer than a doctor's certificate that our sight is keen?

There are some people who take in everything the contrary way. While everybody stands upon his feet with his head up, in India you may see faqirs and Yogis who stand upon their head with their feet in the air; they wish to know what experience they may have by seeing in this way. Everybody is born with an inclination to certain things, an inclination to sleep, to eat and to drink, an inclination to comfort; in this too these faqirs take the contrary way. They sit or stand in one position for hours and hours; they fast, they do not drink for days and weeks; they torture themselves in these ways. It is not that there is any virtue in this, it is not that God is pleased with their torturing themselves, nor that their self, their ego is pleased with it. It is only that they wish to see what experience they get by this.

We all have the tendency to see faults in another; they try to see faults in themselves. They see virtue in sin, and sin in virtue. The world says, "That man is bad, he has done this, he has done that". They do not call anyone bad, they see what good there is even in the one who is called bad. Therefore Christ, because he was a dervish, did not condemn the sinner. He said to those Jews who thought themselves righteous, "Your father is the devil", that is: the *nafs*, the ego. In every virtue, in everything appearing in the garb of virtue, there is sin, or at least conceit: "I am virtuous, I am moral, I am religious". This is the worst of virtue. Therefore Hafiz says, "Show me the way of the free-thinkers. Suitable it appears to me, for the way of virtue and piety seems very far off and long".

We all like to be honoured, to be esteemed, to have attention paid to us; these faqirs and Yogis wish to know what experience there is in disgrace. They call the living dead and the dead living. Praise, consideration from people is nothing to them; they think it is praise from the dead, creatures of four days. The plant, the fire, the wall, things that to us are dead, speak to them, reveal everything to them. In the jungle every tree, every stone speaks to them.

If there is a chair, a table, a piano in the room, we say there is something; if not, we say there is nothing. To them this space which we call nothing is full of everything; in it is everything. They call everything nothing, and in what to us is nothing they see everything.

What is learning without seeing? Christ did not have a degree from a university – he saw. Learned people are always disputing. One says, "There are five elements"; after ten years another comes and says, "No, there are twenty elements"; after twenty-five years another comes and says, "I have discovered the true thing: there are seventy-five". Seers from the first day till now have never differed in the truth which they all hold.

2

The seer sees more than the astrologer can see; he sees much more; there is no comparison. But the difference is that the seer does not speak about it. If he did so, he would become just like the astrologer. For the seer every person's soul is just like an open letter, but if he would begin to say this his sight would become dimmer every day, because it is a trust given to him by God. If he were to divulge it, it would become dim. With spiritual trust they are entrusted who can keep the trust, who can keep a secret.

CHAPTER XII

Does the Consciousness see with the Physical Eyes?

WHETHER THE consciousness sees without eyes, or whether it needs the eyes to see, is a question that comes to the mind of all metaphysicians. If the consciousness can see alone, without the help of the eyes, why were these eyes created? There are people who can see things that are happening at a distance of many hundreds of miles and things that will happen many years later. They see what may be happening not only in their sleep but at all times.

Some time ago there was in Delhi a murshid whose name was Shah Alam. One day he was having his hair cut, and was looking in a little looking-glass while the barber was cutting his hair. In India the haircutters use such little looking-glasses. Suddenly – God knows what he saw in it – the murshid dashed the mirror on the ground so that it broke into pieces. His mureeds who were with him were astonished; the barber also was amazed, wondering what had caused him to throw down the mirror with such violence.

At that time one of his mureeds was travelling by sea from Arabia to India, and his ship was in a great storm and in great danger. He called upon his murshid for help; the murshid saw his peril and saved him. Afterwards the mureed told the others what had happened.

In Hyderabad there was a dervish who had the habit of smoking very strong hashish. When he let the smoke out of his mouth he used to look into it and to answer any questions that were put to him. If someone asked him, "Where is my uncle at present?", he would say, "Your uncle? Calcutta . . . such and such bazar . . . now I turn to the left . . . the second house. Your uncle is sitting in his room. His servant is at his side and his child is standing before him". Whatever he was asked he answered. Did he see it without eyes? No, his consciousness had not its external self before it and therefore it was able to see through the eyes of another – through the eyes of the uncle or any other.

When I was in Russia there was an African, a very

ordinary man, not a man of any education. His condition was such that at night when he was asleep, he knew who came into his room, what they said, what they did. This was because his soul was in and about the house and it saw through the eyes of whoever came there.

In the same way the universal Consciousness sees through the eyes of every being on earth. It is looking through the eyes of all the millions of beings upon earth at the same time. The thief may steal something, hide it, carry it off and think, "No one sees me". He cannot escape the sight of that Consciousness which is within himself, looking through his eyes. It is not that God from a distance looks down and sees all creatures upon earth. No, he sees through the very eyes of the beings themselves.

The faculty of seeing exists in the Consciousness from the beginning. Therefore among the names of God are *Basir* the Seer and *Sami*, the Hearer. *Basarat*, the faculty of seeing, becomes more definite, exact and concrete the nearer it comes to manifestation.

One may ask, "Is God not limited by this, made helpless, dependent?" If it seems so to us it is because we deduct from God a part of His Being. We occupy a part of the ground and call it ours, our self. Really it is all God, the One Being. A Hindustani poet has said,

What shall I call 'I'? Whatever I see it is all Thou.

Body, mind, soul – all are Thou. Thou art, I am not.

CHAPTER XIII

Seeing

ONE CAN see, one can look, and one can observe. These three words denote the same action, yet each word suggests something different. By observing we understand something about that which we see, by seeing we take full notice of it; by looking – whether we understand it or not, whether we take notice of it or not – we have at least cast our glance on something. So there are three conditions: looking at a thing on its surface, seeing a thing properly, and seeing a thing with complete observation, understanding it while looking at it.

Every person notices things in these three ways. That which interests him most he observes keenly; that which attracts his thought he sees, he takes notice of; that upon which his glance falls he looks at. There are therefore three different effects made upon man by all that he sees: a deeper effect of that which he has observed fully, a clear effect of that which he has seen, and a passing effect of that which he has glanced through. So naturally among all those who live under the sun there are thinkers, there are seers, and there are those who have two eyes.

There is another side to this question: a person who is walking has a certain experience of the way he has gone through; the one who goes the same way in an automobile has a different experience, and the one who flies through the air in an aeroplane has a still different experience. Perhaps the one who was walking was not able to reach his goal at the same speed as the one in the automobile and the one in the aeroplane, but the observation he made, the sights he saw, and the experience he had are not to be compared with those of the other two.

In this way our minds work: there is one man whose mind works at the speed of the aeroplane, and there is another man whose mind works at the speed of an automobile. The one whose mind works at the speed of a man walking will perhaps not think as quickly as the other persons, but what he thinks he will think thoroughly, what he sees he will see thoroughly. It is he who will have insight into things, it is he who will understand the hidden law behind things, because the activity of his mind is normal.

Of course quick thinking does not always depend upon the quick activity of the mind: sometimes it is a quality of the mind. An intelligent person also thinks quickly, but that is another thing. As there is a difference between two stones, a pebble and a diamond – both stones, the one precious, the other dull – so these are two different qualities of the mind: one person thinking quickly and intelligently, the other thinking quickly and being always mistaken. The latter is mistaken because he thinks quickly, the former has that quality of mind which, even in quick thinking, makes him think rightly.

The rhythm of thinking has a great deal to do with one's life. When the three, who have travelled the same way on foot, by automobile and by aeroplane, meet together and speak of their experiences, there will be great differences. And so it is that people who have gone through the same life, who have lived under the same sun, who have been born on the same earth, are yet so different in their mentality. The reason is that their minds have travelled at different speeds. Their experiences are quite different though they have gone the same way.

A seer is the one who has not looked, but who has seen. And how has he seen? By controlling the impulse of walking quickly, by resisting the temptation of going to the right or to the left, by going steadily towards the object that he has to reach. All these things make one a seer.

There are wrong interpretations of the word seer. Sometimes people say, "This person is a clairvoyant or a spiritualist, he sees fairies, ghosts or spirits". But that is a different kind of person; he is not a seer. The seer need not see the world unseen. There is much to be seen here in the visible world; for there is so much hidden from the eyes of every man which he could see in this objective world that, if all his life he was contemplating upon seeing in this objective world, he would find sufficient things to see and to think about. It is a childish curiosity on the part of some persons when they want to see something that no one has seen. It is out of vanity that they tell they see something which others do not see; it is to satisfy their curiosity that they see something which is not to be seen in this world of objects. The world seen and the world unseen, both are one and the same, and they are here. What we cannot see is the world unseen, and what we can see is the world seen. It is not that what we cannot see hides itself from our eyes, it is because we close our eyes to it.

Then there is long sight, short sight and medium sight. There are some who can see far beyond, far back, or long before things happen. These also are forms of sight. Another person only sees what is immediately before him, what is next to him, and sees nothing of what is behind him. His influence is limited, because everything that stands next to him influences him; he cannot see far behind, nor can he see far before him. There is another person who reasons about what he sees; this is medium sight. He reasons about it as far as his reason allows. He cannot see beyond his reasoning; he goes so far and no further. Naturally when these three persons meet and speak together, each has his own language. It is not surprising if the one does not understand the point of view of the other, because each one has his own sight, and according to that sight he looks at things. No one can give his own sight to another person in order to make him see differently.

If in all ages spiritual people have taught faith, it was not because they wished that no one should think for himself and should accept everything in faith which was taught to him. If they had had that intention they would not have been spiritual people. Nevertheless, however clever a person may be, however devoted and enthusiastic, if he is without faith the spiritual persons cannot impart their knowledge to him, for there is no such thing as spiritual knowledge in the sense of learning. If there is anything spiritual that can be imparted to the pupil it is the point of view, it is the outlook on life. If a person already has that outlook on life he does not need spiritual guidance, but if he has not then words of explanation will not explain it to him, for it is a point of view, it cannot be explained in words.

However much a person might explain the sight he saw

when he was on the top of a mountain to a man who never climbed the mountain, that man will hear it and perhaps refuse to believe all that the other says; or if he has trust in this person who explains to him what he saw from the top of the mountain, then perhaps he will begin to listen to his guidance. He will not see the sight, but he will listen and he will benefit by the experience of the one who has seen it. But the one who goes on the top of the mountain will see it for himself, he will have the same experience.

There is still another side to this question, and that is from which height one looks at life. When a person looks at life standing on the ground his sight is quite different from that of a person who is climbing the mountain, and it is again a different outlook when a person has climbed on to the top of the mountain. What are these degrees? These are degrees of consciousness. When a person looks at life as "I and all else", that is one point of view. When a person sees all else and forgets "I", that is another point of view. And when a person sees all and identifies it with "I", that is another point of view again. The difference these points of view make in a person's outlook is so vast that words can never explain it. One gets an idea of what is called *Nirwana*, or cosmic consciousness, by reaching the top of the mountain, and an idea of communicating with God a person gets when he has climbed the mountain, and the idea of "I and you and he and she and it" is clearer when a person is standing on the ground.

Spiritual progress is expansion of the soul. It is not always desirable to live on the top of the mountain, because the ground also is made for man. What is desirable is to have one's feet on the ground and the head as high as the top of the mountain. A person who can observe from all sides, from all angles, will find a different experience seeing from every angle; looking at every side will give him a new knowledge, a knowledge different from what he had known before.

Then there is the question of seeing and not seeing. This is understood by the mystics. It is being able to see at will and being able to overlook. It is not easy for a person to overlook, it is also something one must learn. There is much that one can see, that one must see, and there is much that one may not see, that it is better one does not see. If one cannot see, that is a disadvantage, but there is no disadvantage in not seeing something that one may not see; because there are so many things that could be seen, one may just as well avoid seeing them.

That person lacks mastery who is held by that which he sees. He cannot help seeing it, although he does not want to see it. But the one who has his sight in his hand sees what he wants to see, and what he does not want to see he does not see. That is mastery. As it is true of the eyes that what is before them they see and what is behind them they do not see, so it is true of the mind: what is before it it sees and what is behind it it does not see. And so a person who sees may see one side, while always the other side is hidden. Naturally therefore, if this objective world is before his eyes, the other world is hidden from his sight, because he sees what is before him; he does not see what is behind him. And as it is true that what is behind him a person can only see by turning his head back, so it is also true that what the mind does not see can be seen by the mind when it is turned the other side. What is learned in esotericism, in mysticism, is the turning of the mind from the outer vision to the inner vision.

You might ask: what profit does one derive from it? If it is profitable to rest at night after a whole day's work, so it is profitable to turn one's mind from this world of variety in order to rest it and to give it another experience, which belongs to it, which is its own, which it needs. It is this experience which is attained by the meditative process. A person who is able to think and not able to forget, a person who is able to speak but not able to keep silent, a person who is able to move and not able to keep still, a person who is able to cry and not able to laugh – that person does not know mastery. It is like having one hand, it is like standing on one foot. To have complete experience of life one must be able to act and to take repose, one must be able to think, and one must be able to keep silent.

There are many precious things in nature and in art, things that are beyond value, yet there is nothing in this world that is more precious than sight, and that which is most precious is insight: to be able to see, to be able to understand, to be able to learn and to be able to know. That is the greatest gift that

God can give, and all other things in life are small compared to it. In order to enrich one's knowledge, in order to raise one's soul to higher spheres, in order to allow one's consciousness to expand to perfection – if there is anything that one can do, it is to help oneself in every way to open the sight, which is the sign of God in man. It is the opening of the sight which is called the soul's unfoldment.

CHAPTER XIV

The Different Stages of Spiritual Development

IN SANSKRIT three distinct words are used: *Atma* which means the soul or a soul, an individual, a person; *Mahatma*, a high soul, an illuminated being, a spiritual personality; *Paramatma*, the divine man, the self-realized person, the God-conscious soul. As you have read in the Gayan*, "If you only explore him, there is a lot in man"[5], so man – taken as every man – has in the spiritual spheres a very wide scope of development, a scope of development that an ordinary mind cannot imagine. The term "divine man" has always been connected with man, and very few realize that it means God-man. The reason is that certain religiously inclined people have separated so much from God that they have filled the gap between man and God with what they call religion, a faith that stands for ever as a dividing wall between God and man. To man all sins are attributed, and to God all purity. It is a good idea – but far from truth.

Now as to the first word that I have used, *Atma*, which means man: mankind can be divided into three principal categories. In one category man is the animal man; in another he can be the devil man, and in the third he can be the human man. A Hindustani poet has used two different words to distinguish this idea. He says, "There are many difficulties in life, for it is even difficult for man to be a person".

The animal man is the one who concerns himself with food and drink, and whose actions are in no way different from those of an animal, who is content with the satisfaction of his natural appetites.

The man who represents devilish qualities is the one in whom the ego, the self, has become so strong and so powerful – and therefore so blind – that it has almost wiped away from him any sense of gentleness, of kindness, of justice. He is the one who takes pleasure in causing harm or

Gayan, or "Notes from the Unstruck Music" – a book with poetry, aphorisms and prayers.

hurt to another person, the one who returns evil for good done to him, the one whose pleasure it is to do the wrong thing. The number of those belonging to this category is large.

Then there is the human man, in whom sentiment is developed. Perhaps according to the physician's idea he may not be the normal person, but from the point of view of the mystic a person who has balance between thought and sentiment, who is awakened to the feeling of another, who is conscientious about everything he does and the effect it produces upon others – that person is beginning to be a human person. In other words, even for man to be a man is not an easy thing. Sometimes it takes a lifetime.

Then we come to the *Mahatma*, an illuminated soul. This soul looks at life from a different point of view, his outlook becomes different. He thinks about others more than about himself. His life is devoted to actions of beneficence. He expects no appreciation or reward for all that he can do for others. He does not look for praise and he is not afraid of blame. On one side connected with God, on the other side connected with the world he lives his life as harmoniously as possible.

There are three categories of *Mahatmas*. One *Mahatma* is busy struggling with himself and struggling with conditions before him and around him. One may ask, "Why this struggle?" The answer is that there is always a conflict between the person who wishes to go upwards and the wind that blows him downwards. The wind that blows a person downwards is continually felt. It is felt at every moment by the person who takes a step on the path of progress. It is a conflict with the self, it is a conflict with others, it is a conflict with conditions – conflicts that come from all around, till every bit of that *Mahatma* is tested and tried, till every bit of his patience is exhausted and his ego is ground. A hard rock is turned into a soft paste – then appears the personality of a *Mahatma*. As a soldier in the war has so many wounds, and still more impressions which remain in his heart as wounds, such is the condition of this warrior who goes on the spiritual path. Everything stands against him: his friends, who may not know it, his foes, conditions, the atmosphere, the self. And therefore the wounds that he has to experience through this struggle, and the impressions that he receives through it, make him a spiritual personality, a personality which becomes an influence, a power, a personality which is difficult to resist, which is overwhelming.

The next category of *Mahatma* is the one who learns his lesson by passivity, resignation, sacrifice, love, devotion and sympathy.

There is a love that is like the light of the candle: blow, and it is gone. It can only remain as long as it is not blown, it cannot withstand blowing. There is a love that is like the sun that rises and reaches the zenith, and then sets and disappears. The duration of this love is longer. And there is a love that is like divine Intelligence, that was and is and will be. The closing and the opening of the eyes will not take away intelligence; the rising and the setting of the sun will not affect intelligence; the lighting and the putting out of the candle does not affect intelligence.

When that something which through the winds and storms endures and through the rise and fall stands firm – when that love is created – then a person's language becomes different; the world cannot understand it. Once love has reached the Sovereign of love, it is like the water of the sea that has risen as vapour, has formed clouds over the earth, and then pours down as rainfall. The continual outpouring of such a heart is unimaginable; not only human beings, but even birds and beasts must feel its influence, its effect. It is a love that cannot be put into words, a love that radiates, proving the warmth it has by its atmosphere. This resigned soul of the *Mahatma* may appear weak to someone who does not understand, for he takes praise and blame in the same way and he takes all that is given to him, favour or disfavour, pleasure or pain – all that comes – with resignation.

For the third category of these high souls there is struggle on the one hand and resignation on the other, and this is a most difficult way of progress: to take one step forwards, and another step backwards, and so to go on. There is no mobility in the progress, because one thing is contrary to the other. On one side power is working, on the other side love; on one side kingliness, on the other side slavery. As the great Ghaznavi said in a Persian poem, "I, as an emperor, have thousands of slaves ready at my call. But since love has kindled my heart, I have become the slave of slaves". On the one hand activity, on the other hand passivity.

The first example of the *Mahatma* may be called the master, the next the saint, and the third the prophet.

With the *Paramatma* we come to the third stage of the awakening of the consciousness, and the difference that it makes is this: an ordinary person, *Atma*, gives a greater importance to the world and a lesser importance to God; the illuminated person, *Mahatma*, gives a greater importance to God and a lesser importance to the world; but the third person, the *Paramatma*, gives and does not give importance to God or to the world. He is what he is. If you say, "It is all true", he says, "Yes, it is all true". If you say, "All is false and true", he says, "Yes, it is all false and true". If you say, "Is it not true?", he says, "Yes, it is not true". If you say, "All is false and not true", he says, "Yes, all is false and not true". His language becomes gibberish, you can only be puzzled by it, for communication in language is better with someone who speaks your language. As soon as the other person's word has a different sense, his language is different; it is a language foreign to what you speak in your everyday life. The *Paramatma's* "yes" may be "no", his "no" may be "yes": a word means nothing to him, it is the sense. And it is not that he has got the sense, he is the sense: he becomes that which the other man pursues.

The Buddhistic term *Nirvana* means the stage where a person arrives at God-consciousness or all-consciousness. It is at this stage that a soul arrives. And why should not man have that privilege? If man has not that privilege, how can God have it? It is through man that God realizes His perfection. As man God becomes conscious of His Godship, and it is in this gradual progress – to begin as a soul and to arrive at that realization which makes that soul a divine soul – that lies the purpose of life. The whole creation is purposed to bring about that realization. It is that realization which is recognized by the name *Rasul**.

**Rasul* = "the fulfilment of God's purpose".
  (See *Vadan*, chapter *Gayatri*).

You may ask, "If one soul has arrived at this realization, what is it to us?" But it is not the one: it is one and all at the same time.

CHAPTER XV

The Prophetic Tendency–The Prophetic Mission

I WILL give an explanation of two questions which I have very often been asked: What was the object of the prophetic mission? Why is it necessary for man to be taught by another, by his fellowman? Why cannot each one find within himself the way to the light, to illumination?

The prophetic tendency exists in every part of the manifestation. Among the *jinn* and the heavenly beings there is the prophetic tendency and also in every part of nature: in the mineral and vegetable kingdoms, among the animals as well as among men.

There would be no diamond mines in the earth if there were not one spark of a diamond which causes every other atom of the earth with which it comes in contact to become a diamond. It is the same with the ruby. The diamond wants to make everything else become a diamond; the ruby wants to make every other atom into a ruby.

Among the plants in the jungle – not where man has planted and sown, but in the jungle which has not been touched – you will see that if there is one mango tree, it will make a thousand mangoes grow; if there is one fragrant flower, a thousand fragrant flowers will be near it; if there is one sweet fruit, there will be hundreds of sweet fruits.

Among the animals there are many instances of this tendency of which I will tell you some cases that I have seen. Sometimes in India the monkeys come to a village from the forest and break down all the roofs of the houses. There is always one among them who is the leader. When he jumps, all the other monkeys jump after him; when he wants to go back to the forest, they all want to go back to the forest.

In India there are the Jains; their religion is harmlessness: to be harmless to every creature. When the Jains cook their food, they prepare some for themselves, some always for the priest and, if they can afford it, also a little for the animals. In every street of a town we have dogs, ten, twelve, twenty-five dogs, according to the length of the street. The dogs are fed in this way; everyone is their master, and everyone feeds them. Among the dogs there is always one who is the leader. When a dog from another street appears, the dogs all collect behind their leader and when he barks they all bark; when he attacks they all attack, and so they drive the other dog away.

In the Northern provinces near Nainital and in Nepal, at the foot of the Himalayas, there is a jungle in which there are elephants. The people have many ways of catching them, and one way is to dig a small pit and cover it over with branches. Then they hang their swing-like nets up in a tree, and they stay for some days and watch for the elephants. They are happy in the trees, because the climate permits it. Then if a herd of elephants happens to go that way and an elephant puts his foot into the pit, he goes down, he cannot help himself. Then he cries out; the other elephants look on from a distance, but are afraid to come near, and the men have a kind of fireworks with which they frighten them away if they do.

Now in a troop of elephants there is always one who walks in front. He holds a stout branch in his trunk and hits the ground with it before every step he takes to see whether there is a pit. He knows a thousand other dangers and he knows this danger too. Then if the ground is safe he goes forward and all the others follow him. They have such confidence in him that wherever he goes they go too. This shows that the tendency to leadership exists among the elephants, the tendency to self-sacrifice. The elephant who is the leader goes first, thinking, "If there is a pit I may fall in, and the other elephants will be safe". He never goes anywhere where it is not safe, and if some elephant is caught, it is some small elephant which has no sense and does not follow the leader.

In Nepal the Maharaja had an elephant who was a leader of elephants. He was in the Maharaja's house and the Maharaja gave orders that no one should ride him but he himself, because he honoured the elephant, recognizing his qualities. I have seen this. Whenever Maharaja Bir Shamsher went into the forest elephant hunting this elephant was taken too. The Maharaja had named him Bijili, lightning. He was a very small elephant, but when they failed to make a catch he was sent out and, when another elephant saw him, he at once followed him. So Bijili always came back with another elephant – such was his magnetism. He did not like to catch elephants, because he had the quality of mercy. He would never go unless he was forced by the mahouts, and when he saw the other elephants he turned his head away.

Even among the animals there is this prophetic tendency. Sometimes we see this prophetic tendency in parents. Whatever way they themselves may have followed, they wish to train their child the best way for the higher way. Sometimes it is found in a friend. Whatever undesirable way he may have followed himself, he wishes to save his friend from it. It is only the chosen ones, the blessed souls, who have this tendency. It is not in every child's parents that this tendency is found, nor in every friend. To have such parents, such a friend, is the greatest blessing.

To come now to the question what was the object of the prophetic mission I will say that the evolution of men was very much nearer to the animals in ancient times than it is now. They thought only of eating and drinking and of taking the best things from another, caring nothing about the result of their actions, unless they were awakened from this animal existence.

In India, in the villages and small towns there are watchmen who go through every street, calling, "Awake, awake, lest thieves come!" They call at twelve o'clock, at one o'clock, at two o'clock, at three o'clock, all night. The prophets were sent to awaken. When a person cannot wake up in the morning of his own accord, then the alarm-clock awakes him. The prophets were this alarm.

Sometimes power was needed to arouse people; then the prophet was a king, like Solomon. Sometimes beauty appealed most; then Joseph came whose appearance, whose face was so beautiful that all hearts were melted by his magnetism. It has always been the intention of the divine Power to send that prophet whom the time needed. When a venerable life was revered there was Jacob, whose life was so venerable that all bowed before him. When music was most admired David came, who was gifted with a beautiful voice, who played the harp and gave his message in song. Thus every prophet came in the manner that the age could understand.

Man is the aim of the creation and the highest being, because it is man alone who knows the purpose for which he was manifested, the reason why he is here. Cats and dogs do not know this, because their intelligence is not developed enough for this, and also because their self is before their eyes. The prophets had renounced their self: that is why they were prophets. When the self is gone, then all the other selves come. When the self is before the eyes, then the soul is blinded.

Every other being in the manifestation wants to become man. The *jinn* want to become man, the rocks want to become man, the plants want to become man, the animals want to become man. If you go to a riverbed and take up the pebbles, how many pebbles do you not find that show the human face. Sometimes the nose is absent, sometimes the lips are absent, but a partial face you will often find; sometimes they have cracks and lines showing it. What a great thing this shows us: everything is striving to become the human face, to become man.

But it is not man as he is that the divine power wishes to produce. The man we want is not the man eating, drinking and sleeping like the animals. If man wishes to know what he should be, he should compare himself with the animals: if he eats, they also eat; if he drinks, they also drink; if he sleeps, they also sleep. They have their passions and hatred and anger just as he has. If he has only that, then he is not man. It is only in man that kindness, sympathy, discipline, self-sacrifice, meekness, humility, and such qualities are found. And if we see any of them in animals, in dogs, cats, horses and cattle – such as faithfulness in the dog, obedience and courage in the horse – it is only the reflection of man, their association with man.

Then there is responsibility. Man alone has the sense of responsibility. Animals do not have it. About this a Hadith says, "We sent Our burden upon the mountains, and the mountains refused. We sent Our burden upon the plants, and the plants refused. We sent Our burden upon the animals, and the animals ran away at the sight of it. We sent Our burden upon man, and he accepted it". This means that only man has taken the responsibility for his actions.

Then a Sura says, "Verily, man is cruel and foolish". Foolish, because he has taken upon himself that which is God's. There are many who run away from marriage, because they think that a wife and children are a responsibility. They do not think that wife and children are God's and that He takes care of what is His. Cruel, because he uses his will and strength – which are God's – to harm others. Our will, our strength are God's, and yet we say "my" and "mine"; we claim them for ourselves.

The watchman calls from night till morning. In the day the alarm-clock is not needed because it is day. The prophets were sent from night till morning. They came with the same message under different names. The same divine wisdom spoke in each of them, but if a Hebrew had been asked, "Do you recognize Krishna and Rama?", he would have said, "I have never heard of Krishna and Rama. I recognize Moses because that is written in my book" If a Hindu was asked, "Do you recognize Moses or Christ?", he would say, "No, I recognize Rama and Krishna and Vishnu and the Vedanta. You may keep Christ and Moses, I will keep Rama, Krishna and Vishnu". There are some who prefer the Kabbala to the Bible, they recognize the Kabbala. If you ask a Roman Catholic he will say, "If there is any church it is mine". They have all recognized the name, the personality – they have not recognized the truth. They want to keep Krishna in the temple, Christ in the church, and Moses shut up in the synagogue. That is why so many now are seeking for the truth.

In each age the message was revealed more and more – in accordance with the world's capacity to hear it – until the last and plainest revelation, the message of Muhammad, the seal of prophecy. After this no more prophets were needed. The world was awakened to the understanding of the true reality. Now is not the time to wait for the coming of another prophet; now is the time to awaken to the truth within ourselves, and if there is a friend who has gone this way before, now is the time to ask his advice.

The Sufi's work is not to interfere with anyone's religion, nor to force a belief upon anyone. He does not say, "Believe this". The murshid is a friend and a guide. He advises, he does not force anything upon you.

You may be a Christian – I was not born in a Christian family, but no Christian is more touched than I am by the words of Christ that I read. If they are rightly understood, they alone are enough to make you a saint. They say that in the end he was crucified upon the cross, but I say that from his birth onward every moment of his life was a crucifixion. For the souls of the prophets the world is too rough, their hearts are too tender for it.

No Brahmin has studied the Vedanta with more interest than I have. If you know Brahma, if you know God, you are a Brahmin. Whether the Brahmin recognizes you or not is another matter.

The Sufi says, "You wish to know about illumination, about revelation? You wish to know about inspiration? This is the way for you to follow: believe as much as your intelligence allows you to believe, as much as you can reach. Do not believe what your intelligence does not allow you to believe". He recognizes one divine wisdom in all the prophetic messages. He sees the same infinite Being speaking through all in different forms and names through all ages. It is just as if one had the photograph of one's sweetheart at different ages: at twelve, at twenty, at thirty, at forty. The photographs are different, but it is the same sweetheart.

CHAPTER XVI

Points of View held by Spiritual Persons

THERE ARE persons who look at life picturing it as a school, and it is true that life is as a school. How much evolved one may be, there is not one day that one does not learn something new; from the most unevolved person to the most evolved one this can be seen. The more one realizes that life is a school, the more one learns from it, and if one does not learn from it then it is a school just the same. In this way one can justify the divine Spirit in letting every soul grow through different experiences: through the path of pain and pleasure there is something to be learned. One must not think that the divine Being does not teach the one who lives in pleasure. Therein is a teaching for him, and for the one who is in pain there is a teaching in pain.

Very often those who think that they can correct someone, that they can teach someone, that they can guide a person, that they can direct someone, are apt to forget that they may do quite the wrong thing. If a thief was told by his uncle not to steal, not to go and do his work and if he was held back, that only means that he would go and do it the next week. But if he goes and robs, if he is arrested by the police, if he is taken to prison and stays there for three years, then he has learned his lesson. His uncle could not teach him; it is life, it is circumstances that must teach him. It is the experience through which he has to go that teaches man.

Often one feels that it is unjust on the part of destiny to put one into conditions that seem very cruel, and one thinks that it would be kinder on the part of destiny to teach without troubling. But what, after all, is trouble? There are no such things as pleasure and pain; only the comparison between them makes them so. In other words, if there was no pain one would not be capable of enjoying pleasure, and if there was no pleasure one would not be capable of experiencing pain. If that is true, then to the degree to which one is capable to experience pain, to the same degree one is able to experience pleasure. The one who cannot experience pain cannot experience pleasure. The stone has nothing, it has neither pleasure nor pain. It is the relativity, it is the relation, the comparison between two experiences which makes them distinct, but the one cannot be distinct without the other. Therefore there is the necessity of both experiences.

Besides, it is very interesting to see that for one person it is necessary to go through pain and trouble and effort in order to come to a certain success or accomplishment, and for another to come to the same experience there is no pain, no trouble, it is easy. One might think, "Why is it easy for one person and why is it so difficult for the other one?" It is difficult because the soul needs that difficulty; it is the need of the soul, it is the want of the soul. There is a belief that the nightingale sits on a thorn in order to cry so melodiously. If you look into the lives of those who go through troubles and sufferings, you will find that unconsciously they seek trouble, they look for it. Not consciously; consciously they would run away from it, but unconsciously they look for it, because it is good for their souls, it is meant for them. If they did not have it, they would not reach satisfaction.

It is so interesting to watch how every soul is looking for trouble. It is not so interesting that every person is seeking pleasure, but it is most interesting to see how every one is seeking his pain, looking out for it. Tagore says: "When the string of the violin was being tuned it felt the pain of being stretched, but once it was tuned then it knew why it was stretched". So it is with the human soul. While the soul goes through pain, torture and trouble it thinks that it would have been much better if it had gone through life without it. But once it reaches the culmination of it then, when it looks back, it begins to realize why all this was meant: it was only meant to tune the soul to a certain pitch.

Very often the foolish, those who have no responsibility, who have no sense of duty, who have no ideal, who have no principle, seem to enjoy life more than those with an ideal, with principles, with a sincere heart, with a faithful spirit. Those who desire to do good, those who desire to serve – it is they who go through pain and suffering. This only means that it is not the dead souls who are tried; their time is to come, their time will come. But the living souls are tried and tested according to the degree of their development and they are raised to a higher consciousness – even if it was necessary to stretch the string of their souls. In order to tune the string it must be stretched.

Then there is the point of view held by some spiritual persons that life is a puppet show – and that is true also. To-day a person is rich, to-morrow he becomes poor; to-day a person comes to power, to-morrow he is thrown down; to-day he comes to great fame and position, to-morrow he is despised and forgotten. If we look at this world more keenly and with open eyes, we shall find that it is a puppet show. There is a hand behind it which makes one doll a king, another doll a queen or a servant; it is only a night's play, in the morning they are all dolls.

There is a story of a dervish who spoke with a young man who was very interested in his words of wisdom. The young man said, "If I come to your part of the world, I will come to see you. Will you tell me where you live?" The dervish replied, "I live in the place of the liars". This young man thought, "He is a wise man, he makes such a deep impression upon me. I cannot understand that he lives in the place of the liars. It seemed to me that every word he spoke was truth". When he went to that country and asked for the dervish, the people said, "We do not know any place of liars, but there is a dervish living somewhere here". So they took him near the graveyard where the dervish lived. The first question the young man asked was, "Why did you give me a name which is not the name of the place?" The dervish replied, "Yes, this is a place of liars". It was the graveyard. He said, "Come with me, I shall show you. This here is a tomb, they say, of a general. Where is his sword, where is his power, where is his voice, what is he now? Is he a general? Here, this one was called a prime-minister. Where is his ministry, where is his office, where is his pen, where is his power? In the same ground! This person was called a judge. Whom is he judging now? He is in the ground. Were they not liars? Did they not tell a lie saying 'I am so and so, and I am such and such'?" This is the point of view of those who look at life as being a puppet show.

Then there is a third point of view: to look at life as if it was a play going on on the stage, with the actors all dressed up as the king, the servant, the minister, the judge, but when they come away from the stage, they have only performed their part in the story. They are nothing, but while they are on the stage it is their duty to perform the role which they are meant to perform. So one understands that one is performing the role of a king, of a thief or of a judge, of a servant or of a prince. It only means that it is meant so; it is written in the story that it should be performed like this. It is a play that we all perform in the whole universe, and each takes part in this play, a certain part which is given to him — maybe a desirable part or an undesirable part. Only the one who sees it in this light sees that it is a stage on which a play is performed, and the one who does not see it in this light thinks that it is really like this. His life is most difficult.

Then there is again another point of view – that of Hafiz – that every soul is drunken. It has drunk its ideal, its principle, its inspiration, its ambition, its thought, its feeling; it is all a drink. A person who despises another one – it is a drink he has in him; that intoxication makes him despise. A person who loves someone – it is a drink, he has drunk that bowl, he is in that intoxication. If one praises someone, one has drunk the bowl of beauty. If a man has revenge against someone, it only means that he has drunk the bowl of revenge. This life is a wine-press; from that wine-press each person takes that wine which is made for him. The one who looks at it all as a café where everyone is drinking, that person is called sober. He sees each person intoxicated, and he too chooses his wine – but he chooses it, he drinks the wine and at the same time knows that it is wine.

There is another point of view, the point of view of the *madzub*: that every head has a madness, a certain madness, be it of a higher or a lower kind. Why is it madness? Because it is unique, it is distinct and it is different: every head has a different thought, an idea different from others. We call mad someone who has an idea different from others. But every person has an idea different from others. Knowing this the *madzub* tries to act as mad, because he thinks, "When I am among the mad, then I too must act as mad". But the one who tries to act as mad, is not mad; because he is acting as mad it is different.

                    Sufi Teachings

Then there is still another point of view of the spiritual soul, and that is that humanity is to be pitied. The wrongdoer must be pitied for his doing wrong, and the welldoer must be pitied because he does not know how to do better. The foolish one must be pitied because he does not understand better, and the clever one must be pitied because he is not wiser. The spiritual soul thinks that humanity is a process of development of the lower creation, that all that exists in the lower creation is to be found in humanity – passion, anger, wrath, spite, vengeance – and that everyone does not only cause harm to others, but also to himself. One can only enjoy life when one has got rid of all these things and does not harm others by his character. Therefore the one who has this point of view, instead of concerning himself with others, concerns himself with his own being and tries to make himself free of all these things in order to experience the joy that comes from it, proving to the world the teaching of harmlessness.

This same principle is followed by some others who look at it in a different light. They think that to please man is to please God, and to please God is to please man. Therefore in speaking, in acting or in thinking they do all they can to avoid causing hurt or harm to another person. In trying to do everything to please and to serve mankind they think that it is a service to God.

What is lacking to-day in the world is idealism. Where does idealism come from? From deep thought. To-day life in general keeps man so busy in his occupation, in his profession, in his work of everyday life, that he has no time to think deeply and better; he does not find his ideal. Among a thousand persons there is perhaps one person who has an ideal and knows what ideal he has. All the others do not know it, they do not have an ideal. Besides, it is not only to have an ideal, but it is necessary to know the ideal and to attain to the ideal, to develop towards it, to unfold oneself towards the ideal. It is that in which lies life's fulfilment.

Ideals are of five different kinds. There is a certain principle which is a person's ideal, and if he can live that principle he has lived his ideal. There is a certain action which is a person's ideal; if he has accomplished that action then his ideal is fulfilled. There is a belief which is a person's ideal, and if he is able to keep to that belief he has fulfilled his ideal. There is a certain height to which a person wishes to reach, and that mark which he wishes to reach is his ideal. The fifth ideal is a person in whom is a man's ideal, and when all the attributes which that person has are attained then that ideal is fulfilled.

But all these five ideals are as five stepping-stones to the shrine of God. The greatest ideal, the highest ideal is the ideal of God. It is not necessary – and yet it is most necessary – that there should be a stepping-stone to go to the altar of God. Without this stepping-stone many are lost. It is often a very rigid soul who will say, "God is my ideal. I do not care for any other ideal". It comes from his rigidness, for it only means that he does not wish for the ladder; he wishes to jump from the ground to the next floor. The ideal of God is the perfect ideal, and in order to reach it there must be a footstool, there must be a ladder, there must be a stepping-stone which leads to it – be it a principle, be it a belief, be it an action, be it a position, be it a person.

It is the poetic nature that is inclined to have an ideal; it is the artistic nature that has the love of ideal; it is the musical tendency to look for an ideal. Therefore ideal is attached to higher intelligence. The lower a person's evolution the less he is inclined to an ideal; the higher the person is evolved the more he is inclined to an ideal. If those great ones – kings, generals, writers, poets, musicians – have really accomplished something great and made an impression upon humanity, it was because of their ideal. Without an ideal, whatever one has done is nothing. In the first place one cannot accomplish something without an ideal. If one did so, it would be nothing. A machine has finished something: there is no ideal in it. Ideal therefore is like the breath of life; ideal therefore is the lift that takes you upwards.

Then there are some who say, "Yes, I have my ideal in a person, but that person does not come up to my ideal. I am sorry, but I shall turn my back upon him". It will always be like that. What is a person? A person is limited. The ideal is perfect. Therefore in order to retain your ideal you will have to make the person out of your own devotion, out of your love, your sympathy. Give to the person what is lacking, then that ideal is made. For instance, the great teachers of humanity, Buddha, Muhammad and Christ, what are they to those who do not follow them? Nothing. But to those who follow them they are everything. Why? Because their followers have made them out of their devotion; they have taken the name and then they have made their ideal out of their devotion. When a Buddhist says, "Buddha was God, and Buddha was the Lord, and all beautiful attributes were in Buddha", it only means that he has taken all the beautiful attributes of Buddha and has added all kinds of beautiful things. But how much can the idealist add? There is endless beauty. It is only for his own conviction, for his devotion, for his development that he makes his ideal as perfect as possible, and it is the same with the devoted followers of any teacher of humanity.

But if people said, "We are going to analyse what the teacher taught. What he said was this.... Another teacher says another thing and a third one says something else; so it is all different". That again is another outlook. They never have an ideal. Now many study theology in colleges and universities. Do they have that ideal? Never. They say, "What Buddha said is quite right. But there is something else here in the Bible which is different from it. What Muhammad said, well, one cannot apply it to practical life, and he is of quite a different kind". When they begin to analyse the ideal it is an analysing of books. Their ideal is no ideal, their ideal is in the books, and one day they will get above it or beneath it. If they rise they rise above it, and if they fall they fall beneath it. But when one comes to the ideal – it belongs to devotion, it belongs to love. It is the same as what Majnun said about Leila, his beloved girl. When people asked Majnun, "What is Leila? She is not so beautiful, she is like any other girl", Majnun replied, "In order to see Leila you must borrow my eyes". That is what the ideal teaches.

Analysing and idealizing are two different things. If you analyse you are in quite a different sphere. If you analyse something you can say it in words; if you idealize you rise above words. The whole world is going downwards because of the lack of an ideal, and if there is any hope of the betterment of humanity, it is not through better economical conditions; it is not so that, if political conditions were better, the world would be happy. No, never, because that thirst, that hunger for money and that avariciousness will want just the same. If the labour-man came in the place of the government, if the labourer became a capitalist, and the capitalist a labourer, if the whole world became aristocratic, or if the whole world became democratic, that would not take away the trouble of the world. If there is anything that will raise the world, it is the ideal. If the ideal is given in different directions and to different individuals, and if humanity wakens to a higher ideal – that only can be the source of the betterment of humanity.

CHAPTER XVII

Higher Spiritualism

BY HIGHER spiritualism we do not mean that which is occupied with occult, curious or magical phenomena. Such spiritualism keeps man away from progress. Higher spiritualism is that in which the soul is enkindled and illuminated.

The petals and leaves and thorns of the rose are all different, and yet there is one rose; the spirit of the rose is one, these parts are so many aspects of the rose. In the same way all spirits are different, but are the outcome of the one real Spirit. In reality there is only one Spirit and it is only because of a sense of illusion that there seem to be many spirits; every ray of the sun is accounted as separate from every other.

The whole world is wonderful and we need hardly take special steps to find wonders and miracles by going to seek special phenomena. There is no end to the wonders around us! Our life consists of so few days that, if we realized the privilege of life and were thankful for its opportunities, we should devote our time to attaining what every soul really longs for, rather than taking interest in the curious and the occult. After all, those phenomena do not differ from the everyday phenomena we call natural. Human character, human life, the breath we take, our states of pleasure and displeasure, of like and dislike – what are they all but phenomena? The craze for a particular phenomenon leads us to overlook that the whole universe is activity. Christ was not pleased when asked to show a miracle. He did not summon the angels to satisfy the curiosity of his disciples. It was spiritual illumination which was their real need.

However good an education may be, it does not follow that the soul is kindled and, unless the soul is illuminated, how can it illumine another soul? When two such souls should meet it is as lighting a candle. But a match will not kindle a piece of iron; it requires very much heat to do so. So souls which are not awake are very difficult to illumine.

Persons may quarrel and fight over what they believe and disbelieve, but were the soul kindled such fighting would be found to be of no avail.

Forms will always be different; it is the real meaning and essence which is unchanging. Seers are always united in their thoughts because they perceive that the truth is one, and the Spirit is one; other persons have only knowledge of names and forms. When there is only one Spirit and one life, how can there be two knowledges? The spirit of Buddha's teaching, of Solomon's teaching, of Christ's teaching always point to the same meaning, and yet how different their words and how different their lives. Even of one person or of one picture ten persons will have different ideas. This world of variety, always changing as it is, cannot be the basis of unanimity. Only when we come to a knowledge of the One Being can we be led to higher spiritualism.

Those souls who have departed from this life in the absorption of the vision of God, the Only Being, who have directed their love towards humanity so as to draw humanity towards heaven – all these are now not only in the vision of God, but they are bestowing their blessing and bliss upon you. All those blessed souls are linked to one another.

As from one taper every lamp in the world might be kindled, so from the higher Spirit we call God we derive our life, our light, the life eternal. He is the illumination of all the saints; He is the friend and ideal of all. The light which He directs through all the different spirits runs in one current from the souls of the blessed to the souls of the illuminated ones on earth. There can be no higher spiritualism than this.

Since the current is from the one Spirit – even though it reaches us through many, or whether it reaches us from a man, plant, animal, sun or moon, or from whatever apparent source – why seek to differentiate in our search instead of going at once to the source of the current, to the unity rather than among the variety which is illusion?

But only those who have reached a certain evolution can realize the next step in this evolution. It is for us to awake only those who are about to awake and allow to sleep peacefully those who are yet fast asleep. They must not be awakened before their sleep is over; they have not had enough, they will feel inclined to awake some other time. It would be like taking a child to a dangerous electric machine. Not only would the child be hurt, but it would spoil the sensitive mechanism of the machine, or it might even destroy a whole factory. The attempt to reform the whole world because one has found out one aspect of the truth is to try and awaken great numbers of people who are not ready to be awakened. Let them sleep on.

The ultimate end of the sleepers is the same. They cannot go astray; in the journey through the world of changing experiences they can still know they are going on well. The heart will be enkindled and the torch will be given by which to guide them along the higher paths, and some day all will have found the higher spiritualism when they enter into the joy of the Lord.

CHAPTER XVIII

The Process of Spiritual Unfoldment

IT IS not so that only a certain soul who is meant to unfold evolves. Every soul evolves in its own time; only the rhythm of the soul's progress depends upon the speed with which it evolves. Whether a person is inclined to evolve or not, the inner inclination of his soul is to continue its process of unfoldment. Therefore, if among a thousand persons only one can be seen taking the spiritual path, the remaining ones are evolving just the same. It is before our eyes that we see such distinctions as some people going upwards and some downwards, some going forwards and others backwards; in reality all are going forwards, some slowly, others more rapidly.

There are four different ways in which people evolve. One form of evolution is advancing like a drunken man who does not know where he is going, whether he is on the right or on the wrong path. He does not look around, he is enjoying his drink; he is joyful, just passing through life. It is the condition of souls who do not know where they are going and where they have come from. They do not see what is beautiful and what is not beautiful, they do not try to distinguish between right and wrong. Drunken by life's absorption they journey along life's path and, falling down a thousand times, they arrive one day at the same destination.

It is wrong to think that sinners and wrongdoers – whom we make so by our man-made laws – are deprived of the bliss of spiritual attainment. They attain it just the same, only they arrive in their own time, and sometimes a drunken man walks more quickly and may arrive before another person who is not drunken. We cannot always judge who is going to arrive first. Nevertheless, the drunken man may have his own joy, the joy of intoxication, but he is deprived of the other joy that the sober one experiences, the joy of seeing all the beauty that can be noticed on the way, and the bliss of taking every step in life with open eyes. Intoxicated with the wine he has taken and caring little for anything else he is deprived of that bliss. Such is the picture of life: many go along the path of life like drunks without admitting it. Even a drunken man will not say, "I am drunk". He is quite sure of his feet.

Another one is taken to the goal while asleep. Imagine! This person was journeying through a beautiful nature, but instead of looking at the beauty he is asleep. He will arrive at the same destination but has not taken the opportunity of enjoying all the beauty there is to be seen. Nevertheless, he will arrive where he is bound to.

The third form of evolution is that of the person who goes along this path indifferent to it. He also will arrive at the same destination, but because of his indifference he forgets and is unable to experience many things that he could have experienced with sympathy. Many do not notice the beauty that is to be found in the world.

The fourth way is that of the person who journeys with open eyes and heart, enjoying everything he sees. His coming to the goal is a great benefit: he has fulfilled the purpose of life. Therefore it is this particular way that may be called the spiritual path. It is the path one can tread with open eyes and heart, with sympathy and trust. Whether there is sorrow or joy or happiness, one can enjoy all things in life, everything has its beauty.

However much a person seems uninclined to spiritual attainment, yet there is a continual craving going on in the depth of his being. When he feels that irritation he thinks, "What is the matter? Perhaps I have not enough money. That is my trouble." He then goes and works, he wants to collect money in order to be happy. Another one feeling that irritation thinks, "I am lonely, I must find a friend who will make my life happy". A third one thinks, "I should have a big position, a high office. That is what troubles me. If I had it, I would be happy".

No one of them knows the real reason of that irritation and, as by scratching irritation grows more and more, so by trying to satisfy the craving they feel in their soul—the craving to attain something without knowing what they want—it grows too. They have one thing and another and then see that they are more and more dissatisfied; the further they go in the pursuit of satisfaction, the more dissatisfied they become. This is not the case of one or two persons; there is hardly one person among a thousand who, having realized the pursuit of all these different things and having attained them, feels satisfied. These are perhaps means of going forwards, but they are not the goal, they bring no satisfaction. Do you think that a poor man, if money was left to him, would be contented? His irritation would grow more and more in some way or other, because it is caused by something else: it is the craving of his soul to attain a harmonious condition.

There is a story in Arabia of a dervish who came before Alexander the Great asking, "Will you fill my little cup with golden coins?" Alexander thought the little cup was a small thing to fill with gold coins. He asked his treasurer to fill it, but as the treasurer began to do so, the more coins were poured into it the wider the cup appeared. It seemed that it would never be full, always a place was left open to be filled. Alexander was much surprised and thought, "If this continues all my treasure will be taken". He asked, "Oh dervish, what magic cup do you have here? What is it?" The dervish answered, "This is the cup of the desire of man. This cup is always empty and the more you fill it the more empty it becomes; it is never filled".

Desire for wealth, power, position, for pleasure and comfort, for all things belonging to this world, is continuously there. The irritation felt in the soul man attributes to desire, thinking, "The restlessness, the dissatisfaction I feel comes from lack of this or that", and so he spends his time going on from one thing to another. He is wrong, for wherever he arrives, whether he is successful or not, in both cases the irritation never ceases. It continues when a person begins his progress in the spiritual line.

Many people may say to-day, "Oh, but I am practical", which means that they do not believe in dreams or in anything spiritual. Yes, they can say it to-day, but to-morrow they will not say it. It is a condition; one says it when one is drunk, when one is intoxicated, but the moment a person becomes sober he begins to feel a craving which remains unsatisfied. Have I not seen during my travels throughout the whole world how scientists – after having made a great name and after having seen much of the world – understanding the realm of reason and logic were still trying to discover something they did not know, some experience they had not made, to find something they had not explored?

There is a beautiful story of an old scientist who never believed in God, but whose wife had religion. When the scientist became ill and old and his reasoning faculties and the stiffness he had against spiritual things became loosened, he said to his wife, "I wonder if there is anything. I will not believe it, but I should like to know if there is anything else. You never lacked religion, do you think there is something? You are so happy." She said, "I am happy in the belief I have". "I cannot have that belief", answered he, "but I have you and what I can share is your happiness". If one cannot believe directly, belief is taken indirectly. Not only mankind but even birds and beasts are attracted to an illuminated soul. A soul who radiates spirituality, who has realized the meaning of life, can impart his conviction even to the unbeliever who has never believed in soul or hereafter. Even the soul of the unbeliever becomes satisfied, even such a soul is blessed through contact with a person who has realized truth.

When the time comes that the intoxication of life begins to diminish and man begins to look at life differently, what comes first is a kind of depression, a kind of disappointment in things and beings. He thinks that all he had considered valuable has lost its value and importance. He begins to see falsehood behind all he had thought was so real and a kind of depression, of disappointment and bitterness begins to come over him. Be not surprised if a thoughtful person shows disappointment and changes his point of view about things he once considered valuable and important. His looking at things from a different point of view is natural. No doubt those who surround him begin to say, "These are the dishes you enjoyed so much, these the things you valued so much a few months ago. What has happened? Some change has come over you!" It is so, a change has come and the person has taken a step forwards. This change, this sort of disappointment he may show more or less. The more thoughtful the person the less he shows it, and the less thoughtful the more he shows bitterness: it is according to his evolution. One person shows his disappointment in tears, another in smiles. The one who shows it in smiles is superior; it is the way one should take in life.

Another step leads to the stage of bewilderment. He who has arrived at that stage is no more depressed or disappointed, but amazed at things about which ordinarily no one would be amazed. He is amazed because his eyes are open. Others see the same things, but their eyes are closed, so the same experience does not touch them. This person feels it and wonders about it. There is a continual bewilderment, and what causes it most is human nature, every aspect of human nature, its every turn and twist and its many phenomena. He looks at life, and it becomes so interesting. He need not seek solitude, he stands in the midst of the crowd and yet may enjoy every rub and knock. Every experience, all things amaze him and only make him smile and wonder. All such words as kindness, goodness, love, infatuation, connection have a different meaning for him. One might ask, "Does he become critical and cynical?" No, since he understands, he is much beyond cynicism and criticism, but there is bewilderment, continual amazement at his every experience from morning till evening.

Then there is a third stage: as the soul evolves further a man begins to see reason behind reason. So he sees several reasons, one hidden behind the other. There is a reason for everything, whether agreeable or disagreeable, right or wrong. Naturally he then can no more blame one soul in this world; he cannot blame the worst sinner, behind everything he sees its reason. If he sees a thousand reasons in support of someone, whether it is right or wrong, there is nothing for him to say. This makes him naturally tolerant, compassionate, forgiving — not because he thinks that it is kind to forgive, or good to be compassionate or because it is his principle to be tolerant. He is obliged to be so, his inner inclination cannot help being compassionate, cannot but forgive, as in the case of Jesus Christ. When people brought those who were accused of wrongdoings according to the law before the

Master, he said, "God will forgive you". There is not one instance in the life of Christ when he took revenge on anyone, or blamed a person.

When a man has understood the reason of all things and develops still further, then comes the realm of sympathy. Then naturally he has no blame for anybody, and that attitude culminates in harmlessness. Buddha says, "The essence of religion is harmlessness, and the moment you have become harmless, you have understood religion". What is harmlessness? People know so little about it. They think that being harmful means killing someone. But everyone has a meaning of his own for every word. There was a soldier who heard people speaking about kindness and asked, "What is kindness?" They explained to him that it is an attitude and he said, "Once I practised kindness; my horse was ill and I killed it. A feeling of kindness came over me and I killed it".

When one rises above this realm of forgiveness there comes a natural outpouring of sympathy. At that time a person becomes really sympathetic, for then to feel sympathy is no more his moral, it is his nature; it is not felt intentionally but automatically. There will be an outpouring of sympathy towards everyone who comes into the radiance and atmosphere of such a person.

Many people say, "Is it not a weakening of the character to become so gentle and sympathetic? Is it not against practical life where we have to be vigorous, hard and crude in order to stand the hardness of life? Is it advisable to be so fine, kind and gentle that everyone can get the better of us?" Education to-day is quite contrary to this idea. The tendency of education is not to let our affairs or ourselves be shaken by the selfish ones of this world among whom we move and who might get the better of us. This is right, but at the same time if each person prepares himself in this way and harms others, without intervention it must end in battle. The manifestation is not made for battle, but we have made it a battleground.

The meaning of Adam's exile from paradise, when he was sent into the world of toil, is the same. Man was born to enjoy the harmony and beauty of life, to experience what life means, but he has made paradise into a battlefield, into this world of conflict. It is not so that Adam was exiled, Adam turned paradise into a battlefield. Is it not so that we have made life difficult for ourselves? Is it the pleasure of God that life should be so difficult for us? In professional life, in the life of science or art, of business, commerce or politics, in all aspects there is nothing but continual struggle. If one looks with open eyes, one sees that every new born child will have to find this trouble. It is a struggle!

There will come a time before long when it will be difficult to live in this world. Only some few people, very well equipped for strife and struggle and most inclined to conflict, will be able to exist. When to-day we look with wide open eyes we see this aspect more keenly. There is no direction of life where it is smooth; it is more and more difficult every moment of the day. There is nothing but competition and conflict, and when there is one manner of action and one rhythm going on throughout the whole of manifestation, those few cannot help having to go through this same way, because life in the world is a mechanism; we have to run in the same way. Besides, even if we know how disadvantageous life proves to be at the present time, do you think that we can strike another line? Life is put into a mechanism; we cannot make another way out of it.

The number of lives that has been made miserable and disturbed is so enormous that if we thought about it we would be most unhappy to see their condition. There are many who think that a better time may be brought about by making unions, communities and different brotherhoods. But this cannot be brought about by small efforts. Besides, in such unions and parties struggle again begins, one being against the other. What is most necessary at this time is spiritual awakening of the generality, and every effort should be made to awaken this ideal, to lift the spiritual ideal, to bring peace that will remain and last. It is a mission that can be worthwhile. Everyone of us can do it if we think sufficiently about it. In our own lines – be it in business, in politics, or in education – whatever small service we can do we should always render. The main thing we can do is to awake; to awaken ourselves and those around us to a high ideal, to a greater realization of life, and a deeper understanding of truth.

CHAPTER XIX

The Awakening of the Soul

1

THERE IS an awakening from childhood to youth and from youth to mature age and during this development one's point of view, one's outlook in life changes. Also sometimes in one's life, when one has gone through an illness or a great suffering, at the end of it the whole outlook on life has changed. One also sees that a person who has taken a long journey after having come back has quite changed. Also after a friendship, after a pupilship, after a marriage a sudden change comes in the outlook of a person, and we find that there are some cases where the change is so great that we may say that he is an entirely new person. Seeing this we can divide such changes which may be called developments into three classes.

One class pertains to the physical development, another is connected with the development of the mind and the third class with the development of the soul. There are instances in the lives of many – who rarely will say or admit it – that they can recollect experiences in their childhood when in one moment's time their whole outlook on life changed. As ripening is a desired result, it is the result of every object in life to ripen and to develop. Therefore the fulfilment of life's purpose is to be expected in the awakening of the soul.

One may ask what are the signs of the soul's awakening. The first sign of this awakening is just like the birth of an infant. From the time of its birth the infant is interested in hearing something, any sound that comes, and in seeing something, a colour or light, whatever it be attracted to. And thus a person whose soul has awakened becomes awake to everything he sees and hears. Compared to that person everyone else seems to be with open eyes and yet not to see, to be with open ears and yet not to hear. There are many with open ears, but there is rarely one who hears, and there are many with open eyes, but there is hardly one who sees. It is therefore that the natural seeing of the awakened soul is called clairvoyance and his natural hearing clairaudience. In English there is the simple word "seer" which explains that this person not only has eyes, but together with eyes he has sight.

The moment the soul has awakened music makes an appeal to it, poetry touches it, words move it, art has an influence upon it. It no longer is a sleeping soul, it is awake and it begins to enjoy life to a fuller extent. It is this awakening of the soul which is mentioned in the Bible, "Unless the soul is born again it will not enter the kingdom of heaven". Being born again means that the soul is awakened after having come on earth, and entering the kingdom of heaven means that this world, the same kingdom in which we are standing just now, turns into heaven as soon as the point of view has changed. Is it not interesting and most wonderful to think that the same earth we walk on is earth to one person and heaven to another? And it is still more interesting to notice that it is we who change it; we change it from earth into heaven, or we change it otherwise.

This change comes not by study, nor by anything else, but only by the changing of our point of view. I have seen people seek after truth, study in books about it, write many books on theology, and in the end they were in the same place where they were standing before. This shows that all outer efforts are excuses. There is only one thing that brings us before reality and that is the awakening of the soul.

All tragedy of life, all misery and inharmony are caused by one thing and that is lack of understanding. Lack of understanding comes from lack of penetration. The one who does not see from the point of view from which he ought to see becomes disappointed because he cannot understand. It is not for the outer world to help us to understand life better; it is we ourselves who should help ourselves to understand it better.

Then there is a further awakening which is a continuation of what I have called the awakening of the soul. The sign of it is that the awakened person throws a light, the light of his soul, upon every person and every object and sees that object, that condition in this light. It is his own soul which becomes a torch in his hand, it is his own light that illuminates his path.

It is just like throwing a searchlight upon dark corners which one did not see before, and the corners become clear and illuminated again. It is like throwing light upon problems that one did not understand at first; it is like seeing with x-rays persons who were a riddle before.

Since life becomes clear to the awakened soul it shows another manifestation: every aspect of life becomes communicative with him. The idea is that life is communicating, the soul is communicating, but they do not communicate until a person is awakened. Once a soul is awakened it becomes communicative with life.

As a young man I had a great desire to visit the shrines of sages, of great teachers. With every desire of hearing something of them or of asking them something I always held my tongue back. I sat quiet in their presence and had a great satisfaction and felt a greater blessing by sitting quiet there than if I had discussed and argued and talked with them; for in the end I felt that there was a communication which was much more satisfactory than these outer discussions and arguments of people who know not what they discuss. It was enlightening, it was refreshing and it gave that power and inspiration with which one can see life in a better light. Those who are awakened become lights, not only lights for themselves but also lights for others. These may not know it but their light, their presence itself helps to make the most difficult problems easy. This brings us to realize the fact that man is light, as the Scriptures have said, a light whose origin, whose source is divine. And when this light is raised then life becomes quite different.

When the soul is awakened furthermore its condition is then as that of a person sitting in the midst of the night among hundreds and thousands of people who are fast asleep. The picture is that he is sitting among them, standing among them, he is looking at them, hearing of their sorrows, miseries and conditions – hundreds of them moving about in their sleep, in their own dreams, not awake to the condition of the other one who is next to them. They may be friends or relations or acquaintances or enemies; whatever be their relationship, little they know about one another, each one absorbed in his own troubles. This awakened soul standing among them all will listen to everyone, will see everyone, will recognize and realize all they think and feel, but his language no one understands; his thoughts he cannot explain to anyone; his feelings he cannot expect anyone to feel. He feels lonely and nothing else can be felt. No doubt in that loneliness there is a sense of perfection, because perfection is loneliness.

When it was said that the apostles knew all languages at the descent of the Holy Spirit, it did not mean knowing the languages of all countries. They knew the language of the soul; for there are several languages which are spoken in different lands, but numberless languages are spoken, as each individual has his particular language. That brings us to realize another idea of very great importance: the outer language can convey only outward things and feelings to one another, but there is an inner language, a language which can be understood by souls who are awakened. It is a universal language, a language of vibrations, a language of feeling, a language which touches the innermost sense. Heat and cold for instance are different feelings which are called by different names in different countries, but inwardly they are the same feelings. So there is love and hate and kindness, harmony and inharmony which are all called by different names in different countries, but their feeling is the same experience for all men.

When in order to know the thought of another we depend upon his outer word then no doubt we fail to understand, for perhaps we do not know that person's language. But if we can communicate with him soul to soul we can certainly understand what he means, for before he says a word he has said it within himself, and that word reaches us before it is expressed outwardly. Before the word is spoken the expression says it; before the thought has formed, the feeling speaks of it. And this shows that it is a feeling which forms a thought, a thought which comes as speech. Even before this a feeling existed, and even there it can be caught when one is able to communicate with the soul. This is what may be called communication: to communicate with the innermost being of a person. But who can communicate? The one who knows how to communicate with himself, the one who in other words is awakened.

The personality of an awakened soul becomes different from every other personality. It becomes more magnetic, because it is a living person who has magnetism; the dead corpse has no magnetism. It is the living person who brings joy, and therefore it is the awakened soul who is joyous. Never for one moment imagine, as many do, that a spiritual person means a most sorrowful, dried-up, long-faced person. Spirit is joy, spirit is life, and when this spirit has awakened all the joy and pleasure that exist are there. As the sun takes away all darkness, so spiritual light takes away all worries and anxieties, sufferings and doubts. If spiritual awakening were not so precious what would be the use of seeking it in life? It is a treasure which nobody can take away from you, a light that will always keep and will never be extinguished. That is called spiritual awakening which is the fulfilment of life's purpose.

Certainly, the things a person once valued and considered important become less important. They lose their value, and things which are beautiful lose their colour. It is just like seeing the stage in the light of the sun; all the big palaces and decorations on the stage mean nothing. No doubt this takes away the slavery to which everyone is put by the things of this world; the awakened person becomes a master, and at the same time he need not give those things up. Optimism develops naturally, but an optimism with open eyes. Power increases, the power of accomplishing things. Then as long as a person has not accomplished something he will go after it however small it is.

It is very difficult to judge an awakened soul, as they say in the East, for there is nothing outwardly to prove to you, "this person is an awakened soul". The best way of seeing an awakened soul is to waken oneself. No one in the world can pretend to be awake when he is still asleep, as a little child by putting moustaches on his face will not prove himself to be a grown-up man. All other pretences may be accepted but not the one of being an awakened soul, for it is a living light which no one can pretend to be. If there is any truth it is in the awakening of the soul, for truth is born in this awakening. Truth is not taught, truth is discovered.

Very often people make an effort – but in vain – to awaken

a friend or a near relation whom they love. But in the first place we do not know if that person is not more awakened than we ourselves, and we may be trying in vain. And the other point is that a person may be asleep and needs that sleep. Waking him would be a sin instead of a virtue. We are only allowed to give our hand to the one who is turning over in his sleep, who desires to awake. Only then a hand is given.

This giving of the hand in esoteric terms is called initiation. No doubt outwardly a teacher who is acquainted with this path may give a hand to the one who wishes to journey, but inwardly there is the Teacher who gives a hand who has always given and always gives a hand to awakening souls, the same hand which has received the sages and masters of all times in a higher initiation.

Verily, the seeker will find sooner or later, if only he keeps steady on the path till he arrives at his destination.

2

The words waking and sleeping are familiar to us as we use them in expressing different conditions of life. Really speaking, when we look at it from the point of view of the soul, we sleep and are awake at the same time. For instance when we are looking at a certain thing and our mind is fully absorbed in looking at it, we do not hear things at the same time. And if we are hearing something, absorbed in what we are hearing, when our sense of hearing is focused, our eyes may be open and yet we are not seeing. If that is true it explains to us that when one sense is fully awakened the other senses are asleep. In the same way, when we experience a sensation through the mind the body is absent.

The more we look at sleeping and waking from a psychological point of view, the more we shall come to the conclusion that they are not as we understand them, but that every moment of the day and the night we are awake and asleep at the same time. To give another instance: when a person is asleep and experiencing a dream, he is awake to something and yet asleep to the outer things. To one world he is asleep, to the other awake. So one is always asleep and always awake.

According to the ideas of the mystics there are five stages of consciousness which make one asleep to one stage and awake to another. One state of consciousness is our experience through the senses. In this condition – as we are just now, our eyes ready to see, our ears hearing – we are wakeful to the outside world. This is one aspect of wakefulness. Apart from this aspect which we alone recognize as wakefulness there are four other aspects.

The second aspect of wakefulness is when a person is asleep and yet is experiencing life exactly as he does on this plane of the physical world. This is the dream state. We call it dream when we are awake, when we have passed that dream state. At the time of dreaming that state is as real as this state in the physical world; we do not think it is a dream. Nothing that we can find here is lacking in the dream, and even things we cannot find here on the physical plane we can find in the dream state. All the limitation, all we find lacking in this life is provided for in the dream state. All that we are fond of, all that we would like to be, all we need in our life is easier to find in the dream than in the wakeful state.

If we say that after waking up we find the real life and call the other state a dream, and say therefore that it was an imagination without reality, we think that on this physical plane we are awake, that it is real. But is yesterday as real as to-day? When we look back upon our childhood, from the moment we came on earth all is yesterday; only just now is to-day. All that is past is yesterday and if it is not a dream, what is it? We need not only recognize what we see in the dream as a dream; all that is past is nothing but a dream as well. It is the "just now" which gives us the feeling of reality. What we are experiencing – that becomes real to us; what we are not experiencing, what we are not conscious of even at this moment does not exist for us. Only what our senses are conscious of is all the world, is life to us, and all we are unaware of means nothing, does not exist for us.

In this way each person has his own life and his own world; we all live in the same world, and each has his own world. Man's world is that of which he is conscious and in this way every person has his heaven and his hell made by himself. He need not wait for heaven and hell afterwards, he has already there what he has made for himself, what he is conscious of. If he is conscious of sorrow and depression, tortures and sufferings, pains and agitations, he lives in all that. He has made a fire for himself and is standing in it; he need not wait till death comes, he is already there. The one who lives in beauty, compassion, affection, forgiveness, appreciation for all that is good and beautiful, has heaven here; he need not wait for afterwards. This again shows that we are in the world to which we are awake, and to the world to which we are not awake we are asleep. We are asleep to that part of life which we do not know.

Another experience is that of a man who lives in music, whose thoughts are music, whose imaginations compose music, who enjoys it, to whom music is a language: he lives in the world of music. He lives under the same sun as everybody else, and yet his world is different. It is said that Beethoven who could no more hear with his ears, very much enjoyed the music he read and played, while perhaps another man with good hearing did not hear it. The soul of Beethoven was in music; the music he was playing was in himself, he lived in music and enjoyed it.

There is one experience which we make through our five senses, and that is one world, one plane of existence. Then there is another existence which we experience in the dream, and that is a world too. It is a separate world, its law is separate. Those who consider a dream only as a dream do not know the importance, the greatness, the wonders of it. The dream plane is more wonderful than the physical plane, because the physical plane is crude, limited and poor, subject to death and disease. The other plane which one experiences in the dream is better, purer, one has a greater freedom there.

Dreams can be divided into four different classes. One dream is a confused repetition of the same experience which we had during the day in wakefulness. However confused the dream may be, whether it be a repetition of all we have done or said in our daytime life, yet this repetition has a meaning, a great meaning. It has an influence in life, it has an effect, as every thought and imagination has an effect. We must not believe that what once we think or imagine is lost. Every thought ever born lives without our knowing, whether good or bad, harmonious or inharmonious. Once it is born it is created and left in the world of thought to live and to have its effect. A dream also is a thought and is as living, or even more so, as is thought in the wakeful state. Therefore every dream, however confused it may seem, once it has appeared before us has a meaning and a certain effect upon our lives. Also the dream in connection with someone else in our lives in one way or another has something to do with that person.

There is a second aspect of the dream and that is the contrary dream. It is just like the mirror in which you look short when you are tall, and tall when you are short: just the contrary of what you are. In the same way, if there is unhappiness, weakness waiting for you, you will see yourself in that dream in great glory, and when happiness is awaiting you, you will see yourself in misery. It is a kind of upset condition of the mind that produces quite the opposite to what is going to happen.

The third kind of dream is symbolical and it is most interesting to study this aspect of the dream. If a poet has a symbolical dream it is in the poetical realm. If a fine person has a symbolical dream it has fine symbols, for a rigid person it has crude symbols; it is all according to a man's stage of evolution. The more one studies this aspect of the dream the more one marvels at the phenomena of dream-land.

The fourth kind of dream manifests from the spirit and is exactly the picture of the future. It may be a picture of something going to happen the next day, next month, next year, or perhaps ten years later. The law of these dreams is that first a person sees a picture of what is going to happen after twenty years. When he advances this comes closer and closer: something going to happen after five years, after one year, after six months, and so on. And then he sees to-night what is going to be to-morrow. That is the realistic dream.

The first kind of dream explains the condition of everyday life. That dream comes to a person who is engrossed in his work and has no concentration of mind. He is just like a machine working all day long, and at night he sees his work reproduced before him. The second kind of dream, showing the opposite of what one is, comes to the person whose mind is upset, confused, troubled and puzzled. The third kind of dream, the symbolical dream, comes to a person who is intelligent, intellectual, etherially evolved. The fourth kind of dream comes to someone who is already evolved, spiritual, devotional, loving, kind, forgiving by nature, tenderhearted, of gentle nature. This again tells us that man's reward and punishment is not to be anticipated after death, but given to him every day, every hour of life.

Now coming to the third stage of consciousness – this stage lies between spirit and matter. It is this state of consciousness which we experience as the condition of sleep which we call fast sleep, deep sleep, when we do not even dream. There is so little said about it and very few think about it. Once a person studies this question of sleep he will find that it is the greatest marvel in the world. It is a living phenomenon. The rest and peace, vitality and vigour, intelligence and life that come to a man during that time of sleep is beyond explanation. Yet man is so ungrateful, he is never thankful for this experience given to him every day. He is only unhappy when he has lost it; then nothing in the world can satisfy him. No wealth, no comfort, no home, no position, nothing in the world can replace that experience which is as simple as sleeping, which means nothing and yet is everything.

The further we study the phenomenon of deep sleep the more we shall come to understand the mystery of life. It gives a key to the mystery of life, because it is an experience of consciousness which divides our spiritual consciousness between the physical and the spiritual world. It stands as a barrier between two experiences: one in this world and one which is reached by spiritual attainment. Our great poet of Persia, Rumi, who has inspired millions of people and whose works are considered in the East as the foundation of higher knowledge, has written about sleep, "O sleep, it is thou who makest the king unaware of his kingdom; the suffering patient forgets his illness, and prisoners are free when they are asleep". Imagine how all pains and sorrows and limitations of life, all the tragedy of life, all sufferings and agitations are washed away when one experiences that deep sleep.

It is a great pity that the mechanical and artificial life we live to-day in this world is depriving us of that natural experience of deep sleep. Our first fault is our gathering and living in one city, all crowded together. Then there are motorcars, there are houses of twenty storeys shaking every moment of the day and night, every vehicle shaking it. We are a race at the present time which is unaware of the comfort and bliss of the life known to the ancient people who lived simply, who lived with nature, far removed from this mechanical and artificial life. We are so far away from natural life that it has become our habit; we do not know any other comfort except the comfort we can experience in this kind of life we live. At the same time it shows that the soul is capable of attaining to greater comfort, pleasure and joy, to greater peace, rest and bliss only by living naturally.

These three stages of consciousness, physical, dream and deep sleep, are each nothing but an experience of the soul in an awakened state. For instance, when a person is awake outwardly he is conscious of the outer world; when he is fast asleep he is awakened to that particular plane while asleep to both dream-land and the physical state.

Now you may ask, "If a person who sleeps deeply is awakened to a certain consciousness, why does he not remember it? We think that he is asleep, for if he was awake he should know something about it; if he remembers nothing it means that he was asleep and certainly not awake. To be awake means experiencing something; during deep sleep one does not experience".

When we are looking at a bright light and that bright light is shut off then we see darkness. In reality there is no darkness. If there had not been bright light first there would not be darkness but light; it is the comparison that makes it darkness. Therefore the experience we have in our deep sleep is an experience of a higher and greater nature. It is so fine, so subtle and unusual – our consciousness being accustomed to the rigid experiences of the physical world – that the experience we have in that state is too fine to be perceived, too fine to be brought back to the physical world.

Every experience can be made intelligible by contrast. If there were no straight line, we could not say high and low, right and left; it is the straight line which makes us recognize them as such. If there were no sun we would not be able to say south, north, east and west. Therefore with every conception there must be some object to focus upon which helps to form our conception. In order to understand deep sleep we have nothing in the physical existence to compare it with and therefore that experience of deep sleep remains only as a great satisfaction, joy and upliftment, as something that has vitalized us and has created energy and enthusiasm in life. This shows that there is something we receive; we do not come empty-handed from there, we have attained something we cannot get here from the physical plane. From there we receive something that we cannot interpret in everyday language – more precious, more valuable and vital than anything from the physical and mental planes.

There is a still higher plane or experience of consciousness, different from these three experiences which everybody knows more or less, and this fourth experience is that of the mystic. It is an experience of seeing without the help of the eyes, of hearing without the help of the ears, and experiencing a plane without the help of the physical body – an experience similar to that of the physical body and at the same time independent of it. As soon as one arrives at this experience one begins to believe in the hereafter, for it gives one the conviction that, when the physical body is thrown off, the soul still remains – independent of the physical body and capable of seeing, living and experiencing even more freely and fully. Therefore this stage of experience is called the consciousness of the mystic.

Perhaps you have read in books of Eastern philosophy the words *nirvana* and *mukti*, and you have become frightened! *Nirvana* means to become nothing. You may say, "I do not want to become nothing". Everyone wants to become something, no one wants to become nothing. Those who want to be something – although that can be taken for nothing! – are so frightened of that idea. I have seen hundreds and thousands who were interested in Eastern philosophy, but when it came to being nothing they found it a difficult idea to grasp and they found it frightening to think, "One day this 'I' shall be nothing". But they do not know that it is the solving of this question which allows one to be; for what man identifies himself with is a mortal thing that will one day expire, and he will no more find himself to be as he had thought himself to be.

Nirvana therefore is the fifth and highest consciousness which I am explaining now. The experience of this consciousness is of a similar kind to that of a person in deep sleep. But in the deep sleep one is asleep outwardly, which means in the physical and in the mental body, while in the condition of *nirvana*, or highest consciousness, a person is conscious all through: he is conscious of the body as much as of the soul. Then the consciousness is so evenly divided – while yet he keeps to the highest stage – that at that time the person lives fully.

To conclude: what does the soul's awakening mean? The body's awakening means to feel sensation. The mind's awakening means to think and to feel. The soul's awakening means for the soul to become conscious of itself. Everyone is conscious of his affairs, of his conditions of life, of his body, of his mind, but not of his soul. In order to become conscious of the soul one has to work in a certain way, because the soul has become unconscious of itself; by working through its vehicles – body and mind – it has become unaware of its own freedom, of its own beauty.

In the East there is a custom and a belief that the one who sleeps must not be awakened. This is symbolical. Those whose soul is asleep may just as well sleep. If one awakens them they will be sick. It is not their time to awake. If they awake too soon they will be confused, they will act wrongly, speak wrongly. It is therefore that an untimely education of the philosophy of truth always proves to be undesirable.

The other day in London a friend of mine came from Ireland. I told this person to stay in a pension near my place which was a pension of the Theosophical Society. My friend came next day to me very surprised and troubled. She said, "I am quite confused. In that pension someone came to me and said, 'In my last incarnation you were my aunt'. Then someone else came and said, 'You were my sister'. Everyone there was my aunt, or friend, or somebody in a past incarnation, and everyone is claiming to have been a king. No one wishes to have been a poor man". I said – you know that Indians like humour – "They must have committed a great sin to have come this time as simple people".

That shows how, when we give untimely philosophical education, everything of subtle nature is made simple and is spoiled. Do you think that they speak very much in the East? They have respect, they do not talk, do not argue. All that is of a sacred nature, aspirations that belong to a higher world, they keep among some few who understand them and do not speak about these things. Therefore there is that custom never to awaken those who are asleep. When their time comes then you can give them a hand and they will awake.

The first stage in the awakening of the soul is a feeling, "Is there not something else that I could know". He feels dissatisfied with all he knows, with all the knowledge he may have, science, art, philosophy, or literature. He comes to a stage where he feels, "There is something else I must know that books, dogmas and beliefs cannot teach, something higher and greater that words cannot explain. That is what I want to know". It does not depend upon the age of the person. It may be a child who has that inclination or one who has reached age – and yet does not feel like it. It depends upon the soul. Therefore in the East they call a child an old soul when it begins to show that inclination, when it is not satisfied with the knowledge of names and forms and wants to know something else, although it may not know what it is.

Then there comes a second stage, and that stage is bewilderment. Imagine, an evolved person being more bewildered than an unevolved one! And yet it is so, for he begins to see that things are not as they seem to be but as they are. So there comes a kind of conflict: "What shall I call it: this or that, good or bad, love or hate?". There comes a time when all that was accepted in his mind, all that he believed to be so, appears to be quite the contrary to what it seems to be. His friends, his relations, those whom he loved, wealth, position, all things he had followed, change their appearance and sometimes become quite the contrary to what he had thought.

I will give you a little example of this bewilderment. The other day in Chicago a lady came to see me, trembling, in a very sorrowful state of mind. I asked her what was the matter and she said she had had an accident. The house in which she lived had been burnt, she had had to break a window in order to get out, she had hurt her hand, and it had all made a great upset in her life. But then she said, "It is not all that which makes me so upset". I asked, "What else?". She said, "The way how all my friends and neighbours whom I loved and liked acted at the time when the fire was on, has impressed me so that the whole world is quite different now". What does this mean? That friendship, relationship, love, devotion may not be the same as they appear when it comes to the time of test. Then there comes a time when a person begins to look at things differently.

This reminds me of a word from the Prophet Muhammad, who says in a kind of poetic form, "A witch followed me in the hereafter and I was frightened. I asked, What is this, Lord, that is frightening me? And the answer came, It is the same world that once you adored and worshipped and pursued and thought so much of". That shows that our consciousness changes our outlook in life; it changes as soon as our soul has opened its eyes. Our whole life changes. We live in the same world, and yet we do not; it is quite a different world then.

The next stage after this bewilderment is the stage of sympathy. We begin to appreciate things more and sympathize more, for so far we had walked on thorns and did not feel them, but in this stage we begin to feel them. We see that others are walking on the same thorns, so we forget our pain and begin to sympathize with them. The evolved ones therefore develop sympathy, a natural outgoing tendency. Troubles, sufferings, limitations everyone has to go through, everyone has to face the same difficulties. Not only the good ones, the wicked one has a still greater difficulty: he lives in the same world with his wickedness, he has a great load to carry. So naturally the evolved one becomes forgiving and sympathetic towards him.

As one goes further in the soul's unfoldment one finally arrives at the stage of revelation. Life begins to reveal itself, the whole of life, each soul becomes communicative – not only living beings but each thing. They say that the twelve apostles knew all languages. It does not mean that they knew English, French and Italian, but that they knew every soul's language, as every soul has its own separate language. They began to perceive vibrations and so every evolved soul will feel the vibrations of every other soul, and every condition, every soul, every object in the world will reveal its nature and character to him. Sa'adi, the Persian poet, has said, "Once a soul has begun to read, every leaf of the tree becomes as a page of the sacred book of life".

3

The word awakening is merely used for convenience, to make you see it more clearly. In reality the soul is always awake, the soul is never asleep. Day and night are two diverse conditions, they are not conditions of the sun. The sun neither rises nor sets. It is our conception; it is more convenient to speak of the rising and setting of the sun, but if anything rises and sets it is the world, not the sun. So day and night are not conditions of the sun, they are conditions themselves. When the world turns its back to the sun it is night, and when the world turns its face to the sun it is day. It is the same with the soul's awakening. The soul is always awake, but what is it awake to? Someone may be looking with open eyes, but what is he looking at? Upwards or downwards or sideways? He is looking in a certain direction and is conscious of that direction. To speak of the soul's awakening therefore is for the sake of convenience.

What part in us is it that may be called soul? Is it our body with its flesh and bones and veins and blood? Is it our mind with its thoughts, imaginations, feelings and emotions? Neither of these. Then what is it? It is something which is beyond the body and beyond the mind. When one asks, "Is it conscious", the answer is that it is, but its consciousness is not as we understand it, for we know it as intelligence, as being conscious of something. Everyone does not know what it conscious of something. Everyone does not know what consciousness means, but everyone knows what he is conscious of.

For instance, a mirror with a reflection in it is not only a mirror, but it is a mirror in which something is reflected. This means that it is occupied, it is not empty. When a person says "consciousness", he does not think of the original condition of it; he thinks only of the consciousness which is conscious of something. As soon as we distinguish between consciousness and that which it is conscious of we separate them, we see them as two things, just as we can separate the mirror from what is reflected in it.

As soon as we realize this we will come to the conclusion that the soul of the wise and the foolish, of the sinner and the virtuous, is one and the same. The wickedness of the wicked and the goodness of the good, the ignorance of the foolish and the wisdom of the wise are apart from the soul; the soul is only conscious of it. At the time when the soul is conscious of it one says, "Here is an ignorant soul", but the soul is the same. It is not the soul which is ignorant or wise; what is reflected in it is ignorant or wise, wicked or virtuous. At the same time we should know that if an elephant looks into a mirror, the mirror is not the elephant, but one can see an elephant in the mirror. If a man does not know what a mirror is he can say, "Here is an elephant", but it is only its reflection; free from this reflection it is only a mirror. The moment the reflection is removed, the mirror will be a mirror as it always has been.

So it is with the soul. Man makes it miserable, wicked, ignorant, wise or illuminated by being conscious of these things. The soul is neither the one nor the other. The soul is only soul. However there is the difficulty that very often people, having a certain conception of the soul, do not see the idea of the mystic and say, "a wicked soul, a bad soul, a foolish soul". But the soul cannot be that, the soul is the soul, it is beyond any attributes.

Now one will ask, "Where does the soul come from? If it is conscious what is it then?" And the best explanation that can be given is: the soul is the essence of all things, it is life – but not life in the sense we understand it. What we call life is a suggestion of life. The soul is the real life. The reflection, which is only a suggestion of the soul, we call life and one who moves and sees and hears and acts we call a living being, but what is living in him is the soul. The soul is not seen, therefore life is not seen. Life has touched the person; so one sees the effect of that touch in the person and one says, "He is living, it is life". But what we see is a suggestion of life which appears and disappears. Life is life, it never dies.

When one asks, "What is intelligence?", we have the same problem as with consciousness. One knows intelligence as something which is intelligent, but there is a difference between intelligence and intelligent. The intelligence which has the reflection of a certain knowledge becomes intelligent. But intelligence need not know: it is the knowing faculty; just as consciousness need not be conscious of anything: it is consciousness itself, it cannot witness it.

For instance, if one keeps a person in a dark room with beautiful colours and pictures he cannot see them. His eyes are open, his sight is open, but what is before him is not reflected in his sight. What is there is sight, nothing reflected in it. So it is with consciousness, and it is the same with intelligence: intelligence which is consciousness, and consciousness which is the soul. Why do the materialistic and spiritualistic view differ? A materialist to-day says that even biology shows how man comes from the animal kingdom. There is a gradual awakening of matter to become conscious and through the awakening to consciousness matter becomes fully intelligent in man. So far science goes.

A mystic does not deny this. He says, "It is quite true, but where does matter come from, and what is matter?" Matter is intelligence just the same, there is only a process. Just like the seed – which is the root – manifests within the heart of the flower, so in man intelligence manifests through the development of matter. But intelligence which is intelligent begins with intelligence and finishes in intelligence.* Spirit is the source and goal of all things; if matter did not have spirit in it, it would not awaken, it would not develop. Matter shows that life unfolds it, that life discovers it, that life realizes it: that consciousness which was so to speak buried in matter for thousands of years. By a gradual process it is realized through the vegetable and animal kingdoms, and in man it unfolds itself and takes its original condition. The only difference is that in this finishing of the spirit, this fulfilment of the spirit which manifests in man, there is variety: such a large number of human beings, millions and billions – and in their origin is one being. Spirit is one when unmanifested,

---

*just as the seed begins as seed and finishes in seed. (editor's note).

and many in the realm of manifestation. Therefore the appearance of this world of variety gives man first the impression of many lives – which produces what we call illusion and keeps man ignorant of the human being. The root from where he comes, the original state of his being, man does not know. He is all the time under the illusion of the world of variety which keeps him absorbed, interested and busy, and at the same time ignorant of his real condition as long as he is asleep to one side of life and awakened to the other, asleep to the inner and awakened to the outer side of life. Awakening of the soul is what the mystic calls awakening to the source; it is the condition to awaken to the reality of life.

You may ask how one awakens to this reality, what makes one awaken, and whether it is necessary for one to be awakened. The answer is that the whole of creation was made in order to awaken. This awakening is chiefly of two kinds: one kind is called birth, the birth of the body, when a soul awakens in a condition where it is limited in the physical body. This is one awakening and by this man becomes captive. There is another awakening, which is to awaken to reality, and that is called the birth of the soul. First is the birth of the body, next the birth of the soul, as it is said in the Bible. One awakening is to the world of illusion, the other to the world of reality.

One must know that for everything there is a time, and when this is not considered one makes a mistake. When one wakens a person at two o'clock at night his sleep is broken; he ought to sleep all night, it was necessary for him. Not knowing this, people very often try to wake a person up, their wife, husband, friend or relation, their child or father. They are very anxious to awaken the other; often they feel too lonely and think, "This person is close to me, he should be awakened too". It is the same with the one who smokes or drinks: he likes others to have the same experience, just as it is too dull for a person in a cheerful mood if the other one is so dull that he cannot laugh and see the joke. Naturally therefore the desire, the tendency of those who awaken to the higher life is to awaken others. They cannot help it, it is natural.[6] But very often one is too impatient with people and unreasonable. Very often we make great mistakes wanting to awake a person before it is time – when he ought to have a sleep. Also we sometimes presume to be more awake than another, while in reality the other may be more awakened.

There is a story of a wife who was religious and devotional. One day she arranged a feast and her husband asked, "What is it for? Is it a religious day?". "It is more than a religious day", she said, "It is the greatest day in my life. There was something which always kept me anxious and it has left me now". The husband asked what that was, and she said, "Since I married you I thought that you had no inclination to anything spiritual or religious". "Then what makes you think otherwise?", asked the husband. She said, "To-day I have realized, now I understand, that you are spiritual". "Do you? How do you know?" "Well", she said, "do not ask me". "No, tell it to me". She then told him, "I heard you say the name of God while turning over in your sleep". "Did I", said he, "Alas". He fell down and died instantly. The mystery was too sacred to him, something he could never say in words. His feeling of devotion and worship was so great that no church could contain it, it was vaster than any church, greater than the universe. When that mystery was broken it was as if a sacred seal was broken. He could not stand it and died.

The other day I was touched to see a play in which a student of the light of the higher ideals says the Word, the sacred Word, and dies. The beautiful part was that there was a prophet in the play who saw it and said, "He saw beyond and died".*

What does death mean? Turning. The soul is always awake, so it is always living. What is death? Death is turning: the soul turns from one side to another. If a beautiful voice comes from behind to which it wishes to listen then it turns, it is attracted to another direction. This is called awakening, awakening to a certain sphere to which it was asleep.

It is no use trying to awake everybody; everyone is awakening to something – if not to higher truth, then to lesser. The one who has the privilege of being awake can give a hand to

*Hazrat Inayat Khan refers to Ansky's play "The Dybbuk" (editor's note).

the one who is trying to awake – to whatever plane it may be. In the language of the mystic giving a hand is called initiation.

In order to get a clear idea of awakening I should like to bring to your thought the condition which we call a dream. Many give little importance to it. When one says, "This person is dreamy", it means that he is conscious of something which is nothing. But is there really anything which we can call a dream? The real meaning of dream is that which is past. Yesterday is as much a dream as the experience of the night: it is past. When a person is dreaming, does he think that he is in a dream? Does he think that it is unimportant? At that moment does he give it less importance than his everyday life? He looks at it as a dream when he is awakened to the other sphere, but while in the dream sphere he will not call it a dream. When a person is asked, "What about the experience of yesterday?", he will say, "It was a dream, everyday life was a dream".

The more one thinks of it, the more one glances into the hereafter, and the more one will realize that what is behind the veil of death, is awakening to another sphere as real as this, even more real than this. What is real? Real is the soul, the consciousness itself. What is past is a dream, what will come is hope. What one experiences seems real, but it is only a suggestion. The soul is real, its aim is to realize itself. Its liberation, its freedom, harmony and peace, all depend upon its own unfoldment. No outside experience can make the soul realize the real.

Why cannot we see the soul? We can see the body and from our thoughts we can think that we have a mind, because thought manifests to us in the form of a mental picture. Why do we not see the soul? The answer is that as the eyes can see all things but themselves so it is with the soul. The soul is sight itself, it sees all, but the moment it closes its eyes to all it sees then its own light makes it manifest to its own view. It is therefore that people take the path of meditation, the path by which they get in touch with themselves, with their soul. They realize the continuity of life which is immortal life, they realize the independence of life by getting in touch with their soul.

Now one may ask, "What about those who come in this

world in a miserable condition, while others come in good conditions? Is it not something innate in the soul?" No, it is something that the soul has carried along with it like the load on a camel: it is on its back, not within it. So it is with the load of the soul.

Another question is, "If the soul is awakened, how does it awake, and who awakens it?" We see that the time for nature to awake is the spring. It is asleep all winter and it awakes in the spring. There is a time for the sea, when the wind blows and brings good tidings, as if it awakes from sleep; then the waves rise. All this shows struggle, it shows that something has touched it and makes it uneasy, restless; it makes it want liberation, release. Every atom, every object, every condition and every living being has a time of awakening.

Sometimes there is a gradual awakening, and sometimes there is a sudden awakening. To some persons it comes in a moment's time – by a blow, by a disappointment, or because their heart has broken through something that happened suddenly. It seemed cruel, but at the same time the result was a sudden awakening and this awakening brought a blessing beyond praise. The outlook changed, the insight deepened; joy, quiet, independence and freedom were felt, and compassion showed in the attitude. A person who would never forgive, who liked to take revenge, who was easily displeased and cross, a person who would measure and weigh, when his soul is awakened, becomes in one moment a different person. As the emperor of India Mahmud Ghaznavi has said in a most beautiful line, "I, the emperor, who have thousands of slaves awaiting my command, the moment love has sprung in my heart consider myself the slave of my servants". The whole attitude becomes changed. Only, the question is what one awakens to, in which sphere, in what plane, to which reality.

Sometimes after one has made a mistake, by the loss that mistake has caused, the outlook becomes quite different. In business, in one's profession, in worldly life, a certain experience just like a blow has broken something in a person and with that breaking a light has come, a new light. However, one is not always to be awakened by a mistake. No doubt awakening very often comes by a blow, by a great pain, a painful condition, but at the same time it is not necessary to look for a blow. Life has enough blows for us, we need not look for them.

There is a story of a peasant girl who was passing through a farm while going to another village. There was a Muslim offering his prayers on his prayer-rug in the open. The law is that no one should cross the place where anyone is praying. When this girl returned from the village this man was still sitting there. He said, "O girl, now what terrible sin have you committed!" "What did I do?" asked she. "I was offering prayers here, and you passed over this place". The girl asked, "What do you mean by offering prayers?" "Thinking of God", he replied. The girl said, "Yes? Were you thinking of God? I was thinking of my young man whom I was going to meet, and I did not see you. Then how did you see me while you were thinking of God?" That shows what awakening means, what sleep means. She was asleep to the Muslim and awake to the one she was going to meet. And he was awake to something else than to the object of his prayer. He was asleep to his object and she was awake. One's heart is where one's treasure is. If it values a treasure it is awakened to it. If it is not awakened to a treasure it may be awakened to some misery. If its treasure is on earth the heart is awakened rather to the earth than to something else.

In spiritual awakening the first thing that comes to man is the lifting of a veil and this is the lifting of an apparent condition. Then a person does not see every condition as it appears to be, but sees behind every condition its deeper meaning. Generally man has an opinion about everything that appears before him. He does not wait one moment to look or to have patience, he immediately forms an opinion about every person, about every action he sees; whether wrong or right, he immediately forms an opinion without knowing what is behind it, ready to contempt. It takes a long time for God to weigh and measure; for man it takes no time to judge! But when the veil of immediate reason is lifted, then one reaches the cause, then one is not awakened to the surface but to what is behind the surface. There comes another step in awakening when a man does not even see the cause, but comes to the realization of the adjustment of things: how every activity of life, whether it appears to be wrong or right, adjusts itself. By the time he arrives at this condition he has lost much of his false self. That is what brings him there, for the more one is conscious of the false self, the further one is removed from reality. These two things cannot go together. It is dark or it is light; if it is light there is no darkness. As much as the false conception of self is broken up, so much more light there is. On this path therefore a person sees life more clearly.

Another form of awakening is the awakening of the self; one begins to wonder, "What does my thought mean, what does my feeling mean, what does wrong and what does right mean? What is it after all?" A man then begins to weigh and measure all that springs within himself. The further he goes the more he sees behind all things, not only living on the surface of life, but attached to all planes of existence. This is a new awakening. Then a person has only to be awakened to the other world; he need not go there. He need not experience what is death, but he can bring about a condition where he rises above life. This brings him to the conclusion that there are many worlds in one world. He closes his eyes to the dimensions of the outer world and finds within his own self: "You are the centre of all worlds". And the only thing necessary is turning; not awakening, but turning.

Man has become motionless, stagnant by fixing himself to this world in which he is born, in which he has become interested. If he makes his soul more subtle in order to turn away from this world he can experience all that is said of the different worlds, of the different planes of consciousness. He will find the whole mystery within himself only by being able to make his soul so subtle that it can turn and move.

One may ask, "How can we make the soul subtle?" The character of the soul is like water. By being stagnant it becomes frozen like ice which does not move, and so it is with the soul bound to the world of which it is conscious. It is not unable to move, but that consciousness holds it; it is like captivity. A Sufi poet shows the way out of it when he says, "You yourself have made your self a captive, and you yourself will try to make your self free".

CHAPTER XX

The Dance of the Soul

1

ONE OFTEN wonders what it is in the lower creation, in a horse coming from a good race, in a peacock and more animals, which gives them the tendency to dance. What we generally call a beautiful horse is a horse which shows that tendency and those who understand the qualities of animals judge them by their tendency to dance. Once I was looking at a procession of the Maharaja of Nepal. When the whole of the procession had passed and the horse of the Maharaja approached, it seemed as if the horse by his dancing tendency was answering the eagerness of the people to see the Maharaja and pay homage to him. A person standing near me made the remark, "It seems as if the horse were conscious of his master". In that remark lies the secret of the dance.

This tendency is found throughout the lower creation, although it be an unconscious one; it is as it were the rising of the deepest part of being. If there are two horses, one with an inclination to dance every moment, the other with an inclination to stand still like a log of wood, we may say that the deepest self of the latter is covered and the deepest self of the former is open and wanting to express the vibration which animates it. The desire to dance arises in the peacock because it is impressed by beauty, which it also shows in its own wings and feathers. The whole nature expresses its deep touch with its own source. Life is a swing; there is one swing where life touches its innermost being and brings that out to the material world, striking every heart. In the waxing and waning of the moon, the changing tides of the sea, the alternate seasons there is a period when nature breathes downward and dives up something that is most beautiful and appealing to the heart.

When we consider the human race we find that the whole nature represents itself in an individual being, and this individual being reflects the whole nature. The infant has moments of smiles when it is happy and moves its hands and legs while there seems to be no reason why it should do so. Although every man is not a philosopher, every soul is a philosopher, and in the East it is said that when a child smiles it sees the angels. As the sun gives joy by its reflection, so that inner spirit when reflected in a human being produces joy and happiness. By that smile of the infant everybody is drawn; it is a magic for everyone who looks at it. Words can never explain what the child feels. Grown-up persons lose that touch through their artificial life, yet they are drawn to the child's happiness. As the infant grows into a child it still has its moments when it is moved to sing and dance, not knowing where that tendency comes from, but enjoying paradise on earth. It wants a mind that is in touch with the infinite to perceive that joy invaluable in comparison to all other sensations of life in this world.

There is a Sura in the Qur'an which explains this a little, but few understand its true meaning: "Have you known the night of power? During that night angels descend, spirits are attracted, trees and mountains fall in prostration, submitting to the divinity of God". From the beginning to the end of that night there is inexplicable joy and profound peace. The prostration of trees and mountains means that they do not exist for the soul at that time. The soul has risen above them, from all worries and anxieties the mind is empty. Then the night of joy comes. An artist may paint pictures all his life, but there will only be a few moments when without making any effort his brush does what the soul wants it to do. The greatest musicians like Beethoven, Bach, whose music always has a living influence on the heart of man, did not create their music from the brain; it was not merely a play of technicality, there was something else. They are the musicians who caught the moments of the dance of the soul and responded to it.

In a musician the soul dances in the realm of music, in a painter the soul dances in the realm of colours, in the poet it dances in the realm of poetry. In sculpture and architecture we also find that it was the dance of the soul which produced it; the Taj Mahal in India for instance was a product of the dance of the soul. In all these aspects the soul shows its beauty, and in all these different realms the dance of the soul is one and the same. When one bell is rung, by the sound of that one bell other bells will also vibrate. So it is with the dancing of the soul; it produces its reaction and that again will make other souls dance.

How can we get to the secret of this dance? We want the key to be able to wind the soul to make it dance. A story of Tansen, the singer of king Akbar, tells that Akbar said to him, "You are such a great musician. I wonder how great your teacher must be". Tansen answered, "There is no comparison, my Lord, we are different. He is infinitely greater". Akbar was very much inclined to hear this master's music, but Tansen told him that his master lived in a cave, that it was a very long journey, and even then he did not know if his master would sing before a king. Akbar however was persistent and arrived with Tansen at the cave. The master saw who was his visitor but did not mind, and when he felt moved he began to sing. As he sang Akbar and Tansen went into ecstasy and both lost their consciousness. The master disappeared and they found themselves alone and as in a dream. When they had recovered their senses they went home. Akbar asked, "Why has the master disappeared?" And Tansen answered, "So that next time you might not know him". Akbar then asked Tansen to sing again the song of the master, but Tansen was not able to produce the same effect. He explained this to Akbar saying, "While I sing to thee, my master sings to God"

This explains our condition of to-day. In music, in painting, in poetry man's first thought is, "How will it take? What will the people say of it?" When inspiration is sacrificed to the material world how can the soul ever dance – for the dance of the body is death to the soul. In his absorption in the external world man has lost touch with his own self.

Looking at this subject from a metaphysical point of view the soul is dancing when it is charged with the battery of infinite life. In the life of the infant, of the bird, free from responsibility, we find the natural life which is in touch with the battery of infinite life, and they become charged by it. As man grows, the more he is successful in worldly affairs, the more he loses contact with his inner being; he is kept in the spider's web he spun himself. Inharmonious conditions, the artificiality of life cause unrest, man is confused and knows not where lies his happiness. The battery which is the depth of every life may be called the divine Being, or divine Life. Every soul is connected with this battery, but when it is not responding to it, not conscious of it, it loses its chance.

In Krishna's dance, spoken of in every house in India as it is considered a sacred story, the secret of this philosophy is hidden. Krishna was a most charming youth, popular in his village. Every girl wanted once to dance with him and he promised that on a full moon night he would dance with everyone of them. When the night came all the girls arrived at the place where they were to dance and the miracle is told that really Krishna danced with every girl, for so many girls as there were, so many Krishnas appeared to dance.

Krishna is the innermost spirit whose life rises and dances through the artist. The different minds are represented by the *gopis*, the girls, and Krishna is the source of life within the individual. The different minds are considered as *gopis*, because the mind must already have its own beauty to be able to reflect that greater beauty. For instance, if a man had no idea of language and his soul began to dance no *gopi* would be there, no possibility for poetry to flower from him, as his mind was not prepared. Our souls are only created to dance; it is their nature to dance and it is the tragedy of life when the soul is kept from dancing. Our craving for comfort and outward satisfaction, our ambition, our desires are nothing but the longing to experience that dance – as we know it. Paradise is pictured by every teacher as a place where there is music and dance. Music itself is dance, poetry is the dance of words, singing the dance of the voice. Only when inspiration comes naturally it is a life coming from the depth of the individual.

The Hindus speak of Indra as the king of paradise; the dancers in his court are called *apsaras*. A much loved story in the East tells us of a dancer of the court of Indra who loved a being of the earth and brought him with her to heaven. Indra's wrath was aroused; he separated them and they were sent into the desert. The reason is that the dancers who were especially for Indra were not supposed to neglect their duty for the love of other beings. Our souls are dancers to God; born to dance to God they must enjoy beauty in its perfection. When we forget that dance in our absorption in earthly joys we neglect our duties for which we were created.

The object in the life of the Sufi is to keep his heart like a compass pointing to one goal, the centre, Indra for whom every soul is created to dance. We need not go to the forest or the wilderness; we can be in a crowd, but we should be like the compass, always pointing to the one goal of our existence.

Studies and practices are given to prepare the pupil to look at that goal. It is known to many that there are people in the East who for thousands of years have given their whole life to the search of the truth. The Sufi message represents that thought which can draw East and West together in the understanding of life. An opportunity has been given to the friends of these thoughts to bring man home to this secret of life.

2

We see in the life of an infant that there comes a moment when it smiles to itself and moves its little feet and legs as if dancing, bringing delight to the one who looks on and creating life in the atmosphere. What was it that sprang into being in the heart of the tiny infant, ignorant of the pains and pleasures of life? What is it that suddenly springs from its heart, that gives expression to its eyes, that inspires its little movements and voice? In ancient times the old people said, "This is the spirit coming". They thought it was an angel or fairy speaking to the child, but in reality it is the soul which at that moment arises to ecstasy which makes all things dance. There are many delightful experiences in life, but joy is something greater and deeper than delight, it springs from the innermost being. There can be no better description of the springing of joy than the dance of the soul.

One finds in the life of every person, sorrowful or happy, wise or foolish, that there are moments when he begins to sing or move. Joy may be expressed also by a smile, it may even be expressed in tears of joy, but in one and all it is the dance of the soul. This heavenly bliss is not only for mankind, it comes to all beings. Man lives his life in an artificial world and seldom has a chance to see the beauty of nature. This ecstasy is to be found in the forests, in the wilderness where the great Yogis, sages, saints, seers and prophets received their inspiration. If you could only see what is called in the East the dance of the peacocks, the peacocks expressing the impulse of joy, inspired and blessed by the sublime beauty around them. Birds and animals all have their moment of joy, and in these moments you can hear their words, their song, but the greatest expression is in their dance. To nearly every animal there come moments when the blessing of heaven descends upon them, and they respond in dance.

This blessing is revealed in every aspect of life, even in inanimate objects, in trees and plants; even there we see in the spring the rising of life. Flowers and plants are but different expressions of the one life, the source of all beauty and joy and harmony. Someone asked the Prophet for a definition of the soul, and he answered in one sentence: "The soul is an action of God". There could be no more expressive words to explain this philosophy. It is the action of the inner or divine Life, and when this shows itself in any form it is the reaction to the action of God; it is this which may be called the dance of the soul.

It is this which has inspired the great musicians and poets. Why do the music of Wagner or Beethoven and the words of Shakespeare live so long and continually give new joy and inspiration? Why has not all music and poetry the same effect? Because poetry is one thing, and the dance of the soul another. The dance of the soul is beyond mere poetry, and when music expresses itself as the dance of the soul it becomes something higher than music. Man becomes so accustomed to external knowledge! He wants to learn and understand this thing and that, but beauty does not come so naturally because beauty is beyond all knowledge: it is intended to prepare man to express his soul.

How often do we confuse these two things, inspiration and education. Education is the preparation for inspiration.

Education prepares the mind to be a better means for the expression of the natural spring in the heart. When education becomes a hobby and inspiration is forgotten then the soul becomes choked, and where there is no life man is mechanical, unreal. He may write poetry, compose music and paint pictures, but they are all lifeless, for he himself is a machine. The soul in itself is life, knowledge and beauty.

As an instance I will speak of two poets in India. Kalidasa was the most learned poet of the Sanskrit age and was never educated. As far as language goes Kabir's language was most ordinary and yet, when the people in India who laid importance on the delicacy and convention of Hindi heard his words, they forgot conventions, for his poetry brought life, it sprang from the soul, it was spirit. Grammar was faulty, but nevertheless the verses made that impression. Why? Because the words were living, the soul was dancing.

The purpose of life is to become more living, to allow the soul to live more, and that is the limit given by Christ when he says, "Raise your light high". This means allowing the soul to express itself. It does not matter what your life is, what your pursuit is; in order to fulfil the purpose of life you need not be in a temple or a church. Whatever your life's pursuit – art, poetry, sculpture, music, whatever your occupation may be – you can be as spiritual as a priest or clergyman, always living a life of praise. Your work in life must be your religion; let the soul express itself in every aspect and it will surely fulfil the purpose of life. The soul's life comes naturally if we open ourselves for the spirit to rise.

There is an old story in India that expresses this philosophy. In the belief of Hindus there is a heaven or paradise called *Indraloka* where the God Indra is king, and there are angels or fairies whose work is to dance before Indra. There was a fairy from *Indraloka* who once descended on earth and loved an earthly being. By the power of her magic she brought this earthly being to paradise. When this became known to Indra she was cast out from paradise and they were separated.

This legend is symbolic of the human soul, which originally belonged to *Indraloka*, the kingdom of God, the sphere full of peace, joy and happiness. Life there is nothing but joy, it is a dance. Life and love come from God and raise every soul till it dances. It is therefore that the Yogi term *atma* means the soul of man as joy itself. In its pure condition it is a joy, and when it is without joy its natural condition is changed: it depends upon the names and forms of the earth and is deprived of the dance of the soul. Therein lies the whole tragedy of life. The wrath of Indra, the God of paradise, is nothing but breach of law*, as it is natural that the soul is attracted to the Spirit and that the true joy of every soul is the realization of the divine Spirit.

Absence of realization keeps the soul in despair. In the life of every poet, thinker, artist or scientist there come moments when ideas or words are given to him; they are given at that moment and at no other. This is the moment when unconsciously the soul has an opportunity to breathe. Man does not usually allow his soul to breathe; the portal is closed up in the life of the earth. Man closes it by ignorance, he is absorbed in things of much less importance. So when the door opens and the soul is able to breathe even one breath, it becomes alive in that one single moment, and what comes out is beauty and joy making man express himself in song or dance. So heavenly beauty comes on earth.

The things that catch man's mind are always living things. The poems of Rumi which are called *Masnavi*, have lived for eight hundred years, they are living, they bring joy and ecstasy whenever they are sung or recited. They are ever-living life, expressing an everlasting beauty. It is the power of God, and for man ever to presume it possible to produce that by study is a mistake. It is impossible. It is the power of God above which brings out the perfection of beauty. Man can never make the soul dance, but he can make himself a fit instrument for the expression of his soul. The question is, in what way can he so fit himself?

It appears that the soul is the Spirit of God, and the Spirit of God lives within the shrine of the heart; this shrine can be closed or it can be open. There are some things in life that open it and some that close it. The things that close the heart are those which are contrary to love, tolerance and

---

*the law that the highest love must be for God alone. (editor's note).

forgiveness, such as coldness, bitterness and ill-will, and a strong element of duality. The world is more upset to-day than ever before; in many ways man seems to go from bad to worse, and yet he thinks that he is progressing. It is not lack of organization or of civilization; both these things he has. What he lacks is the expression of the soul. He closes his door to his fellow-man, he closes the shrine of the heart and by doing so he is keeping God away from himself and others. Nation is set against nation, race against race, religion against religion. Therefore to-day more than ever before there is a need for the realization of this philosophy. What we need is not that all religions should become one nor all races; that can never be. But what is needed is undivided progress, and making ourselves examples of love and tolerance.

By talking about it, by discussing and arguing it will not come, but by self-realization, by making ourselves the examples of what should be, by giving love, taking love, and showing in our action gentleness, consideration and the desire for service for the sake of God in whom we can all unite beyond the narrow barriers of race and creed.

PART II

THE DEEPER SIDE OF LIFE

CHAPTER I

The Deeper Side of Life

1

LIFE CAN be looked at from two points of view: from the point of view which sees the outline and from the point of view which sees the detail. With the point of view by which one sees the general outline of life one soars upwards continually and one attains to the knowledge of life's synthesis. This is the view of life of the one who is looking from the top of a high mountain. As to the one who sees into life's details, naturally his horizon becomes smaller, his outlook narrower. He makes the analysis of life and so becomes acquainted with the details of life.

The former point of view gives insight into a wider horizon and lifts the consciousness to a higher realization, whereas the latter point of view gives knowledge in the details of life, which one calls learning. Therefore learning is one thing, knowing is another thing. Learning without knowing is incomplete knowledge, knowing without learning is not satisfactory either. The knower can best explain his knowledge if he has learning.

The mystics of all ages have raised their consciousness to view the outline of life in the wide horizon and have felt upliftment being raised high above all the miseries of life. Those who have ever reached that stage of consciousness have only reached it by right meditation under the guidance of masters of spiritual culture.

2

In these modern times people consider an intellectual life or a life of manual labour a normal life. A practical man is considered a man of common sense, and common sense reaches no further than its limited boundaries. A practical man is the one who knows best how to guard his material interests in the continual struggle of life. Common sense sees no further than it sees. Many call it positivism only to believe in all that proves to be realistic to our higher senses and in all that can be perceived, felt and experienced by our mind.

For this reason, in spite of great and unceasing progress in the material world, we have closed the doors to another world of progress, a progress that can only be made by opening the doors to the deeper side of life. Man, by his form and features, by his physical construction, looks at one side and covers the other side with his own self. Man sees before him, but not behind him. As he is made so by nature and it happens to be his nature, he therefore cannot look into the deeper side while absorbed in the life on the surface.

Since there is faith these days, but absence of inner life, there seems to be a greater need of the inner life than there has ever been before. It is the head quality which is developed and it is the heart quality which needs to be developed in order to bring balance in life. Life, so balanced, is then prepared for the inner culture or spiritual life. Many consider sentiment something quite unimportant, something that should be kept aside from the central theme of life to-day which is intellectuality. No one who has given a thought to the deeper side of life will deny for one moment the power and inspiration that manifest themselves once the heart is kindled. A person with heart quality need not be simple, he need not discard intellect; only, the heart quality produces that perfume in the intellect which is as fragrance in a flower. Morals learned from logic are dry morals, a fruit without juice, a flower without fragrance. It is the heart quality that as a course of nature produces virtues which no one can teach; a loving person, a person with sympathy in his heart, teaches morals through himself. It is the balance of mind and heart, or the balance of thought and feeling that makes the ground ready for sowing the seed of the inner life.

There are three steps which one must take in order to come to spiritual life.

The first step is knowledge of the nature and character of man. A seeker takes his first step in the path of truth when he is able to understand his fellow-man fully and when he is able to find the solution to his problems.

The next step is to have insight into the nature of things

and beings, to understand cause and effect and to be able to find the cause of the cause and the effect of the effect, to be able to see the reason of the reason and the logic of the logic. When a person is able to see the good of the bad and the bad side of the good, and when he is able to see the wrong side of the right and the right of the wrong, then he has taken the next step on the spiritual path.

The third step is to rise above the pains and pleasures of life, to be in the world and not of the world, to live and not to live at the same time. Such a one becomes a living dead person, in other words: a dead person living for ever. Immortality is not to be sought in the hereafter; if it is ever gained it is gained in one's lifetime. In this third stage of development one is able to attain happiness, power, knowledge, life and peace within oneself, independently of all things outside.

The spiritual knowledge which has always been sought by the wakened souls will always be sought by them. In ancient times the seekers looked for a guide on this path, the guide who initiated them into the mysteries of the deeper side of life, and once the secret was revealed it no longer remained a mystery for them. The man who is not yet awakened to the inner side of life has not experienced life fully. He has only seen one side of life – perhaps the more interesting side, but the less real. The one who has experienced both sides of life, the outer and the inner, has certainly fulfilled the purpose of his life on earth.

CHAPTER II

Man the Seed of God

1

THERE ARE various ideas and beliefs as to the relation between God and man, and it is natural that there should be various beliefs, for every man has his own conception – his own conception of God. There is no comparison between God and man. The reason is that man, being limited, can be compared with another being; God, being perfect, is beyond comparison. The prophets and masters in all ages have tried their best to give man some idea of God's Being, but this has always been difficult, for it is impossible to define God in words; it is like trying to put the ocean into a bottle. However large a bottle, it can never accommodate the ocean. The words that we use in our everyday language are the names of limited forms, and for our convenience we give a name to God – the one who is above name and form. If there is any possibility of understanding God and His Being – it is only possible by finding the relation between man and God.

Why is this lecture called "Man the seed of God"? Because it is this picture which gives to some extent that idea of the relationship which exists between man and God. There is a root, there is a stem, there are branches and there are leaves – there comes a flower. But in the heart of the flower there is something which tells the history of the whole plant. One might say that it is for the flower that the plant was purposed, but really speaking it is the seed coming into the heart of the flower which continues the species of the plant. It is that seed which is the secret of the plant, which is the source and the goal of that plant. It is that seed which was the beginning; it is from out of that seed that the root came, that the seedling came out – and so it became a plant. Then that seed disappeared, but after the coming of the leaves and branches and the flowers it appeared again. It appeared again – not as one seed but as several seeds, in multiplicity, and yet it is the same, and it is this seed which told us the story that first was the seed, and then the whole plant appeared. Towards what goal? For what result? In order to come again as the result of the whole plant.

The man of simple belief, the man who believes only in his particular idea – for him there is no relation between God and man. But the man wo wishes to understand the relation between man and God – for him the proof of this argument is to be found in everything. It is this idea which is spoken of in the Bible in the words where it is said, "In Our image We have created man". If the seed out of which the plant came and which appeared in the result had said, "Out of my own image I have created the seed which will come forth from the heart of the flower", it would have been the same thing. Only that seed out of which the plant came could have said, "I shall appear in plurality, although in the beginning I am one grain".

It is this idea again which tells us the reason why it is said, "We have created man in Our image", when the whole of manifestation, the whole of creation has come from God. The leaf, the branch, the stem – all have come out of the seed, but they are not the image of the seed. The image of the seed is the seed itself; and not only this, but the essence of the seed is in the seed. No doubt there is some energy, some power, some colour, some fragrance in the flower, in the leaves and in the stem, but at the same time all properties that are in the stem, flower, petal and leaves are to be found in the grain. This shows us the result: that man is the culmination of the whole creation, and in him the whole universe is manifested. The mineral kingdom, the vegetable kingdom, the animal kingdom are all to be found in the being, in the spirit of man. It not only means that the different properties such as mineral and vegetable are to be found in the physical body that is made for man, but also his mind and his heart show all the different qualities.

The heart is just like a fertile soil or a barren desert: it shows love or lack of love, the productive faculty or destructiveness. There are different kinds of stones; there are precious stones and there are pebbles and rocks, and so among human hearts there is a still greater variety. Think of those whose thoughts, whose feelings have proved to be more precious than anything the world can offer: the poets, the artists, the inventors, the thinkers, the philosophers, and then the servants of humanity, the inspirers of man, the benefactors of mankind. No wealth, no precious stone, whether diamond or ruby, can be compared with these, and yet it is the same quality. Then there are rocklike hearts: one may knock against them and break oneself – yet they will not move. There is a waxlike quality in the heart and there is the quality of the stone; there are melting hearts, and hearts which will never melt.

Is there anything in nature which is not to be found in man? Has he not in his feelings, in his thoughts, in his qualities the picture of running water, a picture of a fertile soil and a picture of fruitful trees? Is there not in the heart of man the picture of plants, of fragrant flowers? The flowers that come from the human heart live longer, their fragrance will spread throughout the whole world, and their colour will be seen by all people. How delicious are the fruits that human hearts can bear; they immortalize souls and lift them up!

There are other mentalities wherein nothing springs up except the desire to hurt and harm their fellow-men, thus producing the fruits and flowers of poison, hurting others by thought, speech or action – and they can hurt more than thorns. There are some whose feelings, whose thoughts are like gold and silver and there are others whose thoughts are just like iron and steel. The variety that one can see in human nature is so vast that all the objects one can get from this earth are too small in number if compared with it.

Does man show in his nature, in his qualities, in his body, in his thought and feeling only the heritage of this earth? No, he also shows that of heaven. Man has the influence of the planets, he has the influences of the moon, of the sun, of heat and cold, of air, water and fire: of all the different elements which make this whole cosmic system. All these elements are to be found in his thoughts, in his feelings, in his body. One can find a person with warmth, representing fire; another person is cold, he represents water. There are human beings who in their thought, in their feeling represent the air element; their quickness, their restlesness show the air element in them.

Does not man represent the sun and moon in his positive and negative character, and does not duality of sex show this? Not only this, but in every man and in every woman there is the sun quality and there is the moon quality, and it is these two opposite qualities which give balance to the character of man. When one quality is most predominant, and the other not to be found, then balance is lacking somewhere.

If one goes still further in the thought of mysticism one will find that not only all the visible manifestation is to be found in man, but also all that is invisible. If angels or fairies or ghosts or elementals – anything that man has imagined – can be found anywhere, it is in human nature. In all times one finds pictures of angels in the image of man.

If all that exists in the world and in heaven is to be found in man, then what remains? God Himself has said in the scriptures, "I have made man in My own image". In other words, "If you wish to see Me, I am to be found in man". How thoughtless on the part of the one who, absorbed in his high ideals, begins to condemn man, to look down upon man, however low and weak and a sinner man may be! Since in man there is the possibility of rising so high as nothing else in the whole manifestation can rise – whether something on the earth or any being in heaven – none can reach that height which man is meant to reach. What point of view, therefore, had the mystics, the thinkers of all ages? One can see their point of view in their manner: a respectful attitude to all men. In the example of the life of Jesus Christ, the master of mankind – what compassion one can see when a sinner was brought before him, someone who had done wrong – what forgiveness the master showed! There was tolerance, there was understanding. A man can be called religious or pious, but he cannot be called truly spiritual or wise when he has contempt towards his fellow-man, whatever be his condition.

The man who has no respect for mankind, has no worshipful attitude towards God — he may be the most religious person. The man who has not recognized the image of God in man, has not seen the Artist who has made this creation; he has deprived himself of this vision which is sacred and most holy. A person who thinks that man is earthly does not know where his soul comes from. The soul comes from above; it is in the soul of man that God is reflected. The man who has hatred, contempt, whatever be his belief, faith, or religion, has not understood the secret of all religions which is in the heart of man. And certainly, however good a person, however virtuous he may be, if at the same time he has no tolerance, no forgiveness, if he does not recognize God in man, he has not touched religion.

No doubt there is another side to the question. As man evolves, so he finds the limitations, the errors and the infirmities of human nature, and so it becomes difficult for him to live in the world and to withstand all that comes. Also it becomes very difficult for man to be fine, to be good, to be kind, to be sensitive, and at the same time to be tolerant. What then comes as a tendency is to push away everything, and to find oneself away from everybody and every being. But the purpose of being born on earth is different. The purpose of being born on earth is to find that perfection which is within oneself. And however good and kind a man may be, if he has not found the purpose for which he is born on earth, he has not fulfilled the object of his life.

There are as many different aspects of that purpose as there are people in the world, but behind all these different aspects there is one purpose. It is that purpose which may be called the purpose of the whole creation. That purpose is accomplished when the inventor looks at his invention working. When the great architect builds the house which he has designed, and enters it and sees how nicely it is achieved, the purpose is accomplished. When a producer of a play has produced the play he desired and looks at it, that is the purpose.

Every man seems to have his purpose, but this purpose is nothing but a step to that which is the one purpose, which is the purpose of God. Our small desires, if they are granted to-day, to-morrow we will have another wish. Whatever be the desire, when it is granted, next day there is another desire. This shows that the whole of humanity, that every soul, is directed towards one desire, and that is the object of God: a fuller experience of life within and without, a fuller knowledge of life, the life above and below. It is the widening of the outlook: that it may be so wide that in the soul, which is vaster than the world, all may be reflected; that the sight may become so keen that it may probe the depths of the earth and the highest of the heavens. It is herein that lies the fulfilment of the soul. And the soul who will not make every effort possible, with every sacrifice for the attainment of this, that soul has not understood religion. What is the Sufi message? It is esoteric training, working and practising through life towards that attainment which is as the fulfilment of the object of God.

2

Man the seed of God – it is in this secret that man finds the key that has been lost. This loss shows why the religions of the world seem to be losing their hold upon people, in the Eastern part of the world as well as in the West. Why is there an increasing number of ungodly? Why is materialism ever on the increase? The answer is that man has lost the key which opens the secret of life. It is God who is the key to this secret. During my travellings of some years throughout the Western world I found in every part of the civilized world people getting tired not only of religion but also of belief in God. It seems that the deity's name is repellent to an advanced thinker. He thinks that this is something which was a creed of the past: "The ancient people who did not know life better had some certain idea and now we are too advanced to hold on to the ideas of the past". Very few admit it and many will not say it, but almost all know it. In the East perhaps it is different, but the whole world moves on in the same direction. If the direction of humanity is a material one then the whole world goes in this material direction; if it is a spiritual direction naturally the whole world must go in the spiritual direction.

In spite of all material progress which has raised the value of civilization so high in the eyes of the new generation, it could not keep to its pedestal; it fell down during the war. It has made the thinking world consider, at least for a moment, that the civilization it had thought to be the best has not proved to be the best. No just person, a person with some thought, will deny the fact after having reflected upon it. If we ask ourselves, "Has the world advanced?", no doubt the answer will be, "Yes". The new inventions which have brought about the miraculous phenomena that have brought all countries closer in communication by telegraphy, telephone and wireless all show that humanity has progressed – but only progressed in a certain direction, a progress which cannot bring all satisfaction. It can only bring outer happiness and pleasure, but the inner happiness remains to be found. It might seem to be the saying of a simple believer that in belief in God is the remedy of all diseases, but I should declare that even the wisest person can claim the same after having arrived at a certain realization of life's secret.

Now coming to our subject "Man the Seed of God". If we ask ourselves what is the definition of the seed, we find that the seed is not only the beginning of the plant, but the seed is the end of the plant's destiny too, because the plant is meant to bring out the seed. When we consider the whole manifestation as a plant then in all the different grades in which it has manifested we find that the final thing was the bringing out of man. One may say in connection with a plant that the stem sprung up first, then the leaves, then came the flower, and from the flower came the seed. One may say the same thing in connection with the whole manifestation: there was the mineral, then the vegetable, then the animal, but in the end it finished in man.

Scientists to-day say to have discovered that human life comes from the animal life, but hundreds of years earlier, in the scriptures of Persia, we can find statements which give the proof of them having known this idea. What does this idea tell us? It tells us that this whole creation was intended to bring about a certain purpose, one purpose. But because every man is not capable of understanding this purpose this incapability brings about life's catastrophes. If a majority understands the purpose then the minority follows, but if those who know the purpose are in minority then the majority may have their thought.

If I were to explain the picture of the material conditions of the world which directed man to such occupations as war and disasters and bloodshed, besides the hatred between nations and races, one would understand that these all come from the lack of understanding of that one secret. Knowing this the great souls like Buddha and Krishna have all tried their utmost to explain it. For instance in the Lord's Prayer one reads, "Thy will be done on earth as it is in heaven". If only one could understand the meaning behind these words! It is the whole of philosophy, for it makes one know and understand that this only means that, if every man has his purpose separate from that of another, there will always be lack of order and peace, both outwardly and inwardly. Why do wars come? Why do differences arise? Because of the differences of purpose. When nations have their different purpose, when every individual has his different purpose then there will be no unity. At the same time it is unnatural too, for the purpose of every tree is to bring about the seed, and so the purpose of all nations and of each individual – the final purpose – is to bring about that seed which is the source of this whole manifestation.

It is not the trees which have declared God, nor the mountains; neither have the birds taught the gospel, nor the animals preached religion. If ever this has been taught, if ever God has been brought to the idea of mankind, it has been brought by man. It is not only one man's right, but it is the right of everyone to bring about that source, the source out of which all has come. Do not think that I mean by this that one must not carry out one's occupations in life. What I mean is that one must think with every occupation, everything one does, that the finishing of it is not the only aim. Man's aim is to bring forth in his life that seed which is the source of his whole life.

The modern psychologist says, "Well, any idea like this is acquired". It must however be remembered that teaching has made this idea clear, but the God-ideal is the inborn tendency of man. The best explanation of the word God is to be found in the Persian word *Khuda*, because this is not only a name, but it is the meaning of the idea: it means self-revealing. This itself shows that, if God is self-revealing, then man is not always depending upon the teaching of another; his natural longing is for God.

Very often I have met people without belief in God, but I

have always found that there is some craving behind. In spite of their denying it the craving is there all the same. Besides this, man by nature is vain and once his vanity has taken up the idea of disbelief it is very difficult to make his vanity believe what his soul craves for. A person sometimes feels proud to think, "I do not believe as everybody believes, because I am more intelligent and I am different from others". At the same time many among those who all their life denied the idea of God, after having a kind of sorrow, a heartbreak, a disappointment, or after having gone through life, in the end have begun to search for something somewhere. I was much interested to see how a great materialistic scientist often depended upon his wife who was a believer in the God-ideal. She was a kind of healing during his illnesses, and during his fits of depression she was a consolation. Whenever she said, "You do not believe in God, so how can you be happy?", his answer was, "But you believe in God and I believe in you; so that is the same".

By this I do not mean that belief in God is sufficient for our lives. Belief in God is only a first step; it is the first step towards the accomplishment of the purpose for which this whole universe is formed. If a person with his belief in God is content – there are millions and millions who believe in God and who are not all saints, nor are they the best of people. One may find perhaps among those who seem to be unbelievers more true and just people than among those who have such belief. Nevertheless, for a thinker, for a wise person, the God-ideal is the key to life's secret. The person who only stands on his belief is like a man standing on a step instead of walking on the staircase. But the person who climbs the stairs is the one who is reaching to a realization which can only come by belief in God. Therefore there are many people whose feet are, so to speak, stuck in the path of truth. Neither are they in the world nor in heaven; they become stuck in their belief and do not move from there.

The first thing we have to learn by belief in God is to know the source. As soon as we know the source we begin to feel differently from the average person. The difference between the person who is wise in God and the person who is worldly wise, if both happen to be good, is this: the person of the world will say, "If I do good to another it is a pleasure for me and the other one will learn to do good too". But the man who is wise in God will say, "When I do good to that person it means that I am doing good to myself". This makes a great difference, for when a person realizes the source he becomes one with another, and when he does not meet with another in the realization of that source then another person is another. There are two ideas in this: there is an idea of unity and there is an idea of duality. The idea of unity comes from the realization of God which is the ultimate truth. The idea of duality comes from the absence of this knowledge, and if one has not attained, through the idea of God, that idea of unity, one's realization is not complete. If one has belief in God, but has not arrived at the idea of unity, one has not accomplished the purpose of life.

Therefore the destination of the Sufi movement is to serve humanity towards this end. It is not a new religion, it is not a certain cast or creed. It is only awakening people of all different religions or of no religion to the divine ideal; to awaken humanity to the understanding of truth, which is to be learned by the understanding of God – especially after such a time as humanity has gone through, while the hatred that exists in the heart of men for one another is ever on the increase. People know about different diseases, but they do not know that the worst disease of the world is the disease of the heart, and it seems that this plague is vastly spreading: the bitterness in the heart. If one could only think what psychological effect the thought of prejudice, of hatred, of bitterness has on man! It is not only outward reasons that make persons ill, but a great many illnesses come from inner reasons. To take in bitterness and to keep it in the heart is worse than keeping a drop of poison in the body.

Now the time has come that humanity, after its contemplation on material gain, must contemplate on another gain. Material gains are taken away in a moment's time and leave man in his grave alone without any of them. This earth has not even kept the wealth of the Pharaos, so near to their heart; after so many years the wealth which was buried with them has been taken from them. It shows that this world has never allowed anyone to have his belongings for ever. It is a disappointing world; the true consolation of man does not belong to the earth or its knowledge. This does not mean that the knowledge of the world is useless, but the knowledge of the world does not suffice the whole purpose of life. There is only one thing from which true satisfaction can come, and that is the knowledge of the deeper side of life, the knowledge of the source and goal of all things. It is the realization of that knowledge which can be called divine light, and if there is any happiness, any peace ever to be found, it is in this; in the absence of it all the good that the earth can offer will not suffice man's life's purpose. Whether a man is young or old, whether he is wise or not, every person's life has a need of spiritual guidance, and the only object that man has to accomplish to-day is to become acquainted with his own self by knowledge of himself in belief in God.

CHAPTER III

Sufi Philosophy

1

Manifestation–Gravitation–Assimilation–Perfection

THE ABSOLUTE in its manifested or unmanifested condition is intelligence and the different manifestations of this intelligence may be called light, life and love. It is the dense form of the intelligence which is light. As the sun is the source of the moon, of the planets, of the stars, of fire, of the flame, of the glow – of every aspect of light – so the supreme Spirit is the source of all aspects of manifestation.

The sun is the centralizing of the all-pervading radiance. In other words the all-pervading radiance has gathered itself together in order to centralize in one spot, and this has become the source of the creation, the whole physical manifestation. So the omniscient Spirit by centralizing in one spot has become the source of the whole seen and unseen manifestation. It is therefore that in all ages the wise have worshipped the sun as the symbol of God, although the sun is only the outward symbol of God.

A minute study of the formation of the sun and its influence in all things of life illuminates us so as to understand the divine Spirit. Heat, gaslight, electric light, coal fire, wood fire, the burning candle, the flame rising from an oil-lamp, all these different manifestations of light have their source in the sun; it is the sun which is showing itself in all these different forms. Often we separate the sun from all other aspects of light. So it is with the supreme Spirit which is manifested in all forms, in all things and beings, in the seen and the unseen worlds, and yet stands remote as the sun stands remote from all other forms of light. The Qur'an says, "God is the light of heaven and of earth", and in reality all forms, however dense they may be, are a certain degree of radiance belonging to that Spirit which is all light. All the different colours are different degrees of that light.

The supreme Spirit, the source of all things, has two aspects: audible and visible. In its audible aspect the Spirit is the Word, as the Bible says, or sound, as the Hindus say calling it *Nada*. In its physical aspect the supreme Spirit is the light, in its finer aspect the light of intelligence, and in its dense aspect the radiance of all objects. The manifestation is the phenomenon of light playing in three directions. This is really the meaning of Trinity. One direction is the light that sees, the other is the light that is seen, and the third is the light that shows all things. More plainly speaking: the eyes which see and the object that is seen and the light that enables the eyes to see the object – all three are different plays of one and the same light. In the Hadith it is said, "I have made your light and by your light I create the universe". In other words, the all-pervading Spirit says to the centralized aspect of Himself, "I made you first, and of you I have made the whole universe". In this is the key to the whole creation.

The process of manifestation is like the projecting of rays out of the sun. Why does the sun shoot out its rays? Because it is its nature. And to the question, "Why does the supreme Spirit manifest?", I will give the same answer: "Because it is its nature". No sooner has the all-pervading light centralized in one spot and formed the sun, than the rays begin to shoot out. In the same way, the moment the omniscient light centralized itself in one spot, it began to shoot out its rays. These numberless rays shot out are the various souls – the souls of the good and the wicked both coming from the same source.

As these rays go forward the first plane they strike is termed the angelic plane; the second plane they strike is termed the plane of the genius and the third plane is called the physical plane. Now rises the question, "Have these rays left the supreme Spirit in order to come to the angelic plane, have they left the angelic plane in order to come to the plane of the genius and have they left the plane of the genius in order to come to the physical plane?" No, they have passed through, but while passing through they have received all that is to be received from there, learned all that is to be learned there, gathered all there was to be gathered on their way – and they still are in those planes. They do not know it, they are only conscious of that plane in which the ray has opened its eyes. In other words, we are sitting in this room, we see what is before our eyes, but we do not see what is behind our back. Thus every soul has behind its back the angelic plane and the plane of the genius, but before its eyes there is this physical plane. Therefore the soul is only conscious of the physical plane and unconscious of the planes from which it has turned its eyes.

The souls who have opened their eyes fully to the angelic plane and became interested in that plane have remained there, and the inhabitants of that plane may be called angels. The souls who did not open their eyes fully there only passed through it, and if they became interested in the plane of the genius they remained there. The ancient people called them *jinn* or genii. The souls who went still further towards manifestation and reached the physical plane, the ultimate call of their destiny, opened their eyes there and became interested in the physical plane. Among all living beings human beings are the most widely awake.

A person who has left America for Europe and has gone from Europe to the Orient has brought something from America with him to Europe and has taken something from Europe to the Orient. So every soul who has come on earth has brought with him something of the angelic plane and something of the plane of the genius, and he shows in his life on the physical plane that which he has brought from these two planes of existence. Innocence, love of beauty, deep sympathy, love of song, a tendency to solitude, love of harmony, all these belong to the angelic plane. Inventive genius, intellectuality, reasoning, law, justice, love of poetry, of science, all these belong to the planes of the genius. It is therefore that, without knowing this, people say of those who show any of these qualities, "Here is an angelic person", or "Here is a genius".

Now coming to the subject of gravitation: gravitation known to science is the material gravitation. All that belongs to the dense earth is attracted to the dense earth – but it is the same theory to say that all that is attracted to the spirit belongs to the spirit. Therefore man is pulled from both sides. Man is pulled more so than any other creature, for he is closer to the spirit. On one side the earth demands his body, on the other side the spirit asks for his soul. If man gives in to the attraction of the earth then the body drags the soul towards the earth. If man gives himself to the attraction of the spirit then the spirit drags the body to the spirit. In this way man is subject to the law of gravitation from both sides, from the earth and from the heavens.

As to the subject of perfect assimilation, I have just explained how the soul passing through the different planes has borrowed from each of them things that belong to that plane: qualities, tendencies, ideas, thoughts, feelings, impressions, flesh, skin, bone and blood. That which the soul has borrowed he must give back when it has done its work; it was borrowed for a certain time and for a certain purpose. When the purpose is fulfilled, when the time is finished, then every plane asks for that which the soul has borrowed from it, and one cannot help but give it back to that plane. It is this process which is called assimilation. Since man is born greedy and selfish he has taken all things willingly, enthusiastically – he gives them back grudgingly and calls it death.

Assimilation therefore is to give back the physical matter which one has used on this physical plane – to give it back to the earth. It becomes assimilated by the earth and the soul becomes free of that burden which it once carried. It begins to experience a greater liberty and a greater ease, for going beyond is only releasing the soul of limitation and of a great captivity.

Life in the world of the genius is longer compared with life on the physical plane. It is this life which may be called the life in the hereafter. But there comes a time when all that was borrowed from the plane of the genius has to be given back to that plane too, for it did not belong to the soul. It is according to the same theory that our body will not have what does not belong to it; it will throw it out or, if the body cannot throw it out, it will be thrown out of life. So no one can carry the substance of another plane beyond. Each substance has its own plane and must be returned to that plane. This is the only way the soul can be freed from that plane in order to rise above it.

When the soul soars higher it must also give up the angelic

qualities. They will be assimilated in the angelic plane before the soul can dissolve into the great Ocean, the supreme Spirit: that dissolving which is called merging into the real Self. One most important thing is to be learned from this process: every soul coming from the source towards manifestation gives what it brings from the source to the souls who meet it – the souls returning from the manifestation to the source – and receives from these souls certain impressions to which it is attracted. It is this exchange which is the cause of the various conditions of life in which a man is born on coming on earth. One is intelligent, another is simple, one is born in a rich family, another in a poor family, one is healthy, another weak, one will have a great purpose, another does not know what he must do. It is all determined. By what? A soul coming from the source has collected impressions on its way from souls returning to the source.[7]

For instance a business man was going to Jerusalem in order to lead a retired life. He met someone in Europe who, coming from the East, was going to the United States, and he said to him, "For forty years I have been in business in the United States. If you are going there to do some business I can tell you of my experience. I have a business established there, I can give you my heritage, I can give you all help if you continue that business. I will give you letters of introduction to help you to find sympathetic surroundings". Another man, also coming from the East, met someone who never had luck and who said to him, "Are you going to the United States? I have been there for sixty years without one friend, with nothing but ill luck". This disappointed the man. He came there and found the same ill luck of the person he had met, while the first one came in the midst of friends; all was prepared for him, he had only to continue the thing he was sent for.

Now we come to the final question: what must be the purpose of the whole creation? Is there anything to be gained by it? Yes, what is to be gained by it is the realization gained by the experience of life. What does divine experience mean? It means the soul's experience when this experience has led it to that height where it is no longer only an individual soul, but where it is conscious of all planes of existence, of the source and of its limitation both. When all the inspiration and power latent in man are within his reach, then that realization is called perfection and it is that perfection of which Jesus Christ has spoken in the Bible, where it is said, "Be ye perfect as your Father in heaven is perfect".

Question: Are not those planes rather mental conditions than places?
Answer: Yes, they are. But what we call a place also is a mental condition. Because it has a rigid physical appearance we think of it as a place, but really speaking it is a mental condition. Therefore those who have understood this have called it an illusion.

Question: Is one direction better than another?
Answer: One thing leads to another. As in life one success brings many times more success and one failure brings more failures, so the interest in one direction leads to a deeper interest in the same direction. People say that nothing succeeds like success and that it is money that can make a person rich. That law always is the same; if a person has knowledge then he is directed to greater knowledge. In the same way if a thief goes to a large city he will be the first to find thieves. Another person who is perhaps ten years in a large city will not find one thief, but I would not be surprised if the first man the other person met was a thief. Like attracts like, every impression gathers with that same impression. If a person goes towards happiness, success, riches, knowledge, wisdom, he goes deeper and deeper into it because it interests him. It is the same with all wickedness when a person is attracted to it. A little inclination towards wickedness, towards evil, leads him more and more towards it. Whether he loves it or not he gets accustomed to it and goes on in the same direction.

Question: Does cremation free the soul more than decomposition?
Answer: No, the condition of the body has nothing to do with the freeing of the soul. Only, cremation can shock the soul more than burying in the earth; since the body is made of clay it belongs to the earth.

If a person says that a body belongs to water too – water is in the depth of the earth; it belongs to earth just the same.

2

Sufism is religion, philosophy, science, art and mysticism at the same time. The greatest scientists of to-day will agree with the Sufi conception that the origin of life is motion. The Sufi sees this motion in two aspects: audible and visible. Motion is first audible, then visible. Therefore we read in the Bible – which hints at this idea – that first was the Word and then came light. From a metaphysical point of view it means that motion or vibration originating in the Absolute first became manifest as the Word, audible, and after that became visible in the form of light.

What is the sun? The sun is the centralization of the all-pervading radiance; the light which was spread all around functioned in one spot. There it became more radiant, more glowing, more powerful than the radiance that was left in space. This light again functioned in the moon; its different currents functioned in different planets and stars. This is exactly the picture of the origin of the creation: the all-pervading light of intelligence first centralized itself, thus making itself the Spirit of the whole universe, and from there it began to manifest. The reason why in ancient times people worshipped the Sun-God was that the sun is the exact simile of God, the Spirit of the whole universe; this Spirit of the whole creation formed itself in the same way as the sun.

As there are many rays of the sun, so there are many rays of the Spirit of intelligence, in other words of God, the real Self, and each of these rays is a soul. The ray therefore is the manifestation of the sun; man therefore is the manifestation of God.

The rays spread forth and reach far, yet they are still connected with the sun. The law of gravitation, compared with the law which governs the relation between the sun and the ray, is a similar law. The ray never leaves the sun; its inner tendency is to reach far and to withdraw and to come towards the sun, in other words to merge into the sun. The same is the inclination of the soul. However much the body depends upon the dense earth and the mind revels in the intellectual spheres, the soul's continual inclination is to withdraw itself to its origin. Since the physical manifestation speaks loudest and the mind makes its own noise, the gentle cry of the soul remains unheard. Nevertheless, as it is said in the Qur'an, "All have come from God and to God is their return".

Coming from its origin towards the manifestation and going back to the goal is the soul's journey. In order to come to the physical plane the soul has to pass through two principal planes: first the angelic and then, before it reaches the physical plane, the plane of the genii. The condition of each of these planes is that, in order to pass through or to exist in it, the soul must borrow a body belonging to that particular plane. So the soul cannot pass through, cannot exist in the angelic plane unless it adopts an angelic form, and the soul has to adorn itself with a body from the plane of the genii in order to exist there. On coming to the earthly plane the soul has to adorn itself with the earthly body. This means that the soul has put on an inner garb and an outer garb, and the mantle that it puts over it shapes the soul completely as a human being belonging to the physical plane.

One garb is hidden in another garb. One might think that the garb of the plane of the genius must be smaller in size than the physical garb and that the garb of the angelic plane, covered under the garb of the plane of the genius, must be still smaller, but this is not necessarily true. All that is visible to our physical eyes must have a certain rate of vibration: the physical vibrations of matter make it visible to our eyes. The vibrations of the garb of the plane of the genius are so subtle that our physical eyes cannot see it, but therefore it is not necessarily an under-garb; as much as it might be an under-garb, so much is it an outer garb. Its size need not be as small as the size of our physical form or frame. Its size is incomparably larger.

It is the same with the garb that the soul has adopted from the angelic plane: it is not necessarily so small as to be covered by the two garbs just described, but it is even larger and finer. Only, the eyes of this plane cannot see it; its rate of vibration is greater. We see things because of their vibratory rate; if they are invisible it is not because they are invisible by nature, but because they are invisible to our sight. Since we are dependent upon our physical eyes in order to see, that which the physical eyes cannot see we naturally say is unseen. It is only unseen because we cannot see it as a form.

So it is not an exaggeration to say that man is at the same time genius and angel, for he has passed through these two planes. He does not know it, but he shows the qualities of these two planes. The love quality in man, love of beauty, joy, aspiration, all these tendencies, besides the innocence of human nature, come from the angelic plane. The purity in the face of an infant gives us proof of its having just arrived from the angelic plane; its smiles, its friendliness and its readiness to appreciate everything beautiful, its love of life, all these things show the sign of the angelic spheres.

As a soul remains longer on earth he loses the angelic qualities and adopts new qualities. An infant shows the angelic quality, and a child the quality of the genius by his love of knowing names and forms, by asking questions to his parents with great curiosity. When that stage is passed he seems to be full of miseries, worries, helplessness.

Do we not see in some people the angelic quality predominating? They are good, kind and innocent, forgiving, pure-hearted, righteous, virtuous, lovers of beauty, always inclined to high aspirations. If we studied human nature more keenly we would find a great many examples of the angelic nature. Also there are poets, composers and intellectual people, writers and inventors who show the quality of the genius – in an Eastern language called *jinn*.

Those who show the human quality are still more in number. They can be divided into three classes: there is the humane quality, there is the animal quality and there is a devilish quality. This is shown by the rate of their vibrations and their rhythm. Intense rhythm produces the devilish quality, moderate rhythm shows the animal quality, even rhythm shows the humane quality. The form of these rhythms may be explained thus: the humane quality is mobile, the animal quality is uneven, the devilish quality is zigzag.

Death is nothing but the taking off of one garb and giving it back to the plane from which it was borrowed, for the condition is this: one cannot take the garb of the lower plane to the higher plane. The soul is only released when it is willing – or compelled – to give its garb to the plane it has taken it from. It is this which releases the soul to go on in its travel. And as it proceeds to a higher plane, after its stay there it must again give its garb back and be purified from it in order to go further.

If people knew this they would look at life from a different point of view; they would understand the meaning of the moral: you cannot get away with anything that does not really belong to you. And they would come to realize after the study of philosophy that even their body does not belong to them; it is a borrowed property and must be returned one day. Therefore the wise disown it before they are obliged to give it up. All the spiritual exercises given by teachers are practised for this purpose: that we may begin to disown our body from to-day, that we may not have the remorse of having lost something we thought to be most precious.

This knowledge also throws a light upon the question of death. Death is not really death; it is only a passing stage, it is only a change, as changing clothes. One might think, "Do we not become less by dying?" It is not so. We become more by dying, not less, for once the physical garb has been thrown away the soul enjoys a greater freedom, a greater liberation for the reason that the limitation of the physical body is great. The physical body weighs heavy on the soul and the day when this burden is taken off, the soul feels lighter, its faculties, tendencies, inspiration and power, all manifest more freely. Therefore death is no loss.

Now we come to the question: what is it that brings about death? Either the body, owing to weakness, is not capable of serving the soul properly, or the soul has finished its mission in that plane; it no more wants it. The body clings to the soul and the soul holds the body: that is the position. When the body is too feeble it naturally loses its grip on the soul and gradually loses it more and more till it can no longer hold the soul. Or the soul holds the body as long as it has to accomplish something, and when the soul sees no purpose then it loses its hold upon the body and so gradually the body drops out of the hands of the soul. It is by this process that death is brought about.

What about birth? Human bodies are the clay needed to make a body for the soul. The soul has to knock at the door of the physical plane and a body is given to it. Cupid is the symbol of this idea, of this philosophy.[8]

There is give and take in the two planes through which a soul has to pass, a give and take between the souls who are going from the source towards manifestation and the souls who are returning from manifestation towards the goal. As a traveller coming from Asia to America and a traveller going from America to Asia who meet in Europe exchange money and thoughts with one another, so those souls take upon themselves the debts of one another, the knowledge of one another, the happiness, the misery of one another. In the same way we experience our life on earth. One soul, without knowing it sometimes, may take a route which leads him to riches, to success. Another soul may take a route that leads him to failure, to errors. It all depends upon what route they have taken from the beginning. Hafiz has described this idea in a beautiful way, saying that each person has his own wine, and his love is according to the wine he has taken. If it is the wine of happiness, if it is the wine of joy, if it is the wine of sorrow, if it is the wine of misery, if it is the wine of courage, of fear, of trust, of distrust, of faith, of disbelief, it is in the intoxication of this wine that he acts, presenting the effect of the wine to the world. So we each have our own wine.

In this exchange of souls going from the source to manifestation and souls coming back from the manifestation to the source, one takes the wine of selfishness, another of unselfishness. A Persian poet says, "Before dawn the wine was poured out. No sooner I opened my eyes than a glass of wine was given to me. O *Saqi*, thanks for whatever wine you gave, for it intoxicated me and made me lose myself". The dawn that the poet expresses as birth is the time when the soul began its journey from the angelic plane. The first cup it drank determined its life afterwards.

It is not true that, as they say, a man when he goes higher in evolution is richer in knowledge. No, higher evolution itself is a knowledge. The knowledge one gains from earthly sources is not a coin that is current in other planes. The coin of this plane, a plane so small, is as limited as this plane – and man makes so much of it! It is amusing when a person comes to me and says, "I have read so many books on occult science, I think I am quite ready to be initiated". It amuses me very much. Imagine! Reading occult science should entitle someone to spirituality! The language of that country is different and intellectual knowledge is not current there. Learning that language is unlearning what we have learned here. Therefore the question of spiritual attainment is quite different and must be dealt with from quite a different point of view.

What I have to say in conclusion about Sufi philosophy is that what we call individuality is a momentary state, and this conception of individuality as it is found to-day – do not think that it will be the same to-morrow.

Omar Khayyam says,

"O my beloved, fill the cup that clears
to-day from past regrets and future fears.
To-morrow, why to-morrow I may be myself
with yesterday's seventy thousand years."

As soon as the soul has awakened, it no more gives much importance to individuality – a thing made of garbs borrowed from different planes; it is a doll of rags. All importance we give, we should give to the soul which is real, which comes from the real and seeks after the real.

Question: Is the soul not attracted by action?
Answer: The condition of the soul is likened to a mirror: it mirrors so long as it reflects the object which is standing before it. Yet that object is not engraved in the mirror, it occupies it at the moment it veils it. So the soul is covered by experiences. In other words, our experience may delude the soul, cover it, bury it, but at the same time cannot penetrate it.

CHAPTER IV

The Gift of Eloquence

WHEN WE consider the four kingdoms – the mineral, vegetable, animal kingdoms and mankind – we see that not man alone but also every other being has the gift of expression. The rock expresses least and we feel least for it; we strike it and break it and quarry it. We make use of it in every way and we do not sympathize with it at all, because it does not speak to us; it tells us very little. We sympathize much more with the plant. We love it, we give it water, we tend it, and because it has more expression we care more for it. Among the stones there are some that speak more to us; the diamond, the ruby, the emerald we prize very much. We pay thousands of pounds for them; we are glad to have them, to wear them.

The animal has much more the gift of expression than the plant or the rock, and we feel that animals are much nearer to us. The dog by wagging his tail, by jumping about, by every movement says, "I love you", and we care much more for him. We do not want the plant on the chair next to us, but if the dog sits on the chair it is all right. The cat has no words, but by its voice it speaks to us. All the poets of the East have spoken of the nightingale because of its voice, its expression. There are many birds in the forests of which we never think because they have no voice, but the song-birds we all know and we like to have a parrot because it speaks. Allah has made man the *khalifa*, the chief of creation for this one thing, his tongue: man alone has the gift of eloquence.

Among men we see that some are like the rock, others like the plant or like the animal and some have the human quality. The man who is like a rock has not much expression; he has no magnetism. He has only that which is in his appearance, just like the stones have, the emerald, the ruby; when that appearance is gone nothing is left. The man who is like a plant has no intelligence, only some feeling, some personality. Either is there some fragrance of the personality, some beauty, or he is like a thorn, or there is poison. When man is like an animal he has feelings, passions, but he cannot give them expression. Only that man is a human being who has the gift of expression, who speaks out what he feels.

The gift of eloquence is called by the Hindus *Vak Devi*, the goddess of speech. They have distinguished three sorts of beings, *Rakshasa*, the monster, he who is without speech and without feeling, *Manusha*, the man who has feeling but lacks expression, and *Devata* the godlike man, he who has eloquence. It is his eloquence alone that makes him godlike.

The word was in the beginning before the creation of man. Neither the rock, nor the plant, nor the animal could speak out that word which was from the beginning. It is only man who expresses it; he gives expression to that which existed first. When he expresses it he becomes the pen of the divine Being. Therefore in him the creation is perfected and he is the highest of all beings.

To speak and by speech to hurt, to wound the heart, the feelings of another, is the misuse of eloquence. There is a Persian verse, *"Zaban-i-shirin mulke girin*. A sweet tongue wins the world"*. The tongue, like a sword, has two aspects: it wins and it slays. A sharp tongue kills and a sweet tongue conquers the world. The same idea is expressed in the Gospels, "Blessed are the meek, for they shall inherit the earth".

The world is like a dome in which whatever is spoken comes back to us. If we say, "How beautiful", "how beautiful" comes back to us. If we say, "You stupid", the echo comes back, "you stupid". A man may think, "I have so many servants, I am such a great person, I shall say what I please". But some day the echo of his bad words will come back to him.

Sometimes a person does not wish to speak badly to his friend so as to hurt him, but without wishing to speak badly, he does so, because his mind is full of the bad impressions he has stored there. Therefore we should store up only good impressions, and not keep the others with us, that only good may come from us.

There are two ways of speaking on a subject. Before speaking a person may ponder upon a subject and then speak with all the reasonings that come to him. This is parrot-speaking a person may ponder upon a subject and then speak with all the reasonings that come to him. This is parrot-speech; he repeats what he has learned, as the parrot says some words because he has been taught them.

The store of eloquence, knowledge, is always ready within, and the other way of speaking is to depend upon that store, that knowledge. Then the tongue speaks out what is always there in readiness; the knowledge, eloquence, is always there but it is shut off from us. In order to open up that knowledge an arrow is needed. The arrow is the deep feeling that pierces through to that knowledge. If we see a crooked person walking in the street it is very easy to laugh; it is so absurd. But a little feeling will produce pity, and a deep feeling will bring the expression of pity and compassion.

Why do Hindus call eloquence *devi*? Why goddess, why not god? Because the speaker is responsive to the creator, the god within.

CHAPTER V

Evolution of the World

SOME SAY that the world has evolved since the creation, as it is the law of nature to evolve. Others say the reverse, seeing the conditions of the world falling back every day. When the Buddhists say that the universe is always progressing, the Hindus contradict this by pointing out that virtue and truth have diminished with the growth of the world during the periods called *Satya Yuga, Treta Yuga, Dvapara Yuga* and the present *Kali Yuga* – the golden, silver, copper and iron ages. There seem to be some who, seeing the comfort and convenience of modern life together with its new inventions and wonderful researches, admire evolution. There are others who praise the past saying how great were the ancestors of the past who were so high in their morals and ideals and who had such a comfort and peace in their natural life – until gradually everything had become so degenerated that all virtues became a prey to the selfishness and artificiality of so-called civilization.

According to the standpoint of the Sufi both are right and yet both are wrong, for the Sufi applies the law of vibration to his understanding of the world: each note has its finish at the octave, and so there are an ascending and a descending scale. Each strong accent in anything has its weak part to balance it. The sun rises as well as sets, the new moon develops to the full and wanes until it is new again. Each wave of the sea which rises high is drawn back; each helpless child is helpless again when old. This is the nature of evolution.

A certain direction of life develops for a certain period, and before it has fallen back another direction of life begins to evolve. An individual's view is deluded because evolution seems to him to be a straight evolution, and every fall seems to be a continual fall. After a person has developed in his body and that is finished, perhaps thought might begin its development. If he views the reduction of his body he will feel involution, and if he notices the development of his thought he will realize his evolution. In fact in both ideas he is right; it only depends upon his point of view.

One can study this fact by looking at a fountain where one jet of water is rising to reach its height and another is returning from its utmost reach. Neither is the rise constant for the former, nor is the fall lasting for the latter. This is the way of progress and degeneration of science, art, race, religion and nation. Even the world as a whole has its circle to accomplish, and everything therein has its own time of rise and fall. At the same time the rise is for the fall and the fall again is meant to rise.

CHAPTER VI

Every Man has his own little World

EVERY MAN has his own little world, so little sometimes that it is like a doll's house, and in that little world he is not concerned with the world outside or with the universe; he just lives in his small world so full of illness, misery and ill luck. He cannot come out of it, for he has built a little shell for himself in which he lives, a shell of misery. He likes to live in it for it is his own home.

Human beings living in their shells are mostly unaware of the privilege of life and so are unthankful to the Giver of it. In order to see the grace of God man must open his eyes and raise his head from his little world. Then he will see – above and below, to the right and the left, before and behind – the grace of God reaching him from everywhere in abundance.

If we try to thank God we might thank for thousands of years and it would never be enough. But if man stays in his own little shell he does not find the grace of God; he finds misery, injustice, ugliness, coldness.

When one looks down one sees the mud; when one looks up one sees the sun, the moon, the planets. It all depends how we look: upwards or downwards.

Every day we should have a time in the evening or in the morning to think of what we have experienced during the day, to consider how many mercies and gifts of God we have received, and how less worthy we are of them; to think what we have done wrong – not wrong in the sense of religion, but how we may have hurt the feeling of another by inattention, by a kind of insult, by not doing what he wished when it was in our power to do it. We should never say that we are beyond this. We should say that, whether we are a prophet or a saint, we are liable to all mistakes. If you say that you believe in God, there is the wish for a higher path, for a higher knowledge. If you say, "I do not believe in God, I do not care for anything", then it does not matter, because then your experience will be your teacher. But if you believe in God, this is what you should do.

CHAPTER VII

Marriage

MARRIAGE IS the most sacred of all things. It is certainly not in the first place a contract, a business. When we look at marriage from a higher point of view it appears that marriage is the fulfilment of life.

From a physical point of view this life which is full of struggle and strife can be met with greater strength and greater courage and greater capability, when two harmonious forces are united together. There is a saying of a Persian poet, "When two hearts unite, they become powerful enough to remove mountains". Life is a continual struggle, and in order to become capable of meeting this struggle it is necessary to be strong and powerful. When two hearts are united they are more capable, more powerful and greatly blessed.

Looking at marriage from a mental point of view, no matter how wise, how strong, how courageous, how powerful a person may be, he still lacks something. Every individual, after all, has defects. No matter how many merits he has, he needs something better: at the time of doubt, conviction; at the time of anxiety, support from another source; at the time of confusion, a little light; at the time of sorrow, a word of consolation, of happiness. No matter what a person has – wealth, power, rank, position – this will not balance his life. If there is anything that will balance his life it is another soul to provide that which is missing at the moment when he needs it. Therefore from a physical point of view marriage is a power, and from a mental point of view it brings balance.

Lastly there is the spiritual point of view. Among the ancient people the wise gave an answer to the ever-recurring question as to why the world was created. This answer was that God felt lonely. And no matter how many rays of the light of wisdom we may throw upon life, we shall always receive this one answer as the reason for the creation. If anything exists it is only one Being, and that is God.

Therefore the whole of manifestation which is created by Him is in Himself. If God created it, it was only because He felt lonely. It is the same idea that can be seen symbolically in the belief of the ancient people that Eve was created out of the rib of Adam. It only means that this world was created out of God himself, that it is God's own manifestation. He wanted to see in order to remove the monotony of being alone and, if it was the need of God to create something and put it before Himself to remove the monotony of being alone, it is natural that every human being has this inclination too. But this inclination leads to what? To greater perfection – because an individual man is limited, no matter how powerful, how great, how wise and learned he may be, and in order to become greater he must become another person.

Marriage is the first step to becoming another person. The one who formerly thought that he would attain pleasure, comfort, happiness in life and enjoy it for himself, from the moment he is married thinks first of his wife and of how he can give her comfort, for without her he can no longer enjoy life.

When this outlook comes to a person his consciousness changes; it rises and expands and becomes the source of all revelation and bliss. Why is it so? Because by this expansion the spirit of God becomes awakened in man. It removes what stands between his limited and his unlimited self and gradually raises him to a stage where he fully realizes the One who is the source and goal, who is the essence of his being. As Rumi says, "Whether you have loved man or whether you have loved God, if you have loved enough you will be brought in the end into the presence of the supreme Love itself".

From a spiritual point of view therefore marriage is a step forward on the path to perfection, that path by which the ultimate purpose of life is attained.

CHAPTER VIII

Spirituality, the Tuning of the Heart

1

BEFORE SPEAKING of spirituality I must first explain
what I mean by it. There are people who consider spirituality
as orthodoxy or piety: to be religious, to be a priest, a monk,
a hermit, to fast, or to live a life of a certain discipline, to
adopt a certain form of worship. A person may have all these
outer forms without being spiritual, and a person may have
nothing of these and be spiritual. Those who seek spirituality
in such outer forms are mistaken, for it is more than that: real
spirituality is spirit-consciousness. To be spiritual means to
be conscious of spirit, just as a material person means a person
who is conscious of matter. So it is not religion, orthodoxy,
outer forms, or a certain kind of life which means spiritual
life: it is to be conscious of the spirit that makes one spiritual.

There are others who think that those who perform
phenomena, miracles, who work wonders are spiritual. It is
not so. Many who are capable of performing phenomena are
not different from a magician. Then others say that to be
spiritual means to tell fortunes, or to be clairvoyant, to see
wonderful things. It is not necessary to do or to see
wonderful things in order to be spiritual. Others imagine that
to be spiritual means sitting in the caves of mountains, or
roaming about in forests, or to appear and disappear. All
these things are but fancies of the imaginative. To be spiritual
means to be one's self, to be one's natural self.

How many of us are our self? If we were our self we would
all be spiritual. We are not our self, we are far from it! A
great Indian poet expresses this idea in this way, "Apart from
accomplishing things, for man to be a man is the most
difficult thing". It means that for a human being to be human
is the greatest difficulty. He is born a human being; yet the
first thing he ought to be is what he is not, he is anything but a
human being. He is willing to be a sollicitor, a doctor, a
professor, but to be a human being – that is the thing he thinks
of last, and mostly he does not even think of it at all.

People say that nowadays there is a great tendency in the world to discover spiritual truth, that there is an inner spiritual awakening. Yes, I admit it, but what direction does it take? Very often it takes wrong directions. Those searching after truth often think that the best way to find belief in the spirit and the hereafter is mediumship: to become a medium themselves, or to go to a medium and – when they have found proof – to communicate with the dead. Then they think they have found proof of the spiritual. They wreck their nervous system, many go out of balance. In this manner the way that would lead to spirituality leads to destruction.

There are others who wish to pursue the spiritual in the same way as a person in a university or college. They want to read all things in a book. They think, "If there is anything like spiritual attainment one book must tell us about it". If they go to the library and read throughout their whole life all the books there are, they cannot touch spirituality, because it does not come from books. Reading helps one sometimes to awake; yet every person does not know how to read. What is happening to-day is that there are thousands and thousands of people who read one book, then another and still another, until their mind is so confused that they do not know what to believe and what not to believe. Among them there are many who think that the best way is the intellectual way. But what is intellectual? Is reading really intellectual? Are all books the same? Many times they only confuse a person. Very often books with ten errors on the same line puzzle a person's mind so much that he does not know where he is.

Often people come to me and tell me – in order to help me – to have confidence in them, because for ten years they have been reading my books. Instead of having confidence I have to guide them on the path and to erase what they have learned first. Perhaps they are not willing to erase; they think that they have gained this knowledge by reading a hundred books. What knowledge? Is it spiritual?

Besides, very often intellectual pursuit gives them the idea that there are such masters and such *mahatmas* and saints in the Himalayas, in the caves of the mountains. They never think that such a person can be in the crowds. It interests them most when he is in a place where nobody can reach him. They think he cannot be in a restaurant taking his dinner; he must be in a cave of the mountain. Imagine! Why was this world created? Why are we born in this world, in the midst of this world, if this world were not a school to develop the soul and to arrive at the stage which is life's purpose? Man has lost confidence in his fellowmen. He expects spirituality from the dead, from the trees – not from men. He has no confidence in his brothers.

Others are interested in the meaning of symbology: this particular symbol means this, another gives a great revelation, another is a great mystery. Where is spirituality to be found? Is it not in the heart of man? Instead of in their own heart people want to look in different places, or in certain symbols. Yes, symbols are expressive of it, but the direct way is within oneself.

I had an amusing experience one day. Travelling in England near Bournemouth I was brought to a place where they said I should speak. They said it was an important place; so I went there. The man who brought me there said, "Now here in this corner – you can feel that here is the secret". Imagine, in that place was spirituality, not in man!

Those who make their occupation of spirituality take advantage of people's ignorance. They cater for them, they feed them, they say to every person, "You are a medium". So those who take this as a profession tell everyone, "Come along. Be more fanciful, more imaginative, more superstitious". They feed curiosity. Does it lead anywhere? In this way people get lost and will never be spiritual. This is to be found everywhere.

Now coming to the actual subject, the difference between spirit and matter: once a young Italian who did not believe in God or soul was travelling with me in the same ship, and he thought that perhaps I was a priest. He asked, "Do you believe in anything?" "Yes", I said. "What is your belief?" I answered, "It cannot be said". Since he was antagonistic he said, "I do not believe in anything. If there is anything in which I believe, it is in eternal matter". I replied, "My belief is not far from yours. What you call eternal matter I call eternal spirit. What you have named matter I have named spirit".

It is a dispute over words, the understanding is the same. The difference has come by disputing over words. What is spirit is fine matter and what is matter is dense spirit. In other words, there are two names and there is one subject: call it water, call it snow. When it is crystallised it is snow, and if you do not like to call it water, call it snow. If you wish to distinguish you may call it by two names, there is no objection to it, it is a question of choice. If you choose that there is no matter, as Christian Science also says, then matter is spirit just the same. And if you choose to call spirit matter, then spirit is matter just the same. If you say both things that is right too. Truth is in understanding, not in expression.

People have strengthened their truth, they have taught and fought and arrived at nothing. Very often those who do not understand a subject argue for the reason that they want to know about it, but they do not honestly want to know about it. Their way is to argue; then they know the other's idea also. They oppose the other to hear what he has to say; it is a kind of robbery. They have a thirst for argument. He who will not understand will never understand, however much it is true. He who understands – you tell him and he will understand. It is a matter of evolution.

Besides, there is a tendency in everyone to think, "The other one must look at things as I do. If it is a friend, if it is a wife, a husband, a brother, a sister, or a companion, they must understand things as I do". But that is impossible. May be they are at different stages of evolution, they cannot understand. Leave them alone! For some it is good to sleep, for others it is good to awake. It is no virtue to awake everybody; it is the greatest crime to awake those who ought to sleep. To make everyone spiritual is not a right mission. The best thing is to help a person wherever he is and not to try to bring him to a certain pitch. He will come naturally; to put him on the right track is enough. Often people who are interested in spirituality urge it on those in their surroundings. They are mistaken; those urged are sometimes more spiritual. Man is a great mystery and we know so little about it.

I have travelled in India for nine years in the pursuit of the illuminated ones, the living wise men of the East. You would be surprised to know how various illuminated souls live under the guise of an ordinary person, so that no one can ever distinguish them as different from others. Many of them bear themselves in the same way as everybody does, sitting in the same places, saying the same things that anyone else would say; neither do they show any difference in outward appearance, in speech or claims. At the same time – if you could see behind those great beings – they are as different from others as the sky is different from the earth.

I will tell you something about my own teacher. Once I met a learned man, a doctor of philosophy with a great many degrees. I spoke to him on the deeper side of life and he became so interested in me that he thought much of me. So I thought, "If I were to tell him about my teacher, how much more interesting that would be for him. If I make such an impression upon this man, how much more my teacher will be for him, and how much will he appreciate my teacher", and I told him, "There is a wonderful man in this city, he has no comparison in the whole world". "Yes?", said he, "Are there such people? I would so much like to see him. Where does he live?" I told him, in such and such a part of the city. He said, "I live there too. Where is his house. I know all the people there. What is his name?" So I told him, and he said, "For twenty years I have known this man, and you are telling me about him!" I thought, "In a hundred years you would not have been able to know him". He was not ready to know him.

If people are not evolved enough they cannot appreciate persons, they cannot understand them, they cannot understand the greatest souls. They sit with them, they talk with them, there is a contact of the whole life, but they do not see. Another person in one moment, if he is ready to understand, makes a benefit out of it. Imagine, the learned man had known my teacher for twenty years and did not know him. I saw him once, and became his pupil for ever. One might ask, "Was this man not learned, not intellectual?" Yes, he was. Then what was lacking? He saw my teacher with his brain, I saw him with my heart. People pursue spirituality with their brain: that is where they are mistaken. Spirituality is attained through the heart.

What do I mean by the heart? Is it the nervous centre in the midst of the breast, the small piece of flesh that doctors call the heart? No, the definition of the heart is that it is the depth of the mind, the mind being the surface of the heart. That in us which feels is the heart, that which thinks is the mind. It is the same thing which thinks and feels, but the direction is different: feeling comes from the depth, thought from the surface. When thought is not linked with feeling it is just like a plant rising up from the earth, the root of which has not gone deep. A thought without feeling is a powerless thought; it is just like a plant without a deep root. A tree the root of which has gone deep into the earth is stronger, more reliable, and so the thought deeply rooted in the heart has greater power. The heart therefore is the factor through which spirits and spirituality are to be attained.

In man's being three aspects can be distinguished: body, heart and soul. The heart is a globe over the soul and the body a cover over the heart. One might ask: Is the soul so small as to be covered by the heart and is the heart so small as to be covered by the body? It is not so. The soul is within and without. For instance, a light is covered by a globe and the globe by another cover – and yet, is the light covered? It shines out just the same. The light is not under the cover; it seems to be under the cover, but it shines out. Such is the soul. The globe does not shine out, but the light takes the colour of the globe. It is the soul that is larger; at the same time the light is within the globe and the soul within the body. It is exactly like the light within the globe and the globe within the cover. The light is outside the cover, and the power of the globe shines outside the cover. So the power of the heart is greater than the power of the body, and the power of the soul is greater still. As long as one is ignorant of this, one does not realize truth.

Imagine what a power the heart quality has. The little hen, when it is with its young ones and a horse comes or an elephant, is ready to fight them. Otherwise it would run away, but with its young ones it is ready to fight with the elephant. The heart quality is blooming at that time, it is feeling; at that time its power is so great that the little hen is ready to fight with anyone. In India a hunter's story is told about a she-deer that was pursued by a hunter and ran far away into the woods. When she came near her young ones who were waiting for her she did not run further, she forgot the hunter. As soon as the heart quality was awakened in the presence of her little ones she had no fear.

There is nothing one will not sacrifice, accomplish, or face when the heart quality is awakened. All cowardice and weakness, misery and wretchedness come when the heart quality is covered and man begins to live in his brain. Lions turn into rabbits when they are not lion-hearted. Very few understand the power of the heart. Once the heart is awakened there is nothing that one does not accomplish. Besides inspiration and illumination it gives all the force and power one needs to attain anything one wants.

One might ask: Is it not natural to attain spirituality? Does it not come without any effort on our part? And if it is not natural, then what is the use of attaining spirituality? These are right arguments, and my answer is that spirituality is not only for human beings, but also for the lower creation, for every being: not spirituality in the sense we understand, but in that of being tuned to one's natural pitch. Even birds have their moments of exaltation. At the setting and rising of the sun, the breaking of dawn, in the moonlight, there come times when birds and animals feel exalted. They sing and dance, they sit on the branches of the trees in exaltation. Every day they feel this exquisite joy. If we go still further and have eyes to see life in those forms in which others do not see it, in the rock, in the tree, we find that there are times when even the trees are in a complete state of ecstasy. Those who move in nature, who open the doors of their heart, whose soul comes in contact with nature, find nature singing, nature dancing and communicating.

It is not only a legend, a story of the past, that saints used to speak with trees. It is an actual fact, and it is the same to-day as in the past. Souls are of the same nature, they are the same. The only difference is that we have become unbelievers, we have no confidence in life, we have become material, we have closed our eyes to what comes before us. To-day souls can become saints and sages just as before. Are the stars not as before? They communicate also to-day with the one who is able to respond to nature. But we have turned our back to nature, we live in an artificial world; there is no self-confidence in us, no belief. Naturally we have not only become materialistic, we have become matter! Therefore those who ever have attained to spirituality have attained by awakening the quality of heart.

Sufis in all ages, mystics of India, Persia, and Egypt have considered the awakening of the heart quality to be the principal thing in life. For all the virtues that the priest can teach and prescribe, the virtues that one is told to practise in life, come naturally when the heart opens. Then one need not learn virtue, virtue becomes one's own. All virtues as taught by people – how long do they last? If there is any virtue it must come by itself: spirituality is natural. And if animals and birds can feel spiritual exaltation, why not we? But we do not live a natural life. We have tried in our civilization, in our life, to be as far removed from nature and natural life as possible, breathing an artificial atmosphere to withstand climatic influences, eating food that we have prepared and improvised, turning it into something quite different from what nature had made and given us.

Besides that, the deeper we go into the life of the community, the more we find that we are not on the track as we ought to be. We seem to have lost our individuality. We have called it progress – a progress towards a certain condition. And there we begin to feel that we are in a maze. Now has come the time – and more and more so every day – that thoughtful people, wise people who are just and honest realize, "We are not progressing, we are in a maze and we are looking for the door." I spoke with a great scientist, and in spite of all his knowledge what did he say? "We do not know where we are. We have made inventions, but we do not know how to control them to the best advantage of life".

Invention apart, the first question is how to make the best of our life, how to make the best of this opportunity which is passing us by. Every moment lost is incomparably more valuable than the loss of money. As man will realize this he will more and more come to the conclusion that he has gone on and on thinking he was progressing, but that he has been moving around in the same maze. If only he found the door, that door which is called by the wise spiritual attainment! However well educated one may be, however much progress one has made, however much one has collected or accomplished, however much power and position one has gained, only one thing is everlasting and that is spiritual attainment. Without this there will always be dissatisfaction, an uncomfortable feeling. No knowledge, power, position or wealth can give that satisfaction which spiritual attainment can give.

There is nothing easier and nothing more difficult in the world: difficult because we have made it difficult, easy because it is the easiest thing possible. All other things we have to buy and pay for – even water. For spiritual attainment we do not need to pay a tax, it is ours, it is our self, it is discovering our self, finding our self. Yet what one values is what one gets with difficulty. Man loves complexity so much! He makes a thing big and says, "This is valuable". If it is simple he says, "It has no value". That is why the ancient people, knowing human nature, told a person when he said he wanted spiritual attainment, "Very well; for ten years go around the temple, walk around it a hundred times in the morning and in the evening. Go to the Ganges, take pitchers full of water during twenty or fifty years, then you will get inspiration". That is what must be done with people who will not be satisfied with a simple explanation of the truth, who want complexity.

Often having been asked, "Show us a tangible truth", I asked myself how it would be if I wrote TRUTH on a little brick and gave it to people saying, "Hold it fast. Here is tangible truth". Fine people, when they write a letter, expect their friend to read between the lines. Even subtle feelings of the human heart cannot be expressed in words. How then can anyone expect truth to be spoken in words? That which is spoken in words can never be truth. People do not distinguish between the meaning of fact and of truth; they always muddle truth with fact.

Often the greatest error is made when a person who has a crude or insolent nature or a brain of stone says, "What do I care how anybody takes it? I simply tell the truth. It does not matter whether a person is hurt". But truth is the finest thing and most beautiful. If one tells the truth must it hurt? If it hurts anybody can it be truth? Truth must raise a person, must illuminate him, it must be the most beautiful thing on earth, harmonizing, uplifting, inspiring, it cannot be hurtful. If it is truth it is the greatest healing there is. But people interpret truth in the form of facts, and muddle truth with fact, just as they confuse pleasure with happiness.

When people are pleased they say, "I am happy", and when they are happy they say, "I am pleased". But pleasure is far from happiness. A small thing can give pleasure, but in order to be happy one ought to arrive at that pitch where there is everlasting happiness. Pleasure comes and goes; it is the shadow of happiness, it is not happiness.

In the same way people muddle cleverness with wisdom. Of a wise person they say, "What a clever man", and of a clever man they say, "How wise is he." A worldly person is not wise, he is clever, and a wise man is not necessarily clever, although he is perfect wisdom. Cleverness is a shadow of wisdom. Wisdom is light.

In the East no doubt seekers after truth in all ages have sought the direction of those who had already acquainted themselves with the path, in order to tread the path under their guidance. To-day a man comes and says, "I do not wish to follow any guidance or advice. If a book can tell me something I shall read it. Tell me just now what I should do, and I shall do it". Imagine! In order to develop your voice you go to a teacher of voice-culture and do a thousand practices with open mouth and make a thousand kinds of grimaces you would never like to make. In order to develop the voice you have to do a thousand things which sound foolish in order to sing one day. What comparison is there between spiritual attainment and singing? If singing rightly takes so many years' practice and so much concentration and discipline under the orders of a teacher, how can a spiritual teacher tell at the dinner table what spirituality means? People ask, "Would you tell us in one word how we can attain spirituality?" Is it such a simple thing?

Who then can tell it and how can it be told? It is something to discover for oneself. The teacher can only put one on the track to attain to that realization which is called spirituality. No doubt according to the idea of the people of the East the responsibility of the spiritual teacher is still greater than that of parents towards their children. From the time of his birth the parents' thought is centred on the well-being of the child. Even when he is grown-up the child is the same in the heart of the parents; they are interested in everything he does. The child may not care for them, but they will understand. He may be far away, yet from a distance the heart of the mother will always be craving for the welfare of her child. So it is with the teacher. The spiritual teacher under whose guidance a pupil places himself will fulfill to him the place of both father and mother, and even more. His welfare is the teacher's religion, it is his spiritual responsibility; for the spiritual teacher there is no other religion. He is not necessarily a priest; all the duty he has is to be anxious about the welfare and well-being of those who sought his guidance, who come under his direction.

It is therefore that the service of the great ones such as Jesus Christ, Buddha, Moses, Muhammad, or any others who came from time to time to serve humanity in a small or in a great way, has been a service of love and affection in order to raise humanity by their own example, their own ideas, their own love. What they have taught is not so important as what was given beyond words as love and light. That is the sacrament in the church, the same in the form of love and wisdom. What has come in words, or from the lips, is very little – so simple.

There is no comparison between the Bible or any such spiritual book and a writer of to-day, because the value of the book is not in the capability of the writer; its value lies in the personality of the teacher. The wonderful souls who from time to time served humanity helping it to progress – whether known or unknown, whether mankind has forgotten them or still holds them – have done their duty and always do so. Those who take such an opportunity of benefiting by their teaching, by their thought, are blessed ones.

2

Spirituality is not necessarily intellectuality, nor is it orthodoxy or asceticism. Orthodox, ascetic or intellectual pursuit after truth – all these are the ways people have taken in order to reach a spiritual goal, but the way is not the goal. If there is a definition of spirituality it is the tuning of the heart.

In this material age of ours the heart quality is totally forgotten and great importance is given to reason and logic. When we argue with a person, he says, "Argue with reason, be logical". Sentiment and idealism have no place; it is therefore that humanity is getting further and further from spiritual attainment. The main quality, the best in man, is ignored and by ignoring that quality it becomes dead. For instance, if a poet happens to live in a village where no one understands poetry, if an artist lives in a town where no one cares for his pictures, if an inventive genius has no opportunity of bringing out his inventions, these faculties become blunted and in the end they die. So it is with the heart quality: if it is not taken notice of, if it has no opportunity to develop, if it is ignored, then this quality becomes blunted and in the end it dies. As it is said in a song, "The light of life dies when love is gone".

When feeling has become blunted then what remains? Nothing. Then there is no sign of life. What remains is intellectuality expressing itself by the power of egoism. It is difficult to live in the world because selfishness is ever on the increase. Business and industry apart, even in friendship, in relationship the give-and-take has the greatest importance, worldly interest takes part in it. There is a certain fineness that belongs to human nature, a certain nobleness, a certain independence, there is a certain ideal, a certain delicacy, a certain manner that belong to human nature, and all these become blunted when the heart quality is left undeveloped.

I have been travelling for many years seeing people busy in the pursuit of truth and to my very great disappointment I have found many of them, although interested in higher things, yet arguing, discussing, "Do you believe what I believe", or, "Perhaps my belief is better than yours" – always that intellectual side. They said, "We have so many things connected with our life in the world in which we can use our intellect: business, industry, domestic affairs". In seeking God, in attaining spirituality we do not need to use so much intellect, because this does not come by the intellect: it comes by the tuning of the heart.

People will say, "Yes, but all the same there are emotional persons, affectionate and loving people". But I do not always call emotional people loving people. They may be so outwardly, but very often the more emotional they are the less loving, for one day their love is on the rise, next day it is on the fall, one day very loving, next day just moved with emotions like clouds. One day the sky is clear, next day it is covered. One cannot depend upon emotions, they are not love. It is the feeling nature that is to be developed, the sympathetic nature.

Besides, there exists, especially in the Western world, a false conception of the strength of personality. May be many have understood it wrongly; under the guise of strength they want to harden their hearts. For instance, many men think that for a man to be touched or moved by anything is not natural or normal. On the contrary! If a man is not touched or moved it is not natural; he is still in the mineral kingdom and not yet in the human kingdom. To be human and not be touched or moved by something touching or appealing only means that the eyes of the heart are closed, its ears blocked. This heart is not living. It is a wrong understanding of a high principle. The principle is that man must be feeling and at the same time so strong that as much feeling he has, so much strength he must have to cover it. It does not mean he must not be feeling; man without feeling is without life. Those who are afraid of feeling think that the right, the normal thing to do is to keep away from feeling. However much they study psychology, theoretically and methodically, they will not attain to spirituality. Spirituality does not belong to intellectuality, it has nothing to do with it. In connection with spirituality intellectuality is in so far useful that an intellectual person can best express spiritual inspiration.

Many people say, "I had a deep feeling, but that feeling is all gone, it is lost. Now I have no more feeling". That means

that something in them has died. They do not know it, but
something of great importance has died, for they were
affectionate, loving, kind. Perhaps they have met with the
disappointing qualities of human nature and have become
disappointed, and so the feeling heart has taken the bowl of
poison and died. Or perhaps some began to dig the ground in
order to find water, but before they could reach water they
saw mud. Having no patience to go on digging still they
became disappointed with the mud and lost their enthusiasm
to dig. There are others who, out of self-righteousness or
keen perception of human defects or out of their critical
tendency, begin to hate before they can love someone, and so
hate comes first giving no chance to love.

What is necessary is to develop a sympathetic nature and
to sustain its gradual growth. As it is difficult for the student
of voice-culture to practise his voice and not to let it be
spoiled – for even practice may spoil it – so it is with the
sympathetic person: while developing the faculty of
sympathy there is a chance of spoiling it. In other words, the
more loving a person, the more chance he has to be
disappointed. The greater the love, the finer the fragility and
the more susceptible to everything; therefore the greater the
love, the more fragile the heart – at any moment it can break.
The one who walks in the path of sympathy therefore must
take great care that his way may not be blocked. It is his own
perseverance that will keep him from everything that is
trying to block his way.

There is one principle to be remembered in the path of
sympathy: we must do all we can with regard to the pleasure
of those whom we love and whom we meet, but we must not
expect the best from those whom we love and meet, for we
must know that the world is as it is. We cannot change it, but
we can change ourselves. The one who wants others to do
what he wishes them to do will always be disappointed. That
is the complaining soul; all day long, every day of the month,
that soul is complaining. He is never without a complaint; if
not about a human being, then it is the climate; if not about
the climate then about the conditions; if not about someone
else then about himself. Something is hurting that person all
the time.

He must remember that self-pity is the worst poverty. The person who takes life in this way, saying, "My poor self, crinkled, forgotten, forsaken, ill treated by everybody, by the planets, even by God" – that person has no hope; he is an exile from the Garden of Eden. But when one says, "I know what human nature is, I cannot expect any better, I must only try and appreciate what little good comes from it, I must be thankful for it and try and give the best I can to others" – that is the only attitude that will enable man to develop his sympathetic nature. The one who keeps justice on the foreground is always blinded by it; he is always talking about justice, but never knows it. As to the one who keeps justice in the background – the light of justice falls on his way and he only uses justice for himself. When he has not done right to others he takes himself to task, but if others do not do right towards him he says that this is justice also. For the just person all is just, for the unjust everything is unjust. Remember that the one who talks too much of justice is far from justice; that is why he is talking about it.

One may think, "Is there any reward in sympathy if it leads only to disappointment?" I shall answer, "Life's reward is life itself". A person may suffer from illness or disease, be most unhappy and sad, but ask him, "Shall I turn you into a rock?", and he will say, "No, let me live and suffer". Therefore life's reward is life; the reward of love is love itself. Loving is living, and the heart that closes itself to everyone closes itself to its own self.

The difference between human love and divine love is like that between drill and war. One has to drill in order to prepare for war. One has to know the phenomenon of love on this plane in order to prepare to love God who alone deserves love. The one who says, "I hate human beings, but I love God", does not know what love means; he has not drilled, he is of no use in war. A loving person, whether he loves a human being or whether he loves God, shows no trace of hatred, and the one who has hatred in him loves neither man nor God, for hatred is the sign that the doors of his heart are closed.

Is it not a great pity that we see to-day among the most civilized nations one nation working against the other, lack of trust between nations and this fear of war? It is dreadful to think that humanity which appears to be progressing so much is at the same time going backward to such an extent that never in the history of the world such bloodshed has been caused as during the last war. Are we evolving or going backward?

What is missing is not intellectuality, for people are capable of inventing things and imagining governments every day better and better. Then what is missing? It is the heart quality. It seems it is being buried more and more to-day. Therefore the real man is being destroyed and the false part of his being is continuing. A better condition can be brought about by the individual who will realize that the development of the heart and nothing else brings about better conditions.

The other day I lectured in Paris and after my lecture a very able man came to me and said, "Have you got a scheme?" I said, "What scheme?" "Of bettering conditions." I replied that I had not made such a scheme, and he said, "I have a scheme, I will show it to you". He opened his box and brought out a very large paper with mathematics on it and showed it to me saying, "This is the economic scheme that will make the condition of the world better: everyone will have the same share". I said, "We should practise that economic scheme first on tuning our piano: instead of saying D, E, F, we should tune them all to one note and play that music and see how interesting that would be – all sounding the same, no individuality, no distinction, nothing." And I added, "Economy is not a plan for construction, but it is a plan for destruction. It is economics which have brought us to destruction. It is the heart quality, it is the spiritual outlook which will change the world".

Very often people coming to hear me say afterwards, "Yes, all you say is very interesting, very beautiful, and I wish too that the world was changed. But how many think like you? How can you do it? How can it be done?". They come with that pessimistic remark, and I tell them, "One person comes into a country with a little cold or influenza and it spreads. If such a bad thing can spread, can not an elevated thought of love, kindness and goodwill towards all men spread? See then that there are finer germs, germs of goodwill, of love, kindness, and feeling, germs of brother-hood, of the desire for spiritual evolution, which can have greater results than the other ones. If we all have that optimistic view, if we all work in our little way, we can accomplish a great deal".

There are many good, loving and kind people whose heart goes out to every person they meet, but are they spiritual? It is an important question to understand. My answer is that they are just close to spiritual attainment, but unconsciously spiritual. They are not spirit-conscious. Often we meet a mother, a father or a child in whom we see a deep loving tendency; love is pouring out from them, they have become fountains of love. They do not know one word of psychology, of mysticism, but that does not matter. After all what are these names? Nothing but nets for fishes to be caught in, which remain in those nets for years. Sometimes these are big names with little meaning to them, of which much is made by those who want to commercialize the finer things. Very often it is a catering on the part of so-called spiritual workers to satisfy human curiosity and to create sensation even in the spiritual world. But truth is simple. The more simple you are and the more you seek for simplicity, the nearer you come to truth.

The devotional quality needs a little direction; that direction allows it to expand. The loving quality is just like water. The tendency of water is to expand, to spread, and so the loving quality spreads. But if a person is not well directed, or if he does not know how to direct himself then – if instead of deepening that quality flows – it is without root and it becomes limited. The love quality must be deepened first before it spreads out. If not, what generally happens is that those who set out to love all human beings end in hating all human beings. Because they did not first deepen themselves enough they did not have all the strength to draw more.

The Sufis have therefore considered the development of the heart quality as a spiritual culture, and have called it the culture of the heart. It consists of the tuning of the heart. Tuning means changing the pitch of the vibrations. Tuning the heart means changing the vibrations, bringing them to a certain pitch which is the natural one where you feel the joy and ecstasy of life, which enables you to give pleasure to others even by your presence because you are tuned. When an instrument is properly tuned you need not play music on it; just by striking it you will feel a great magnetism coming from it. If an instrument well-tuned can have that magnetism, how much greater should be the magnetism of hearts that are tuned. Rumi says, "Whether you have loved a human being or whether you have loved God, if you have loved enough you will be brought in the end into the presence of the supreme Love itself".

Question: Is there a science of culture of the heart?
Answer: The science of the Sufis teaches that in the mind and in the body a blockage is produced by the lack of development of the sympathetic nature. In the physical body are some nervous centres which are awakened by sympathetic development and by lack of sympathy they are closed. It is therefore that a butcher is less intuitive: everything that keeps man away from sympathy robs him of intuition, because sympathy develops a life in the finer centres, the nervous centres, and the absence of sympathy takes away that life.

So it is in the mind; when the heart is not sympathetic something is missing in the mentality of man, and it is sympathy which opens it. Sufis have the medicine for this disease: it is the practice of a certain art which in our language is called *dhikr* (*zikar*) or *mantram*. By practising that particular art in the right way one works with vibrations on these fine centres. It is a process of vibrations by the help of certain mystically prescribed words; by the repetition of these mystical words the centres begin to vibrate. Very often after six weeks' practice a person feels quite different. Then with that vibration a thought is held in the mind and so concentration is developed at the same time. It helps the love nature or sympathetic nature to be deepened and centralized in the person. As the love nature develops it begins to flow out, and its outflowing creates an atmosphere, a spiritual atmosphere.

That is why in the East you will always find that the presence of a Sufi is sought by Hindus and Muslims, by people of all different creeds, because the Sufi is all. He is not solely a Hindu or a Muslim, he has not any other religion, he is all, and this comes from the development of feeling. During my pilgrimage to the holy men of India I have seen some whose presence could illuminate you more than reading books for your whole life, or than disputing over any problems a thousand times. They do not need to speak, they become living lights, fountains of love. And if there is infection in disease so there is also infection in spiritual attainment. It is infectious, a person feels uplifted, he feels full of joy, ecstasy, happiness, enlightenment.

Of course the one is more impressed than the other; upon one the influence is much greater than upon another. It all depends upon the person. I will tell you an amusing instance. I remember a lady telling me, "Since you have come my husband is very, very nice". I said, "Yes". But eight days after I had left that town she wrote to me that the man was just where he had been before. The effect of influence is very different, because it is just like the effect of fire. The effect of fire on stone, on iron, on wax, on paper, on cloth, on cotton – upon every object – is different. So on every person the effect of a spiritual personality is different.

CHAPTER IX

Optimism and Pessimism

OPTIMISM REPRESENTS a spontaneous flow of love; optimism also represents trust in love. This shows that it is love, trusting love which is optimism. Pessimism comes from disappointment, from a bad impression which is there of some hindrance in the past. Optimism gives a hopeful attitude in life, whereas by pessimism one sees darkness on one's path. No doubt sometimes pessimism shows conscientiousness and cleverness – and pessimism also shows experience. But in point of fact can we ever be conscientious enough if we only think what difficulties we have before us in our life? It is trust which solves the problems in the end. Very often the wise have seen that cleverness does not reach far; it goes a certain distance and there it stands, for cleverness is a knowledge which belongs to the earth. As to experience – what is man's experience? One is only proud of one's experience in life as long as one has not seen how vast the world is. In every line of work and thought no mountain of experience is needed, and the further man goes in experience the less he realizes that he has none.

The psychological effect of optimism is such that it helps to bring success, for it is by the optimistic spirit that God has created the world. Optimism therefore comes from God, and pessimism is born out of the heart of man. From what little experience of life he has man feels, "This will not be done, that will not succeed, this will not go, that will not come right". For the optimistic one, if things will not come right in the end, it does not matter; he will take his chance. And what is life? Life is an opportunity. To the optimistic person the opportunity is a promise, and for the pessimistic person this opportunity is lost. It is not that the Creator makes man lose it, but it is man who withdraws himself from the possibility of seizing the opportunity.

Many in this world prolong their illness by giving a pessimistic thought to it. Mostly you will find that for those who have suffered for many years from a certain illness their illness becomes so real that its absence seems unnatural. They believe this illness to be their nature and its absence something they do not know. In this way they keep the illness in themselves. Then there are pessimistic people who think that misery is their share in life, that they are born to be wretched and cannot be anything else but unhappy, that heaven and earth are against them. In fact they – and nobody else – are against themselves, they themselves are their own misery and their pessimism is their misfortune.

Man's life depends on what he concentrates upon. If he concentrates upon misery he cannot but be miserable. If he has a certain habit or a certain nature of which he does not approve, he thinks he is helpless before it because it is his nature, his own. Nothing is man's nature, except that which he makes for himself. As the whole of nature is made by God, so the nature of each individual is made by himself. As the Almighty has the power to change His nature, so the individual is capable of changing his nature – if only he knew how. Among all the creatures of this world man is most entitled to be optimistic, for man represents the nature of God on earth: God as Judge, as Creator and as the Master of all His creation. So is man master of his own life, master of his affairs – if only he knew it.

A man with an optimistic view will help another who is drowning in the sea of fear or disappointment. A pessimist, on the contrary, if somebody comes to him wo is ill or downhearted by the hardness of life, will pull that person down and let him sink to the depths with him. So on the side of the one there is life, on the side of the other there is death. The one climbs to the top of the mountain, the other goes to the depth of the earth. Is there any greater helper in one's sorrow, in misfortune, at moments when every situation in life seems dark, than that spirit of optimism which knows, "All will be right". Therefore it is no exaggeration if I say that the very Spirit of God comes to man's rescue in the form of the optimistic spirit.

It does not matter how hard a situation in life may be, however great the difficulties, they all can be fought, they all can be surmounted. But what matters is that his pessimistic spirit weighs a person down low, when he has already come to low waters. Death is preferable to being weighed down in misery by a pessimistic spirit. The greatest reward there can be in the world is the spirit of optimism, and the greatest punishment that can be given to man for his worst sins is the spirit of pessimism.

Verily, hopeful is the one who in the end will succeed.

CHAPTER X

Conscience
Questions and answers

Question: What is the origin of conscience?
Answer: Conscience is the cream of the mind. The best that the mind has produced is conscience. It is a product of the mind, and therefore the conscience of a person living in one nation is quite different from the conscience of a person in another nation: it is built in another element. For instance, in ancient times there were communities of robbers. Now there are nations. The robbers used to think that they were entitled to rob the caravans passing by; they had a moral principle and an ideal. If a person said, "All I have I give you, let me go", they said, "No, I wish to see blood from your hand". They did not let him go without hurting him. What was their principle? They thought, "We do not accept anything from you, we are not beggars, we are robbers. We risk our lives for our profession, we defend ourselves risking our lives, we are brave, we are entitled to it, we are courageous". It was the same with the sea pirates; they thought what they did was virtue, and from that thought they became kings. The same people when small were robbers, when great became kings.

Conscience therefore is what we have made. At the same time it is the finest thing we make; it is like the honey made by bees. Beautiful experiences in life, tender thoughts and feelings gather in ourselves and make a conception of wrong or right. If we go against it, it brings and produces discomfort. Happiness, success, comfort in life, peace – they all depend upon the condition of our conscience.

Question: Does not each person make his own law for his necessity?
Answer: That would be nice, but we are living in a community; we are not entitled to live in a community and to disregard its laws. If we wish to benefit, to entitle ourselves to all its advantages we must adhere to its laws. No doubt if we have better ideas than the community has produced, we can make them see that our principle is the right one, but we

must not disregard the principle in which the whole community lives, saying, "We make our laws for our individual being". We can go to the mountains and forests saying, "We live according to our own law"; then we can be entitled to do so. In ancient times there were spiritual people who went into the caves of the mountains and into the forest and lived according to their own laws. But if we say, "As members of the community we must have its privileges", then we must also adhere to the laws of the community.

Question: Is not the disapproval of the conscience due to the soul's memory of unpleasant consequences of actions in the past, added to conventionalities and accepted ideas as to what is right at the present time?

Answer: Does "past" mean yesterday or the day before yesterday, this life or the life before? If no more explanation is given I might say that the whole life of the world is built of conventionalities and accepted ideas, and nothing else. Therefore I do not mean to say that conscience is truth. When we come to the absolute truth there is nothing to be said – but the conscience is made of accepted ideas. The world is *maya* and nothing else. If we accept something as being right, to another it is wrong. What the modern German philosopher Einstein says about relativity is the same thing which many years before the Hindus have called *maya*, illusion: illusion caused by relativity, for everything exists by our acceptance of it. We accept a certain thing to be right, good, or beautiful; once accepted it becomes our nature, our individual self – it is all acceptance. If we do not accept it then it is not. A mistake, if we do not accept it as such, is not a mistake, but once accepted it is a mistake.

Question: But we do not always know if it is a mistake.
Answer: Do we not know it from the painful consequences ensuing? That also is acceptance.

There are dervishes who work against accepted facts, for instance the accepted fact that fire burns. They jump into the fire and come out unharmed. So they give a proof to the religions, saying, "hellfire is not for us. When we can prove that here for us it does not exist, certainly for us in the hereafter it does not exist".

Question: Is not the conscience really the result of the soul's respect for the accepted ideas of a community? If left to oneself would there be any reaction in one's conscience?
Answer: But there is action and reaction in oneself. The reason is that a human being has had different phases of existence. In one phase he is less wise; if he dives deeper in himself he is wiser; if he dives still deeper in himself he is wiser still. What he does in one sphere he would reject in another sphere. Therefore a man has so much in himself to combat and to reject that he has action and reaction even without contact with others.

Sometimes in his mood a person is a devil, sometimes a saint. There are moods, there are times when a person is quite out of reason; there are fits of goodness and fits of badness – that is human nature. Therefore one cannot say that an evil person has no good in him, nor a good person no evil. But what concerns the conscience most is one's own conception of what is right and wrong, and the second influence is the conception of others. Therefore a person is not free.

Question: Is not the role of the conscience very difficult?
Answer: The best way of testing life is to have conscience as a testing instrument with everything – whether it is harmonious or inharmonious. If it is inharmonious, then to think that it will upset the whole environment; if it is harmonious then to think that it is all right.

Question: How can a feeling be controlled by the conscience?
Answer: The conscience – like everything else – if it has become accustomed to handle one's thought, speech or action becomes stronger. If it is not accustomed to do this then it becomes weaker and remains only as a torture, not as a controller. The conscience is a faculty of the heart as a whole which contains reason, thought, memory and heart.

Question: But who is it in the conscience who judges?
Answer: In the sphere of conscience the soul of man and the Spirit of God meet and become one.[9]

Question: In what manner do the soul of man and the Spirit of God meet in the conscience and become one?
Answer: The heart in its depth is linked with the divine Mind. Therefore in the depth of the heart there is a greater justice than on the surface, and a kind of intuition comes, inspiration, knowledge as the inner light falling upon our own individual conception of things, and both then come together. In the conscience is the throne of God; there God Himself sits on the throne of justice.

A person condemned by his conscience is more miserable than the one who is condemned by the court. A person whose conscience is clean, if he is exiled from his country or sent to prison, still remains a lion – even in a cage, for even in a cage there is his inner happiness. But when his conscience despises a person then that is a bitter punishment, more so than any the court can give.

Sa'di says it very beautifully. He sees the throne of God in the conscience and says, "Let me confess my faults to Thee alone that I may not have to go before anyone in the world to humiliate myself".

Question: Why can we only have knowledge of God through the heart? What part of the mind does the heart represent?
Answer: The heart is the principle centre – not the heart in the body, but the heart which is the depth of the mind, for the mind is the surface of the heart. The heart and the mind are one, as one tree: the root is the heart, the branches, the fruits and the flowers represent the mind.

Question: What is the relation between conscience and truth?
Answer: I distinguish between truth and facts. Conscience is made from the cream of facts, but not from truth, because truth stands above all things; it has nothing to do with conscience. It is facts which have to do with conscience. When we come to understand truth – the understanding of truth is just like a spring which rises and expands into an ocean, so that we come even to such a degree of understanding that we say, "All is true, and all is truth".

CHAPTER XI

Justice and Forgiveness
Questions and answers

Question: Is it not very difficult to avoid judging? For in order to become just one has to come to a certain conclusion.
Answer: Yes, but what man generally does is not only that he judges anyone in the mind – he is very ready to give his judgment out. He is not patient enough to wait and analyse the matter and think more about it. As a rule a person is not only ready to judge, but without any restraint on his part he is ready to express his judgment instantly. He will not think, "Have I the right to judge that person? Have I risen to that state of evolution?" – when Jesus Christ himself refused to judge and said, "Whoever is faultless – it is that person's place to accuse or to punish". It teaches a great lesson: even in order to learn justice it is not necessary that we should be ready to judge and instantly to express our judgement, our opinion.

The idea of the Sufis, who see in every form the divine form, in every heart the divine shrine, is that to judge anyone, whatever be his position, his action, his condition, is against their religion, their attitude, for theirs is a respectful attitude towards everyone. And in this manner they develop that philosophy which has first been learned by them intellectually.

Question: Does the fact of not blaming others mean that we do not see their faults any more, that we are above seeing them?
Answer: No, in the first place it is a question of self restraint or self control, of politeness, kindness, sympathy, and graciousness, of a worshipful attitude towards God, the Creator of all beings: all are His children, good or bad. If anybody's child happened to be homely in appearance would it be polite to say before its parents, "Your child is homely"? The Father and Mother of all beings is there, ever present, and knows what is going on in every person's heart; all are

His creatures. When with their faults and their merits before us we are ready to judge and to express our opinion against them, it is certainly against the Artist who has made them – not behind His back, in His presence! It would not be difficult to feel the presence of God everywhere if only we were conscious of this.

Besides this it is not only that we judge the faults and merits of people impartially, our favour and disfavour are always connected with it. Our favour is always inclined to see the merit, our disfavour the fault. Is there any person, however great, without a fault? Any person, however wicked, without a merit? Then if we see more faults it means that we close our heart to the favourable attitude and open our heart to the attitude which is unfavourable in order to criticize.

Now the other question: are we above seeing faults? Yes, there comes a time, after a continual practice of this virtue of not judging, when we see the reason behind every fault that appears to us in anyone we meet in our life. We become more tolerant, more forgiving. For instance, a person is ill, he is creating disturbance in his atmosphere by crying or weeping or shouting. It disturbs us and we say, "How terrible, how bad, how annoying. What a bad nature that person has got!" It is not the nature, it is the illness. If we looked from a different point of view, that reason would make us tolerant. And tolerance can give rise to that forgiveness, that only essence of God which can be found in the human heart.

Question: Will you please speak about the justice of God's judgment?

Answer: By giving you a little simile I will show you what difference there is between man's justice and God's justice. There are children of the same father and they are quarreling over their toys. They have reasons to quarrel over their toys. One thinks a certain toy is more attractive: why should he not possess it? The other says, that toy is given to him: why should he not hold on to it? Both have their reason and both are just, but the father's justice is different from theirs. The father has not only given them the toys to play with, but at the same time he knows what is the character of each child and what he wishes to bring out of that child, and whether that particular toy will help to bring out what he wishes to come out. The child does not know this. It happens perhaps that the toy seems poor to him and according to his sense of justice he cannot understand why that toy was given to him and not to the other. If the child was older he would have accused the father of injustice, but he does not know the justice of his father. He has to grow to that stage of evolution where his father is in order to understand the meaning behind.

The same is with the justice of God and man. Man's justice is covered by his limited experience in life, by his favour and disfavour, by his preconceived ideas, by the learning he has which is nothing compared to the knowledge of God. When one compares the father with his innocent child, their relationship is too near to be compared to the relationship between God and man where there is such a distance; if we counted all the human beings that exist they would be like a drop compared to the ocean. There is no comparison between God and man. Therefore man's justice is imperfect, God's justice is perfect.

If one ever gets a glimpse of divine justice, the only way is first to believe in the justice of God against all the proofs which will contradict His justice. There are many proofs which will contradict His justice. Why is this person rich, why is the other poor, why is this person in a high position, why has that person suffered so much, and why has another lived long and had a pleasant life? If one judged their actions, their intelligence, their stage of evolution one would find no justification. By judging this one will come to a conclusion where one will say, "Oh, there is no justice, it is all mechanical working which is perhaps behind it".

Ideas such as *karma* and reincarnation will satisfy, but at the same time they will not root out God behind them, for then God has no power. God cannot be all powerful if everyone has the power to make his own *karma*. Root out God, then everything is working mechanically. And even if so, there cannot be a machine without an engineer; for a machine there must be an engineer. Is he subjected to his machine? Is he subjected to its power or is he the controller of it? If he is subjected then he is not powerful enough. If he is limited then he cannot be God any more. God is He who is perfect in His justice, in His wisdom and in His power.

If we question the cause of all such happenings which do not give us a justification then we come to another question, and that question is: Can a composer give a certain justification of every note he has written in his composition? He cannot; he can only say, "It is the stream that has come from my heart. I have tried to maintain certain laws, to keep to certain rules of composition, but if you ask me for the justification of every note I am unable to give it. I am not concerned with every note, I am concerned with the effect that the whole produces".

It is not true that there is no law. There is a law, but is law predominant or love? Law is a habit, and love is the being. Law is made, love has never been created; it was, it is and it will be. So love is predominant. What do we read in the Bible? God is love. So God is beyond the law: love is above the law. Therefore if we come to any solution to our ever rising question: Why is it so? – it is not by the study of the law, never. Study of the law will only give increasing appetite which will never bring satisfaction. If there is anything which will bring satisfaction it is diving deep into love and letting love inspire law. That will open up a realm of seeing the law better.

Then we shall see that there is nothing in this world which has no justification. It is inexplicable but it is perceptible that all has its justification, and in the light of perfect justice all life will be manifest. Then we shall not have one word to say that "this is unjust", not even the most cruel thing we saw. A thought like this may shock, but at the same time that is the point the wise man reaches, and he calls it the culmination of wisdom.

Question: How do we know that God forgives more than He judges?

Answer: In the first place justice is born and love has never been born. It always has been and always will be. Of what is justice born? It is born of the sense of fairness. As this sense becomes matured in man he begins to seek for evenness, and what is not even he does not like. But to inspire this sense, to develop it, all must exist first: justice is the outcome of what we see, love is not. Love is spontaneous and is always there, as it is said in the Bible, "God is love". Therefore justice is God's nature, but love is God's very being. Therefore He forgives, because He is forgiveness Himself, and He judges because it is His nature to judge.

Question: So justice comes from God's intelligence, and forgiveness from His divine love?
Answer: God's intelligence in this world of illusion has a limited expression, for when one judges limited things one's intelligence becomes limited also. One is as limited as the object before one; the greater the object, the greater becomes the vision. But forgiveness does not judge, it is only the feeling of love. And therefore whatever be the other's fault, once a person has forgiven, the happiness and joy are shared by both. Justice has not that joy. The one who judges too much is unhappy himself and makes the one whom he judges unhappy also. The one who forgives is happy, he does not keep any grudge in his heart, he makes his heart pure and free from it. Therefore God's greatest attribute is forgiveness.

CHAPTER XII

Pairs of Opposites used in Religious Terms

IN RELIGIOUS terms one makes use of pairs of opposites such as God and devil, heaven and hell, sin and virtue. Man who begins to acquire knowledge by learning through pairs of opposites cannot at once rise to that pitch where he comprehends life without them. In one way it is not correct, it is not right to conceive God who is all-powerful together with the conception of another personality, an opposite power, calling it devil. On the other hand it would puzzle a believer in God, who considers God all good and all beautiful, when he knew that also all that is bad or evil is contained in God. Besides, a devotee, a worshipper of God, whose object is to raise by devotion and worship his ideal of God as high as he can, is hindered in his effort by being made to see that all that he considers wicked and ugly also belongs to God's part. On the other hand one has diminished God, making Him limited, producing before Him a power which – if not equal – exists as a power opposite to God.

No doubt whichever method the wise of the world have taken to guide humanity, whether with the limited idea of God opposed by another power, Satan, or with the other idea that God is all-powerful, the only Being, it has always been wisdom's work to bring man to that pitch where he can understand life more perfectly. No doubt when we give a place to a power for wrong, for evil, when we picture it as a personality and call it a devil, we certainly limit the power of the One whom we always call almighty. Nevertheless, it is picturesque, it is more comprehensible and tangible to believe in the God of good and in the Lord of evil.

As to the idea of what is called heaven and hell – for our comprehension these are two places: one where a person is punished, the other where he is exalted, where he is happy, where he is rewarded. This idea is clear, but where do we experience all unhappiness and sorrow and discomfort, and where do we experience all pleasure and happiness and joy? Is it not on the same earth? It is under the same sun. This explains to us that those two places were shown to us as different because we are capable only of seeing them as two different places. The wise of the world, at any time of the world's civilization, could not do better than to make the subtle ideas of life as simple and comprehensible to man as possible.

For instance, if I were to say that the world of thought and the world of action are different, it would be true. Yet it is the same world in which we live – call it the world of thought – and the very world in which we live is the world of action. It is not only how it is said, but it is also how we look at it. What is said is not wrong but, if we look wrongly at it, it can be wrong. It is not disbelieving in things which is wrong, but believing wrongly is even worse than disbelief: it is the understanding of all things from every point of view which enlightens, not refusing to believe them or to believe them simply. Cannot one's own mind be turned from hell to heaven and from heaven to hell? Cannot one's own life's situation be turned from hell to heaven and from heaven to hell? It is here where one sees the difference and at the same time the oneness of the two.

Now we come to what people call sin and virtue. In all ages they have pointed out, "This particular thing is sin, that particular thing is virtue". Whenever the wise have done it they have done it rightly, and yet they differ from one another. If a greater light is thrown upon this subject it is possible to view sin in the light of sin and also to view sin in the light of virtue. Very often one can also see that under the cover of virtue there was a sin, and under the cover of sin there was a virtue.

When people came to Christ accusing a person of wrong-doing the Master did not think of anything else but forgiveness, for he did not see in that person what the others saw. Looking at right and wrong is not the work of an ordinary mind, and it is amusing that the more ignorant a person, the more ready he is to distinguish between right and wrong. Very often it is the angle from which we view a thing that makes it right or wrong, and therefore the very thing that we would call wrong, if we were able to see it from different angles, we would call right at the same time.

When people say that they distinguish between right and wrong by their results, even then they cannot be sure if in the punishment there was not a reward, or in the reward a punishment. What does this show us? It shows us that life is a puzzle of duality. The pairs of opposites keep us in an illusion and make us think, "This is this, and that is that". At the same time by throwing a greater light upon things we shall find in the end that they are quite different from what we had thought.

Seeing the nature and character of life the Sufi says that it is not very important to distinguish between two opposites. What is most important is to recognize that One which is hiding behind it all. Naturally after realizing life the Sufi climbs the ladder which leads him to unity, to the idea of unity which comes through the synthesis of life, by seeing One in all things, in all beings.

You may believe that the world has evolved, that humanity has always evolved, or you may believe that it has gone up and then down, going round and round in circles, or whatever may be your belief. But in whatever age the wise were born, they have always believed the same: that behind all is oneness, and in the understanding of that oneness is wisdom. A person who awakens to the spirit of unity, a person who sees the oneness behind all things – his point of view becomes different and his attitude therefore changes. He no longer says to his friend, "I love you because you are my friend"; he says, "I love you because you are myself". He says, as a mystic would say, "Whether you have done wrong or whether I have done wrong, it does not matter. What is wanted is to right the wrong".

Question: If I have well understood your philosophy and idea of religion it seems to me that it starts from doubt, not making a distinction between good and evil, sin and virtue, justice and injustice. Do you seek to establish a triangle system on which you seek to find the centre of gravity?
Answer: Yes, you are quite right, but I do not mean that we start by not distinguishing between the two. We do not need to start by it, because life starts by distinguishing between the two; life starts us in this way. If we did not distinguish

between the two and we arrived at that conception of unity of which I have spoken, we would be missing a great deal in life. It is after distinguishing these that, without becoming congested, we may come to the idea of unity which raises us above it all. For instance, when a person says, "I will not look at the fault of another" and closes his eyes, he has missed a great deal. But the one who has seen it and risen above it has really closed his eyes; he is the person who deserves to close his eyes from the other side.

The purpose of our life on earth is to come and see all the distinctions and all the differences, but not to be congested by them and so to be thrown downwards. We should go on rising above them all, at the same time experiencing them all. For instance a man may say, "I have never thought about anyone who has done me any good, and I have never considered any harm that has ever come to me from anyone; I have always had just that one idea before me and after that idea I kept going". He may be advanced, he may be spiritual, he may be pious, and yet he has missed a great deal. But the one who has received all the good that has come to him with grateful thanks and felt it, and who has also felt the harm done to him and forgiven and pardoned it, he is the one who has seen the world and is going beyond with success.

Question: What do you mean exactly by the idea of God?
Answer: Everything in the world can be defined except one, and that is the idea of God. If it could be defined it could not be the idea of God – and that is God. Because God is greater than His name and higher than our comprehension of Him. It is our fault to call Him God, but if we would not call Him God then what would we call Him? By giving a name to the nameless, by making a conception of Someone who is beyond conception we only make Him limited. At the same time when we would not do it, we would not do what we ought to do. The idea is that in order to respect a great man we ought to have a conception of greatness, and this conception is not that person, it is the idea we have made of that person.

If there are twenty admirers of a great personality each one of them has his own conception of that personality, I might say that each one of the twenty has his special great person. Therefore there are twenty great personalities instead of one, and only the one name makes the twenty persons unite in it. If the Hindus have said, "So many men, so many Gods", it was not an exaggeration; it expressed only the idea that every man has his God in his conception, and each one – if he can ever express it – can best express his own conception of God. It is necessary first to have a conception of God in order to reach that stage where comes a realization of Him. If a person does not have a conception of God he cannot have the realization of Him. I mean to say: fuller realization of Him. If a person does not think a personality great, he will not see into the greatness of that personality; he must first have the conception that in him there is something great. In other words we first make our God before we come to the realization of Him.

Question: What do you mean by "God has no opposite"?
Answer: There is the sun and there is the moon, there is man and woman, there is night and there is day. The colours are distinguished by their variety and so are the forms. Therefore to distinguish anything there must be its opposite; where there is no opposite we cannot distinguish. There must be health in order to distinguish illness; if there were no health and only illness then it would not have been illness.

Furthermore in ancient times many have tried to help the imagination of the God-seekers by giving them a belief in a Satan: that God is all goodness and Satan all badness. It was to answer those who could not understand better. In reality badness is only the shadow of goodness; as shadow is non-existent, so evil is non-existent. There is always going forwards. What is left behind – that is less good; what we gain in the journey forwards – that is more good.

When we compare them then we call one thing evil and the other good. Therefore people have called the devil all evil, to whom one should turn one's back, and God all goodness, to whom one should turn one's face. It was a convenient method to teach the people of those times. In reality God has no comparison. No doubt God can be compared if we make God good, as many do. But if we have a wider conception of God we cannot confine God to what we call goodness. What is our idea of goodness? It is very small. Perhaps it is good for us, but it is not something to judge God with.

God is not kind only to a few, to those who are good. We can see that He sends the rain to all the trees and plants, not to a few only; the sun shines upon all, all are given food – because His kindness is perfect.

Question: How could the almighty God allow so much bloodshed in the recent war?
Answer: The answer to this question is that nothing that gives pain and causes harm through life is from God. It comes from the limited, not from the unlimited. In essence it is God-power which is working through all powers, but when analysed it is the power called *Qadr* working through human beings which has been wasted through these wars causing so much bloodshed and disturbance in the whole cosmos and disharmony in all spheres on this planet.

God is not to be blamed for this. It is we human beings who are at fault; instead of seeking the pleasure of God we have sought our own pleasures. It is beyond the power of man to judge the actions of God from his own moral standard and from his limited point of view. A just person will certainly accept the fact that it takes a long time and much practice to develop the sense of justice which after a great many tests and trials makes man just, and it is not the man who is ready to weigh and measure the action of his fellow-man and to form an opinion who is really just. No man with any sense may dare try to trace the cause of war to the divine Spirit of God, when the whole life on earth is laid before us like an open book wherein we can read distinctly its true cause.

Question: As evil cannot come out of good, how came the wickedness and miseries of humanity?
Answer: The miseries and wickedness of humanity did not come from good, but good came out of wickedness and miseries. If it was not for wickedness and miseries and wrong we would not have appreciated what good and right means. It is these two opposite poles which make us distinguish between the two. If there had been just one thing, we would

have called it goodness or wickedness, but it would have been just one. Calling it by two different names helps us to distinguish them.

Many have been cross with God for having sent any misery in their lives – but we always get such experiences! Becoming cross one says, "Why, this is not just", or "This is not right", and "How could God who is just and good allow unjust things to happen?" But our sight is so limited that our conception of right and wrong and good and evil is only for us – not according to God's plan. It is true that, as long as we see it as such, it is so for us and for those who look at it from our point of view, but when it comes to God the whole dimension is changed, the whole point of view is changed.

It is therefore that the wise in all ages, instead of trying to judge the actions of God, have so to speak put aside their sense of justice for the time being and have learned only one thing, and that was resignation to the will of God. By doing this they have come to an understanding which was the greatest blessing in their lives: that they could see from the point of view of God. But if they would express that point of view before the world, the world would call them mad. Therefore they have called themselves *Muni*, which means the people who keep silent.

Question: Why do people who do evil, who do wrong, succeed, while there are people who do right without ever succeeding?

Answer: That is not a rule. The rule is that the one who succeeds through wrong will only succeed through wrong; by doing right he will fail. The one who succeeds by right will always succeed by doing right; if he does wrong he will fail. Furthermore for him who ascends, all – right and wrong – becomes as steps to ascend and for him who descends, all – good or evil – becomes a step to descend. Yet what is consoling is that this takes one to the ideal: there must be an ideal before one in order to ascend; then even one's error will help.

For instance, when a person is to be cured, both taking medicine and not taking medicine will help him towards his cure. And the one who is not meant to be cured, neither medicine nor its absence will help him. It teaches us to find out what we are seeking, what is our ideal. Do we ascend? How do we descend? A picture of this is a person who is climbing a staircase. If he is going upwards and his foot slips, even then he will go upwards because he is bound to go upwards. The one who is going downwards, if he slips, will go down because he is bound to go down. There is no man in this world who can say, "I am faultless" Does this mean that he is not destined to reach what he is bound to reach?

It is a great pity if a person does right or good because he wants to progress or to become spiritual, for what is goodness after all? It is a very small price to pay for spirituality. And the man who depends upon his goodness to attain spirituality may just as well wait a thousand years, for it is just like the picture of a man who is collecting all the sand he can to make a hill in order to mount to heaven. If one is not good for the love of goodness, if one does not do right for one's love of justice, for one's own satisfaction, there is no meaning in doing right, there is no virtue in doing good.

To be spiritual is to become nothing; to become good is to become something. To be something is like being nothing, but to be nothing is like being all things. It is this claim of being something which hinders the natural perfection. Self-effacement is a return to the Garden of Eden.

Question: Is there no risk that a person endeavouring to become selfless will become a prey to all the conditions of life?
Answer: On the contrary, for all strength and wisdom lies in perfection. The absence of perfection is the tragedy of life. The person who holds on to himself is a burden even to the earth. The earth can easily bear mountains upon its back, but the person who is egoistic is heavier. And what happens in the end? His own soul cannot bear that person, and that is why many commit suicide. The claim of the self has become so heavy upon the soul that the soul wants to depart from it. A hint was given by Jesus Christ when he said, "Blessed are the poor in spirit". What does poor in spirit mean? It means the ego that is effaced.

CHAPTER XIII

Insight

THERE IS a stage of evolution in man's life where his every question is answered by the life around him. If there is a living being before him or if there is nature around him, if he is wakeful or if he is asleep, the answer to his question comes as an echo of the very question. As certain things become an accommodation for the air in order to turn it into sound, so for every thought of a sage everything becomes an accommodation in order to help it to resound, and in this resonance there is an answer. In point of fact the answer is in the question itself; a question has no existence without answer. It is man's limited vision that makes him see the question only, without the answer.

There is a pair of opposites in all things, and in each there exists the spirit of the opposite: in man the quality of woman, in woman the spirit of man, in the sun the form of the moon, in the moon the light of the sun. The closer one approaches reality, the nearer one arrives at unity. The evidence of this realization is that no sooner a question has arisen in the heart, than the answer comes as its echo within or without.

If you look before yourself the answer is before you; if you look behind the answer is behind; if you look up the answer awaits you in the sky; if you look down the answer is engraved for you in the earth; if you close your eyes you will find the answer within you. It is only a matter of climbing a mountain; the name of this mountain is WHY. As you have climbed it, then you are face to face to your ideal. It is not study which brings man to this realization; it comes by rising above all that hinders one's faith in truth.

CHAPTER XIV

The Law of Attraction

THERE ARE two great principles: the attraction of like to like and the attraction of opposites.

Looking at nature we see that if there is one speck of dust on the wall all the dust will collect there. Where there is one grain of wheat much wheat grows. Where there is one little roseplant there will be a great many rosebushes. It may be hard for us to find one fly in the room, but if there is one fly we shall see that there are other flies near it. It may be difficult for us to find one ant, but if there is one ant there will be other ants near it. Where there is one sparrow there will be many sparrows. In the jungle where there is one parrot there will be a great many parrots in the same part of the forest. However much dogs may quarrel and fight, where there are three or four of them it is there that they enjoy being. The rabbit does not delight in being among sparrows, nor does the donkey rejoice in being with serpents.

This shows us that like is drawn to like, to its affinity. This is the reason why nations and races have their peculiar characteristics and attributes: for ages people of like character and like qualities have collected together forming one group. The French are unlike the English, the English are different from the Swedes, the Swedes differ from the Germans. It is not difficult for a person whose intelligence is exercised in this direction to tell at once in a crowd a Belgian from a Frenchman, a Rumanian from an Italian.

In India every province, every district has its peculiar character. A Gujerati will always like to be with another Gujerati. Where there are two or three Gujeratis they are happy, they do not want a Punjabi in their company. The Bengali is not like the Madrassi. When a few Bengalis are together they do not want a Madrassi, and the Madrassi enjoys being in the society of Madrassis; he does not want a Bengali to be there. Why? Because each rejoices in his own element.

Families also have their likeness which comes from the like

attributes being drawn to their like. In India where great attention is paid to heredity this is traced very far. The first reason for the attraction of like to like is bloodrelationship. At the present time relationship is much less thought of; we do not know who our relations are. It is however a great bond, as it is said: the blood is the same, the form is made of the same element.

The second reason is the affinity of occupation. A farmer who has been tilling the soil all day, in the evening will want to be with other farmers with whom he can talk about the crops; he does not want to sit among literary persons. A soldier always wants to be with other soldiers. A sportsman wishes to be with sportsmen; he will not like to be among the learned in whose society he feels out of place. A literary person always seeks other literary persons. A musician likes the society of musicians. I have experienced this myself. Sometimes there were Indians among my audience, people from my own province, but they were less appreciative than Western musicians. The Western musician perhaps did not understand the words I was singing, but he was a musician, his interest in the music made him akin to its being.

The third reason is the similarity of qualities. A brave person will like to be with other brave people; he will not like to be with cowards. A kind person will seek other kind-hearted people. The affectionate are drawn to the affectionate, not to the cold-hearted. A quarrelsome person will seek out another quarrelsome person to fight with. Like is always recognized by like. If there are two thieves in a company the one will at once recognize the other. If a thief goes from Paris to New York it will be very easy for him to find a brother there. For another person it will take a very long time, but the thief knows at once, "This is a thief, this is my brother".

A cruel man attracts the cruelty of others. If we deceive another ever so little we shall at once find others who deceive us. Deceit may not be in our nature – but we have deceived. This is the secret of the punishment of our sins. It is not that God gives us a certain punishment, but by our wickedness, by our evil thought we attract the same wickedness, the same evil thought from others to us. The evil that we do brings the same evil upon us from others. A little kindness in us attracts the kindness of the kind. A kind person meets with kindness wherever he goes, even among the cruel. A least little generosity on our part attracts the generosity of the generous. By the repetition of the names of God, by impressing upon our soul the kindness, the mercy of that infinite goodness we create in our soul those qualities and we attract to us the kindness and mercy of that goodness under all forms and names.

Besides the attraction of like to like there is the law of attraction of each to its opposite. There are two great forces in nature: the creative force and the receptive force that answers to it, or the active force and the passive force, *jalal* and *jamal*. This can be understood from the law of rhythm. In every rhythm there is the stronger beat and the weaker beat, the returning. In two-four time, for instance, we count one-two, one-two, the strong beat and the beat that has just as much force as to counterbalance the other.

We can also see this in the forms of protuberance and cavity. The representatives of these two forces in nature are the male and the female. But in every man some qualities are male and some female; in every woman some of the qualities are female and some male.

We can see that the ears receive sound; they do not create. The eyes are creative. The nose perceives the odour; it cannot create. The nose can tell us the flavour of a thing much sooner, much more exactly than the palate. The lips, the mouth, create, and they are attracted to each other. When the ears hear a sound, the eyes at once want to turn to see what it is, from where it comes. The nose at once wants to interfere with what the mouth does. It says, "Do not chew that any longer. I don't want it", or it says, "Do justice to that; I like it; it is nice".

We can see that, when our right hand takes hold of something, the left hand wants to help it. When our right foot goes out, the left foot at once wishes to join it. When we fold one arm, the other arm wants to be folded too. One leg inclines to cross the other. In India there is a superstition that it brings bad luck to sleep with the legs crossed. Everyone knows it, but it is most difficult for anyone to get out of this habit because it is so natural.

Often a person would rather be with his opposite than with one who is nearer his own level. When two who are of nearly equal strength meet they are not harmonious to each other. Students of breath will readily understand this; they know that there is a more active breath and a less active breath, and when both become of equal activity there is a sort of fight. If one person is a great singer and another is teaching voice-production they can agree together. There is no competition between them; the one wants to show himself, to show his voice, the other does not. But if there are two great opera-singers, a tenor and a bass, they will never agree; there is rivalry between them, they both want to be something.

A wise man will rather have a foolish servant than a half-wise one who will interfere in his orders. There is a story of a servant who, when sent to fetch the doctor, went first to the undertaker. He was thinking of the future! If he cannot be among the wise, a wise person will rather be among the foolish than among the half-wise. I have often seen that the simple one with a simple faith can be inspired and become illuminated, while the intellectual is always reasoning and does not advance one step. This is why scientists and mystics never harmonize. The scientist says, "If you know something, I know something too. If you are something, I am something also".

There will always be some societies, some associations that we like and some that we do not like; some that do not like us and some that appreciate us, because we always like only our own element. There is nothing surprising in this and nothing to blame; it is the law of attraction.

The Sufi makes himself harmonious with all; he makes himself the element of all. He activates the element that is within, and that element is love. We can learn this from the Bible which says that God is love. The differences and distinctions are external, but from the beginning man is so trained to see the differences that he does not see the unity underlying. People have said, "We are of this race, we are superior, you are inferior; our religion is superior, yours inferior; our nation is great, yours less". This was the cause of the present war. The nations of Europe had reached the same level; if one made a good airship another made one better still; if one made a good submarine another made one better still. If the one was strong another wanted to be still stronger.

People have said, "By being strong, by a strong rule, we shall unite the world". What a mistake! We can see what happens when we try to rule our family with a strong hand. It will never be united. It is only love that can unite the world. It is the only way in which the union of mankind, universal brotherhood, can be brought about.

CHAPTER XV

The Liberal and the Conservative Point of View

THERE ARE two points of view open to one in everything in the world: the liberal and the conservative. Each of these points of view gives a person a sense of satisfaction, because in both there is a certain amount of virtue.

When a man looks at his family from the conservative point of view, he becomes conscious of family pride and acts in every way so as to keep up the honour and dignity of his ancestors. He follows the chivalry of his forefathers and by looking at the family from this point of view he defends and protects those who belong to his family, whether worthy or unworthy. In this way he helps to keep up a flame, lighted perhaps years ago, by holding it in his hand as a torch to guide his way.

When one looks at one's nation from a conservative point of view it gives one the feeling of patriotism – which to-day is the substitute for religion in the modern world. It is no doubt a virtue in the sense that one begins to consider one's whole nation as one family: one cares not for one's own children only, but for the children of the nation. Man gives his life when occasion arises to defend his nation, the dignity, the honour, the freedom of his people.

The conservative spirit is the individualizing spirit, which is the central theme of the whole creation. It is this spirit which has functioned as the sun; otherwise it was the all-pervading light, and it is the power of this spirit working in nature which keeps many branches together on one stem and several leaves together on one branch. It is again this spirit working in man's body which keeps man's hands and feet together, thus keeping him an individual entity.

But there is always a danger that this spirit, if increased, may produce congestion. When there is too much family pride man lives only in his pride, forgetting his duty towards mankind and not recognizing anything that unites him with others beyond the limited circle of his family. When this congestion is produced in a nation it results in all kinds of disasters, such as wars and revolutions with violence and destruction. The nightmare that the world has just passed through was the outcome of world congestion produced by the extreme of this same spirit.

This shows that it is not true that virtue is one thing and sin another. The same thing which once was virtue becomes sin. Virtue or sin is not an action; it is the condition, it is the attitude which prompts one to a certain action, and it is the outcome of the action which makes it a sin or a virtue.

Life is movement, death is the stopping of the movement; congestion stops it, circulation moves it. The conservative spirit is useful in so far as it is moving, in other words: as it is broadening itself. If a person who first was proud of his family, after having done his duty to his people, takes the next step forward which is to help his fellow-citizens, and the third step which is to defend his nation, he is progressing. His family pride and his patriotism are no doubt a virtue, for they lead him from one thing to another, better than the former.

Congestion comes when a person is set in his interest. If his family causes a man to be so absorbed in his pride and interest in it that nobody else in the world exists for him except his own people, or when a person thinks of his own nation alone – nothing else interests him, others do not exist for him – in this case his family pride or his patriotism becomes a veil over his eyes, blinding him so as to make him unable to serve either others or his own.

In selfishness there is an illusion of profit, but in the end the profit attained by selfishness proves to be worthless. Life is the principal thing to consider, and true life is the inner life, the realization of God, the consciousness of one's spirit. When the human heart becomes conscious of God it turns into the sea and it spreads; it extends the waves of its love to friend and foe. Spreading further and further it attains perfection.

The Sufi message is not necessarily a message of pacifism. It does not teach to make peace at any and every cost; it does not condemn family pride or patriotism; it does not even preach against war. It is a message to make one conscious of the words of the Bible: "We live and move and have our being in God" – to realize this and to recognize the brotherhood of humanity in the realization of God. The natural consequences of this will bring about the spirit of brotherhood and equality and will result in preparing the outer democracy and the inner aristocracy which is in the nobility of the soul whose perfection is hidden under the supremacy of God.

CHAPTER XVI

The Attitude

ALL AFFAIRS of life depend upon man's attitude, and the mechanical work that is psychologically done is such that before man steps forward to work he sees his attitude being reflected on his affair. For instance, a person starts to do something with doubt in his mind – on that affair he sees the shadow of doubt. When a person wants to do something which he knows is not quite just – before he begins to work he sees the phantom of injustice before him.

The heart of man, as the Sufis say, is a mirror. All that is reflected in this mirror is projected upon other mirrors. When man has doubt in his heart that doubt is reflected upon every heart with which he comes in contact. When he has faith that faith is reflected in every heart. Can there be a more interesting study and a greater wonder than to observe this keenly? As soon as man is able to watch this phenomenon in life, it is just like a magic lantern that makes all clear to him. In this light, how foolish would appear the cleverness and the crooked ways of the dishonest who for a moment thinks that he is profiting by them, and who for a moment may seem to be benefited by them.

In this life on earth, in which we cannot depend even on the morrow and in which worldly gains are snatched from one hand to an other, it is not worthwhile making the heart reflect an element that is foreign to it. That which is comforting and consoling through all this life of falsehood is only the feeling of purity in one's own heart, when one feels that one's own attitude in life is right and just. The one who experiences this will certainly say that it is greater than all the wealth of the world. It is the knowledge of this philosophy which seems to be lost from the heart of humanity at the present time. It is therefore that all things go wrong. If there is any preventive which can be used against it, it is to make one's own life as much as one can an example of one's ideal – although to make it perfectly so is most difficult. There is nothing like trying, and having failed once, another time one may be successful.

Someone may say, "Yes, for certain errors made here suffering has now come; I shall bear it". No doubt he is brave and just, but personally I would prefer the man who would resist suffering by realizing that his birthright, as a divine right, is happiness alone. Pain and suffering are foreign to his soul; they do not belong to it. He does not want it, he will not have it.

Question: Is suffering necessary for our evolution?
Answer: Suffering is helpful for evolution, not necessary. Therefore we must not seek suffering in order to evolve. We must avoid it. To a wise person every failure is a teaching, but it is better if he avoids learning in this way.

Question: Would it be possible to gain the same degree of evolution in life without suffering?
Answer: Certainly possible, but most difficult.

CHAPTER XVII

The Law of Life

ALL THAT comes to a person – in reality he arrives at it. By this I do not mean to say that he does not make it, create it, earn it, or deserve it, or that it does not come to him by chance. All that comes may come to a person in the above five ways, but at the same time in reality he arrives at it. These five ways are realms through which a certain thing comes, but what brings it about is the person himself.

This subtle idea remains hidden until one has an insight into the law of life and notices clearly its inner working. For instance, if one said that a person had come to a certain position or rank, or into the possession of wealth or fame by working for it – yes, outwardly it is true, but many work and do not arrive at it. Besides one might say that all blessings of Providence come to one if one deserves them, but one can see so much in life which is contrary to this principle, for there are many in the world who do not deserve and yet they attain. With every appearance of free will there seems to be helplessness in every direction of life. And as to what man calls chance, there is so much against it too, for a deep insight into life will prove that what seems to be chance is not in reality chance. It seems to be chance, as illusion is the nature of life.

Now to explain more fully what I mean by arriving at a certain thing: every soul is so to speak continually making its way towards something, sometimes consciously and sometimes unconsciously. What a person does outwardly is an appearance of action, an action which may have no connection with his inner working. It is like a journey: not everyone knows towards what he is making his way, and yet everyone is making his way. Whether he is making his way towards the goal he has desired, or whether he is making his way towards quite the contrary goal which he has never desired, he does not know. But when the goal is realized on the physical plane then a person becomes conscious: "I have not worked for it; I have not created it; I have not deserved it;

I have not earned it. How is it possible that it has come?" If it is an object desired by him then perhaps he gives the credit of it to himself; he tries to believe: "I have made it in some way". If it is not desirable then he wants to attribute it to someone else, or to suppose that for some reason or other it has happened like that. But in reality it is a destination at which one has arrived at the end of one's journey.

One cannot definitely say that one has created it, or made it, that one has deserved it, or that it has come by accident. What can be said is that one has journeyed towards it, either consciously or unconsciously, and has arrived at it. Therefore in point of fact in his desirable or undesirable experiences no one has departed from the destination at which he was meant to arrive.

Nevertheless, what is most necessary is to connect the outward action with the inward journey, the harmony of which will certainly prove to be a cause of ease and comfort. It is this which is meant by saying that one must have harmony within oneself. Once this harmony is established one begins to see the cause of all things more clearly than in its absence.

One might ask in what way harmony can be established between the inner journey and the outward action. What generally happens is that a person is so much absorbed in his outward action that his inner attitude becomes obscured to his view. The first thing necessary is to remove the screen that hides the inner attitude from one's sight. Everyone is conscious of what he does, but not conscious of his inner attitude. In other words, everyone knows what he is doing, but everyone does not necessarily know towards what he is going. No doubt the more one is conscious of this, the less becomes one's action, for thought controls action — but it only gives a rhythm, a balance to life. Compared with a person who is capable of running without knowing where he is going, he is better off who is walking slowly but knows towards what he is going.

There are two distinct parts of one action: there is an action of our inner life and there is an action of our outer life, the inner being and the outer being. The outer being is physical action, and the inner action is our attitude. Both may be actions of free will, but in a certain way they both prove to be mechanical or automatic actions. No doubt the inner action has a great power and influence upon the outer action. A person may be busy all day doing a certain thing but at the same time, if the attitude is working against him, he can never have success in his work. By his outward action a person may deserve a great prize, but for his inner action he may not be deserving it. Therefore if these two actions are contrary to one another, there is no construction and there is no attainment of the desired results. The true result, the result that is desirable, comes through the harmony of these two activities.

CHAPTER XVIII

The Law of Action

WHATEVER WE do comes back to us. It may not come back from the same side, it may come from another side. But how does it come? Suppose we speak very badly to a servant, we insult him, we hurt his feelings. We think, "I am quite safe; he cannot do me any harm". But subconsciously our mind is impressed by the insult, the unkindness and that impression we take with us; we take it before whomever we meet and it calls forth the insulting tendency, the unkindness of him with whom we come in contact. The element attracts the same element, our coldness attracts his unkindness. We may meet many people who cannot insult us: their situation makes it impossible for them. But when we meet someone who can do so, our superior for instance, he will insult us, he will hurt our feelings.

If we do someone a kindness we ourselves are impressed by kindness and this impression draws out kindness from those before whom we come. The cruel will not be so very cruel with us because of this impression of kindness, and when we meet someone who is kind his kindness towards us will be increased a thousand times.

A sin without its reaction is just like a drop of poison in one's system which awaits its chance until it is developed enough to break out throughout one's life as a disease arising in time from that one drop. And such is the case with virtue, but an unanswered flame of virtue may enlighten one's whole life so that the world may see the illumination.

We make sins and virtues according to our idealization. What we have been taught from our childhood as good, we think good. What we have been taught from our childhood as bad, we think bad. It is not that God, from there, without the experience of manifestation, has made certain things virtues and others sins. It is God who sees with our eyes, who hears with our ears.

Every thing we do, every little good deed or bad deed has its effect upon every soul. It has always been said, "If you wish to see your children happy, do good deeds, give to the poor, be charitable. If you wish to see your fathers, your ancestors happy in the life beyond, do good actions, because the effect of your deeds will reach them, is felt by them."

CHAPTER XIX

The Soul, its Origin and Unfoldment

WHEN WE look at life and the process of its development either from a mystical or from a scientific point of view, we shall find that it is one life developing itself through different phases. In other words, there is one vital substance – call it energy, intelligence, force or light, call it God or Spirit – which is forcing its way out from the most dense aspect of nature towards the finest aspect of nature. For instance, by studying the mineral kingdom we shall find a life in it which is forcing its way out. When we look at it scientifically we shall find that from the mineral kingdom come substances such as gold and silver and precious stones, which means that there is a process by which the mineral becomes finer, finer and finer, until it begins to show that the spirit is radiance, intelligence, beauty, and that it even manifests through the precious stones.

This is a scientific point of view. When we come to a mystical point of view we see that if we go among the rocks, if we stand in the mountains, if we go into the solitude where there is no one else, we are alone and begin to feel an upliftment, we begin to feel a sense of peace, a kind of at-one-ment with the rocks, hills and mountains. What is it? It is that the spirit which is in us is the same in the mountains and rocks. That spirit is buried in the rocks and less buried in ourselves. But it is the same spirit, and that is why we are attracted to mountains. Mountains are not as living as we are, and therefore we are more attracted to them than they to us. Besides, what can we give to mountains? Our lack of peace, discord, our inharmony, our limitations. What can the mountains give us? Harmony, peace, calmness, quietude, a sense of patience, of endurance. What do they inspire us with? The idea that they have been waiting perhaps for thousands of years for an unfoldment which comes by the development of nature from rock to plant, from plant to animal, from animal to man.

It is this whole gradual unfoldment of the spirit which is

buried in all these different aspects of nature and at each step – from rock to plant, from plant to animal, and from animal to man – the spirit is able to express itself more freely, is able to move more freely. In this way the spirit finds itself in the end. What does it show? It shows that there is one purpose working through the whole creation. The rocks are working out the same destiny as man, the plants are growing towards the same goal as man. What is that goal? Unfoldment. The spirit is buried in the creation and wants to make its way out. At each step of evolution there is a new unfoldment, a greater opening.

From the animal, Darwin says, man has come. It might have seemed at the time that it was a new scientific discovery, but it was not so. There are proofs of this in books of Persian poets. A poet who lived seven hundred years before Darwin says in his poetic terms, in a religious form, that God slept in the rock, dreamed in the plant, awoke in the animal, and realized Himself in man. Perhaps this poet has not said in detail from where man has come, but he has given his outlook so many years before. And twelve hundred years ago the Prophet Muhammad in giving the Qur'an has expressed the same: that first was the rock, from that came the plant, afterwards the animals and from them man was created.

Now the difference between the scientifical or biological point of view and the mystical or prophetic point of view is this: a materialistic scientist says, "Here is a rock. By a process of development a kind of life has come to it. Then vibrations increased. From animals came man; man is a developed animal. So from perfect denseness intelligence has developed". The mystical conception is different. A mystic does not trace the origin of life in the rock; he traces it in spirit. One may ask, "What is spirit?" Spirit is intelligence. One might think, "We do not see intelligence in a rock, in animals". The answer is that we must first distinguish between spirit and matter, understand what difference there is between the two. Spirit is finer matter, matter is dense spirit. In other words, water is snow and snow is water. When water is not frozen it is water and when frozen it is snow; when heated again it becomes water. It is the same with spirit and matter. There are many in this world inclined to say, "Matter does not exist". It is easy to say, but difficult to prove. Besides, is that not only a conception? Others say, "Spirit does not exist". What is needed is to understand the relation between the two and the difference beteen the two.

When I was travelling to America there was a young Italian with me on the ship. Looking at me he thought that I was a priest, and being himself an atheist he began to ask me, "What is your belief?" I said, "Nobody can tell his belief, it cannot be put into words. But may I ask what is yours? Perhaps you can explain it better". "Well", said he, "I believe in eternal matter". "Then my belief is not very far from yours. What you call eternal matter, I call eternal spirit. The dispute is over words; if you do not stick to preconceived words there is no difference". [10]

Many in this world argue over words. If one reaches the sense no dispute is left. If someone sees the eternal aspect in matter which is ever changing, let him call it eternal. It does not matter, it is the eternal aspect of life we are looking for.

Now we come to the idea of the mystic's conception of the soul. The mystic sees a development of material life from rock to plant, from plant to animal and from animal to the human physical body. That is one thing, it is a part of the mystical conception. Then there is something else: the divine Spirit, the Light, the Intelligence, the All-Consciousness. The first part makes the earth, the other makes heaven; it is that Sun, the divine Spirit shining and projecting its rays – and each ray becomes a soul. It is therefore not true to say that man has come out of a monkey. One is degrading the finest specimen of nature that God has created by calling it an improvement of a monkey. It is a materialistic, limited conception. The soul comes direct from the divine Spirit, it is intelligence itself, it is consciousness. But it is not the consciousness we know, for we never experience the pure existence of our consciousness. What we know of our consciousness is what we are conscious of; so we only know the name consciousness and do not know what it is in reality.

There is no difference between pure intelligence and consciousness. We call pure intelligence consciousness when that intelligence is conscious of something. But what we are conscious of is something that is before us. We are not that: we are the being who is conscious, not that which we are conscious of. The mistake is that we identify ourselves with what we see, because we do not see ourselves. Therefore, because he does not know himself, man naturally calls his body himself; as he cannot find himself, what he identifies himself with is his body. In reality man is not his body, man is his soul. The body is something man possesses; it is his tool, his instrument with which he experiences life, but the body is not himself. Since he identifies himself with his body, he naturally says, "I live", "I die", "I am happy", "I am unhappy", "I have fallen", "I have risen". Every condition of his limited and changeable body makes him think, "I am this". In this way he loses the consciousness of the never-changing aspect of his own being.

The soul is the ray which in order to experience life needs this instrument: the vehicles of body and mind. The soul with its two vehicles, body and mind, could be called spirit – that other word we use for soul. Through the body it experiences outward conditions, through the mind it experiences inner conditions of life. So the soul experiences two spheres, the physical and the mental sphere: the mental sphere through the mind, and the physical sphere through the body with its five senses.

When we come to the evolution of the world according to the point of view of the mystic, we shall see that it is not man who has come from the plant, the animal and the rock. But man has taken his body, his physical instrument, from the rock, from the animal, from the plant. He himself has come direct from the spirit and is directly joined to the spirit. He is, and always will be, above this instrument which he has borrowed from the earth. In other words, man is not the product of the earth but man is the inhabitant of heavens. It is his body which he has borrowed from the earth. Because he has forgotten his origin, the origin of his soul, he has taken the earth for his origin, but this is only the origin of his body and not of his soul.

Now we come to the law of gravitation, of which many say that it is a theory which was not known to the ancients. I say that the law of gravitation was already explained thousands of years earlier, even by Buddha, and in the Qur'an we find a Sura saying that the soul has come from God and is bound for Him. What science tells to-day is that the body of clay which has come from the earth is attracted to the earth because of the law of gravitation: earth attracts earth. But prophets and mystics and seers and sages always knew and taught that the soul is attracted to the Spirit. In other words, by the law of gravitation the body is attracted to the earth and the soul to the Spirit. When a person is unaware of this he only knows of one attraction which is of the earth. Then he does not know of the other attraction, and that does not help to give release to the soul, for the soul is attracted to the Spirit.

If it were a virtue to be spiritual – if it were only a virtue – I would be the first person to refuse it. But it is the greatest necessity of the soul; we cannot help it. Very often people think, "Is it necessary to be spiritual? What do we gain by it?" We do not need to gain anything by it, it is a natural attraction, we cannot help it! Those who are conscious of it begin to look for it. Those who are not conscious of it are unconsciously attracted to something which they do not know.

During my travellings of so many years through East and West I have met most intelligent people, maybe not at all religious, not interested in spiritual subjects, and at the same time, after having become more familiar with them, what have I found? There was a secret seeking. Outwardly it is out of fashion to think about spirituality, but inwardly they were all the time seeking for it. In schools the name of God and any mention made of religion has been erased from the text-books. Nevertheless, scientists come who after all the research of science begin to think about these things. They themselves would like to avoid it, but they cannot help it. When people ask, "Did you find response during your travellings in the Western world?", I say, "Whether it is West or East, North or South, there is response from every man. Maybe he does not know it, but every man in the world is my customer".

Every man has interest as soon as one tells him about life and its deeper side. No doubt some are sleeping, some are half awake, and some on the point of awaking. It is those on the point of awaking who must be helped. Those who are half awake – let them awake; they will see. Those who sleep – after their sleep is over they will wake up and look for it. It is cruel to wake up a person. If he does not care for food, let him sleep; when he awakes he will feel hungry, he will ask for food. That is the time to give it to him.

Now we come to the question of the soul's natural unfoldment towards spiritual attainment. Spirituality apart, at every stage in one's life – infancy, the time from infancy to childhood, from childhood to youth, from youth to middle age – at every step further there is a new consciousness. Childhood is quite a new consciousness compared to infancy; youth is quite a different consciousness compared to childhood. If that is true then every soul, no matter in what stage of life he is, has gone through so many different unfoldments which have given him a new consciousness every time, whether he knows about it, whether he thinks about it, or not.

There are experiences such as failure in business, or misfortune, or illness, or a certain blow in one's life, whether an affair of the heart or of money or a social affair, whatever it may be – there are blows which fall upon a person and a shell breaks, a new consciousness is produced. Very few will see it is an unfoldment, very few will interpret it as such, but it is so. Have you not seen among your acquaintances how a person with a disagreeable nature, a most uninteresting man to whom you were never attracted, perhaps after a blow, a deep sorrow, after some experience, awakened to a new consciousness and suddenly attracted you, because he had gone through this process? As we unfold at every step in our life, so we do with every experience. The deeper the experience touches us, the greater the unfoldment. In this way we unfold gradually towards that which is called perfection.

Spiritual unfoldment is the ultimate goal of every person. It comes at a moment when a man begins to be more thoughtful, when he begins to remember or to realize this yearning of the soul. Then consciously or unconsciously a feeling comes, "Is this all I have to do in my life: to earn money? Whether I have a high rank or a position, it is all a play. I have become tired of this play. I should think of something else. There is something else I have to attain". This is the beginning; it is the first step on the spiritual path. As soon as a person has taken this first step his outlook has changed, the value of things becomes different and things to which he had attached great importance become of less importance; things with which he concerned himself so much he no longer concerns himself with. A kind of indifference comes. Nevertheless, a thoughtful person keeps to his duty just the same; he is even more conscientious and this brings about a greater harmony, because he begins to pity others.

When he goes another step forward there comes bewilderment. He begins to wonder, "What is it all?. Much ado about nothing!" It gave me much to think about when once I saw in India a sage whom I knew to be very deep, a man of high attainment, who was laughing at nothing. I wondered what he was laughing at. Then I stood there and looked around myself, thinking, "I must see from his point of view what makes him laugh so much", and I saw persons hustling and bustling. For what? Was it not laughable? Every person thinking his particular point of view to be the most important, pushing others away because he finds his action the most important! Is it not the picture of life? It is the way of the evolved and the unevolved. And what do they reach? Nothingness! Empty-handed they leave this world; they come without anything, and they go without anything. It is this outlook which gives the soul bewilderment. He does not feel proud to laugh at others, but it is no doubt amusing. As much as he is amused at others, he is amused at himself.

When a person goes another step forward an understanding comes that changes his outlook and manner. Generally what happens is this: from morning till evening he reacts against every good and bad thing. But good he sees very rarely and bad things he always sees, or he meets someone who is nervous and excited, or dominant or selfish, and so all the time a continually jarring effect comes from everyone he meets. Then without knowing it his continual reaction is of despise, of hatred; the thought to get away is all the time before him. If he can say, "I don't like", "I dislike", he can say it from morning till evening with everyone he meets, for there is rarely one person about whom he will not say such words. And this reaction he expresses in words or thought, by feeling or action.

When one reaches this third stage, the stage of understanding, one begins to understand instead of reacting. Then there is no reaction: understanding comes and suppresses it. It is just like a boat which is anchored; it produces tranquillity, stillness, weight in the personality. It does not move with every wind that blows, but stays like a heavy ship on the water, while a light ship moves with every wave that comes. That stability a person reaches in this third stage of unfoldment; he is ready to tolerate, to understand both the wise and the foolish – all.

Is it not amusing to think that the foolish person disagrees more with others than the wise? One would think that he knows more than the wise one. The wise one agrees with both the foolish and the wise; he is ready to understand everybody's point of view. It may not be his idea, his way of looking, but he is capable of looking at things from the point of view of others. It is not one eye that sees fully; to make the vision complete two eyes are needed, and so the wise one can see from two points of view. If we do not keep away our own thoughts and preconceived ideas, if we cannot be passive and desirous of seeing from the point of view of another, we make a great mistake. This third stage gives a tendency to understand every person we meet.

Then again there is a fourth stage of unfoldment. In this stage we not only understand, but sympathize; we cannot help but sympathize, for we can see that life in the world is nothing but limitation. Whether a person is rich, in a high position, or in a wretched condition – whatever condition he is in, or whatever he is – he has to experience this limitation and that itself is a great misery. Every person therefore has his problem before him, and when we begin to see that every person on this earth has a certain problem and weight to carry through life, we cannot help but sympathize.

The one who can awake to the pain of mankind, whether it is his friend or his foe, cannot help sympathizing with him. Then he develops an outgoing tendency; he has always a feeling that he should go out to every person he meets and then, naturally, by his sympathy he looks for good points, for when one looks at a person without sympathy one will always touch his worst point.

When one goes a step further still, then a way is open to communicate. Just as there is a communication between persons who love each other very much, so the sympathy of a person whose soul has unfolded itself is so awakened that not only every person but even every object begins to reveal its nature, its character and secret. To him every man is a written letter.

We hear stories of saints and sages who talked with rocks and plants and trees. They are not only stories; it is reality. It is also told of the apostles that at the moment when the Spirit descended upon them they began to speak many languages. When they understood so many languages, they understood the language of every soul. It means that the illuminated soul understands the language of every soul. And every soul has its own language. It is that which is called revelation.

All the teachings that the great prophets and teachers have given are only interpretations of what they have seen. They have interpreted in their own language what they have read from the manuscript of nature: that trees and plants and rocks spoke to them. Did nature only speak to those in the past? No, the soul of man is always capable of that bliss if he only realized it. Once the eyes of the heart are open, man begins to read every leaf of the tree as a page of the sacred Book.

CHAPTER XX

The Unfoldment of the Soul

IT IS in unfoldment that the purpose of life is fulfilled, and it is not only so with human beings but also with the lower creation; even with all the objects that exist the fulfilment of their existence lies in their unfoldment. When the clouds gather the purpose of their gathering is shown when it is raining: it is the unfoldment of that gathering of clouds which shows itself in the rain. Not in the gathering of the clouds was a purpose accomplished, it was accomplished in the raining; the gathering was a preparation. One finds the same thing in nature which works the whole year long and brings forth its fruits in the autumn. Not only human beings but even birds and animals can watch and be delighted to see the purpose of nature's continual working fulfilled in the spring.

We learn from this that every being and every object is working towards that unfoldment which is the fulfilment of its purpose. There is a saying of a Persian poet, Sa'adi, that every being is intended to be on earth for a certain purpose, and the light of that purpose has been kindled in his heart.

In all different purposes which we see working through each individual, there seems to be one purpose which is behind them all, and that is the unfoldment of the soul. The ancient Hindus therefore held that object before them in all walks of life. Not only those who sought after truth were seeking for the soul's unfoldment, but an artist, a scientist, a learned man, a man of industry, of commerce, each one thought that through his particular occupation he was to come to that end. The great misfortune we find to-day is that humanity is divided in its different occupations and has lost that thread which binds humanity into one and gives that impetus which results in the benefit of all. When the scientist stands on his ground, strong and firm, the artist in his sphere, the industrial man in his world, and the man of commerce in the world of commerce, it is natural that their souls do not come in contact with one another giving them the force to combine for the betterment of the whole.

Although a degeneration caused by extreme materialism prevails throughout the whole world, yet it is not too late to find examples of personalities who through all walks of life still wish to arrive at the proper goal. Our modern poet Tagore brought out a translation of poems by Kabir, a man who was never educated, who from childhood was a weaver and whose livelihood depended upon his weaving. Through his work he arrived at that goal, and he gave his experience in his ordinary language in a book which to-day is taken by the people as a Scripture. This makes us wonder whether it would not be possible for a scientist to arrive through his scientific occupations at the same truth, or for an artist through the practice of art, or for a man of industry or commerce to arrive at that central truth which concerns every soul.

When we look at humanity we find that we can not only divide it into different races and different nations, but we can also divide it into people of different occupations. In this age of materialism, if there is anything that unites us, it is only our material interest. And how long can we be united by a material interest? A friendship formed in materialism is not a friendship which will endure, for in that friendship the one depends upon the other for his own interest. It is sacrifice which enables us to be friends and to join with one another, and it is in sacrifice that the sign of spirituality is seen. We do not unite together in sacrifice to-day, our unity is in what we can gain by it. It is a matter for distress that in order to unite we are holding on to a lower ideal which will never prove a centre of unity. It is the high ideal which can unite, and that is the hope in which we can unite – if ever we can unite.

Now coming to the main part of our subject: how can the unfoldment of the soul be defined? The soul can be likened to the rose, and as a rosebud blooms so the soul unfolds itself. For the rosebud to bloom five conditions are required: fertile soil, bright sun, water, air and space. And the same five things are required for the unfoldment of the soul.

As a fertile soil is required for the roseplant in order to grow, so it is necessary for the child to be given education in the spiritual ideal from the moment it is born. When a child is deprived of that most important education in its childhood, then the soil is taken away from the roots of the roseplant. How many people there are who, with every possibility, with every tendency to become interested in all that is spiritual, in everything that is lofty and high, yet are afraid of the terminology in which it is expressed. What does this show? It shows that in childhood something was removed from them, and now that they have grown up they feel a desire for it, they want it but, when they look at it in a form they are not accustomed to, they are afraid of it. I have sometimes been amused more than words can express hearing someone say, "I am so interested in all you have to say, but I cannot make myself believe it".

Is there one soul*, however materialistic, which does not wish to unfold? There cannot be. Every soul has been born to unfold itself; it is its innate tendency, it cannot help it. Only, if the soul is deprived of the necessary conditions, then it ceases to develop. There are many people who do not believe in any particular religion, do not profess any particular faith, do not adhere to any form, but who at the same time have great spiritual qualities.

One might ask what is meant by that education. Is it a religious or a moral education that is meant by it? One might say that to-day we give more education than ever, even so much that a child who goes to school is busier than a workman going to the factory. Every year it is more difficult to get a degree in a university. Every year a greater and greater burden is put upon the student, a burden which is of no use to him or to anybody else. Education therefore can be divided into two parts: a real education and a superficial one. An education which comes from book knowledge, from learning is a superficial, outward education. The other education gives a deeper insight into life, and that alone can be called a real education. What we recognize as education to-day, what we mean by it, is the outward education significant of a certain degree or title. But the outward education ends; this inner education never ends because it is unlimited. It is as vast as the ocean, as wide as the horizon. No

---

*Hazrat Inayat Khan, characteristically, often uses the words "man" and "soul" indiscriminately.

soul is too young to receive this education, and no soul is too old to receive it, for it is unlimited. There are mothers, impressed by the modern conditions, who ask advice saying, "What shall I do for my child? He receives all the education that school or college gives. I have not sent him to any religious place fearing that he will receive something different. Will you tell me what I must do to inspire this child which is constantly searching after something higher?" The answer is that for a really important education there is no institution; it is an education which one should acquire oneself and one should impart it to a little child.

Now one may ask what is meant by the water that nourishes the rose. That water is the love element. If that element is kept away in a person's life, with all his intellectual knowledge and with every desire to seek after truth, he will remain backward. And unfortunately this element seems to be missing in the life of culture. A learned man will say that it has no place in the world of reason, and this separates outer learning from the religious ideal which calls God love.

What is it that takes the part of the sun in the life of a person, as the sun takes part in the growing of the rose? It is intelligence. Everyone may not seem to be intelligent, but the soul itself is intelligence. When the intelligence is covered by the mist of impressions and ideas of this earth, that intelligence becomes drowned in something, buried under something. When it is discovered then it is as bright as the sun. The mission of Buddha was mainly intended for that purpose. All Buddha wished to teach his disciples was to discover that pure intelligence which is above all reasoning and which is the essence of all reason.

What place does the air take in the growing of the soul? The air is symbolical of the inspiration which comes to the heart that is prepared for it. It is not only by outward learning, but by what one learns through inspiration, that the soul is elevated towards unfoldment.

What is meant by the space which is needed around the roseplant in order to let it grow? Symbolically it means a wide outlook on life. A person may live a hundred years, and with a narrow outlook will never see the light. In order to see life clearly the outlook must be wide. There is much to fight with in life in order to keep our outlook wide, because the nature of our life in the world is such that it drags us down and puts us in a sphere where we cannot but be narrow. A great person is not great because of his merits, qualities or reputation; the greatest thing that he can show proving his greatness is his vast outlook. And it is wonderful to notice how, even unconsciously, people who have arrived at a stage of being great in whatever walk of life automatically begin to show a vast outlook on life. What manures the plant and makes roses bloom is, symbolically, that teaching given by the great masters of humanity.

How can this development of the soul in which the purpose of life is fulfilled be recognized? What are its indications, its signs? The soul becomes like a rose and begins to show the rose quality. The rose holds together many petals, and so the person who comes to the unfoldment of the soul begins to show many different qualities. These qualities emit fragrance in the form of a spiritual personality. The rose has a beautiful structure, and so the personality which proves the unfoldment of the soul has also a fine structure in manner, in dealing with others, in speech, in action. It is like the perfume of the rose that the atmosphere of the spiritual being pervades all.

The rose has in its heart its seeds, and so the developed souls have in their heart that seed of development which produces many roses. The rose comes and fades away, but the essence that is taken from the rose lives and keeps the fragrance that it had in its full bloom. Personalities who touch that plane of development may live on the earth for a limited time, but the essence which is left by them will live for thousands and thousands of years, ever keeping the same fragrance and giving the same pleasure that once the rose gave.

CHAPTER XXI

Divine Impulse

THE FIRST question to be considered in reference to the subject of divine impulse is: where does every impulse come from? Every movement, every vibration, every motion has one source. One sees a hint of this in the Bible where it says, "The word was God". The word means vibration and vibration means movement. In the Vedanta *nada Brahma* means sound. Vibration was the first or original aspect of Brahma, the Creator. In the Qur'an we read, "Be – He said – and it became". Every impulse, every action on any plane of existence has its origin in the one source. It is also said in the Qur'an, "God is all power; there is no power but God's". In all that is done, what is done is by His power.

Now the question arises: If all the scriptures say this, where does Satan come in? What is the meaning behind the power of Satan? Another power is suggested besides the power of God, and sometimes the power attributed to Satan seems mightier than the power attributed to God. This is a puzzle to many who wonder where the action of Satan comes in. The explanation is to be found in the understanding of metaphysics and of the laws of nature. There is one law, the natural law, and all that comes directed by nature's law is harmonious. The gardens that man has made may seem for a moment to improve upon the forests, but in the end, on examination, the garden with its artificial structures proves limited in beauty and harmony. The inspiration one gets in the forest, in the wilderness is much greater than in the man-made garden, for there man has made inspiration limited, because the life he radiates is limited. Man makes a law and finds he cannot keep it; so he makes another law and is never satisfied, for he takes no account of nature's laws of peace and harmony.

Men say that nature is cruel; yes, but man is far more cruel than the animals. Animals have never destroyed so many lives as man has. All the apparent cruelty of nature cannot compare with the cruelty, ignorance and injustice of man.

Jesus Christ said, "Thy will be done". There is much for us to learn in this. Man makes another world in which he lives, a world different from the plan of God, from the laws of nature, and so the will of God is not done. The prayer teaches man that he must find what is the will of God. It is not necessary for the animals and birds to find out the will of God, for they are directed by nature's impulse, they are closer to nature than man. The life of man is so far removed from the life of nature, and so every movement is difficult. We do not see this at present; with all our knowledge we make life more and more complicated and so the strife becomes greater and greater. For every person, old or young, rich or poor, life is a difficult struggle, for we go further and further from the impulse which comes direct from the source whence every impulse comes.

From the metaphysical point of view there are different rhythms describing the condition of man; they are spoken of in the Vedanta as *sattva, rajas* and *tammas*. *Sattva* is a harmonious rhythm, *rajas* a rhythm which is not in perfect harmony with nature and *tammas* is a rhythm which is chaotic by nature and destructive. Every impulse that comes to man while he is in this chaotic rhythm is followed by destructive results. Any impulse coming to a person when he is in the rhythm of *rajas* is accomplished, but the impulse that comes when he is in the rhythm of *sattva* is inspired and is in harmony with the rhythm of the universe.

The active life of man gives little time for concentration and for putting mind and body into the condition in which he can experience the rhythm that gives inspiration and meets with the will of God. This experience comes in answer to the prayer of Christ, "Thy will be done on earth as it is in heaven". By producing this condition of mind and body one tunes oneself to a certain pitch which is harmonious and heavenly and in which the divine will is easily done, as it is in heaven. It is in this rhythm alone that the will of God can be done.

It was not any prejudice against the world that made the great ones leave the world and go to the forests and caves; they went in order to tune themselves to that rhythm in which they could experience heaven. Heaven is not a country or a continent; it is a state, a condition within oneself, only experienced when the rhythm is in perfect working order. If one knows this, one realizes that happiness is man's own property. Man is his own enemy: he seeks for happiness in the wrong direction and never finds it. It is a continual illusion. Man thinks, "If I had this or that I should be happy for ever", and he never arrives at happiness because he pursues an illusion instead of the truth. Happiness is only to be found within, and when man tunes himself he finds all for which his soul yearns within himself.

The nature of every impulse is such that it goes through three stages and after the process of these three stages it is realized as a result, whether it is right or wrong, beneficient or disadvantageous, as soon as the impulse springs from within. There is no impulse which in its beginning is wrong or purposeless or inharmonious, for in the total sum of all things every impulse has its purpose. It is our limited outlook that judges. The justice behind is so great that in the ultimate result everything fits into its proper place. But in the process through which the impulse passes it becomes right or wrong – not in the beginning or in the end, for the beginning has a purpose and the end has answered the demand.

This is a question of metaphysics and one must study it from different points of view or one will be very much confused. Man with his little knowledge is ready to condemn or to admire, and thousands of times he fails to judge rightly. All great souls have realized this in their attainment. Christ says, "Judge not". Then tolerance comes, and when one realizes what is behind the impulse one says very little.

The first process through which the impulse rises takes place in the region of feeling, and in this region the impulse is either strengthened or destroyed. The feeling may be love or hatred, kindness or bitterness, but whatever the feeling may be where the impulse rises, it gains strength to go forward or it is destroyed. For instance, a person may have a great feeling of kindness; then the impulse of revenge may rise, but it is destroyed. Another person has a great feeling of bitterness, and if the impulse is to forgive it will be destroyed before it ever touches the reason. Or a person is most kind and, when the impulse towards revenge has arisen, he feels very uncomfortable; he will not have to call on thought to judge the impulse, for his feeling will destroy it. Or a person has a great feeling of bitterness and the impulse of doing a service of kindness comes, but it will be destroyed before it reaches the realm of thought. Or if the impulse rises till it reaches the realm of thought, then one reasons, "Why should I help? Why should I serve? Does he deserve it? Will he benefit by it? Is it right?" All these problems are settled in this region. Then thirdly comes the realm of action. If the mind consumes the impulse it goes no further, but if the mind allows it, it comes into the region of action and is realized as a result.

Now one may ask how sages and thinkers have distinguished the divine impulse among the different impulses that arise in the heart of man. First we must understand what the word divine means. Divine means: in a state of perfection. This state is experienced by God through man. In other words, when man has risen to the stage of development where he can be the perfect instrument of God, when nothing of his own being stands in the way of the direct impulse that comes from within – that spirit may be called perfect. That which is most precious, that which is the purpose of man's life is to arrive at that state of perfection when he can be the perfect instrument of God.

Once a man has risen to this stage he at first begins to realize at moments; then, as he develops, for a longer time, and those who develop still further pass most of their time in that realization. Then feeling and thought no longer hinder the divine impulse, for it rises freely and results in a divine purpose. The message of the prophets and teachers of all times has been to teach man how to make peace with God. The fulfilment of life's purpose is in harmonizing with God, and this is done by distinguishing the divine impulse.

How can one distinguish the divine impulse? Just as in music one can distinguish the true note from the false, the harmonious chord from the discord; it is only a matter of ear-training. When the ear is trained one can find out the slightest discord; the greater the musician, the more capable he is of finding out harmony and discord, the true and the false note. Many think that what we call right or wrong, good or bad, is something we learn or acquire. That is true when it is man-made right or wrong, but of nature's right and wrong every little child has a sense. The child feels a wrong vibration at once; the infant feels if its surroundings are harmonious or inharmonious, but man confuses himself so that he can no longer distinguish clearly. For man to learn to know for himself is a great advance along the spiritual path. When man is clear as to the feeling he gets from every impulse, he has advanced far. There are some who say after the result, "I am sorry", but it is too late then, it was not true ear-training.

The divine impulse is an impulse full of love, it gives happiness, it is creative of peace. The difficulty is that not every man observes the beginning of the impulse, he only observes the result. He is like an intoxicated person and so in time, as in the condition of a drunken man, he becomes confused and depressed, and there is struggle and strife. But man was not born for this. He is born for happiness. Peace, love, kindness and harmony are parts of his own being, and when a person is unhappy it means that he has lost himself, he does not know where he is.

Man is seeking for phenomena, he wants wonder-working, communication with ghosts or spirits, he is looking for something complex, and yet the simplest thing and the most valuable thing in life is to find one's true self.

CHAPTER XXII

The Symbol of the Cross

1

THE CROSS which is usually taken as the symbol of the cross on which Christ died has many mystical meanings. It shows a vertical line and a horizontal line: everything that exists extends vertically and horizontally. This may be seen in the leaf: it has length and breadth. All that exists has come from these two lines, the vertical and the horizontal. The cross therefore, in its first meaning, is the symbol of manifestation.

Then, whenever someone begins to speak, to act for the truth, his way is barred, there is a cross against it. Speak the truth before the nation and there comes the cross, the bar from the nation. Speak the truth in the face of the world and the cross comes from the world against you.

You may ask, "If all comes from the One, the Same, why is one thing truth and one falsehood?" Truth is that which lives, which remains, which stands upright. False is that which falls, which is dead. While we are alive we stand upright; when we are dead we have fallen down. What is dead? This false self, this mortal self. This is *fana*, destruction. The cross shows that in *fana* – in the ending of the mortal, of that which is changing, dying every moment, which lives upon mortal food in mortal surroundings – is the immortal life. What is not *fani* the Sufi calls *baqi*. This I can explain as *ba yaki*, oneness. In the death of the mortal there is life, immortality, the one immortal life.

There is another great mystery of the cross which is very little understood. Everywhere without us there is space. We call space that which can accommodate, which can contain. Within us there is space too; the space within extends in another direction. It is always a puzzle for the materialist when he hears of the two worlds, this world and the other, the next world. He says, "This world I know, but the other world I do not know. Where is the other world?" Our eyes can give us an idea, a picture of the other world. These little eyes, not an inch in length, contain so many miles of country, such vast tracts, the sun, the moon, the whole cosmos, millions upon millions of miles. These are not contained in the physical eyes but in the eyes within. The space within is much vaster than the space without; it can contain hundreds and thousands of times all that is in the world without. In this meaning the cross signifies the two worlds.

People have thought that the next world is above the sky, beyond the stars. It is not above but within. This world is contained in it.

2

Many think that this symbol has existed from the time of Jesus Christ, and no doubt it became better known after the time of the master, but in fact it is an old symbol known at different times and at all times known by the mystics. The mystery of the symbol contains a great truth.

There are two sides to this mystery. One side is the journey towards a spiritual ideal, the reaching of a spiritual ideal, and if any picture of this can be given there cannot be a better picture than a cross. The other side of this mystery represents the destiny of a teacher, the life of a teacher, signifying what he has to meet with when delivering the message of truth.

Besides this, the cross is a natural sign that man has always made from his artistic or from his reasoning faculty. It is the nature of light to spread rays, especially when the light is in its perfection. For instance, sometimes by looking at the sun – at the setting sun in particular – one finds lines forming on the sky and on the earth: first there is one straight line and if one watches that first line minutely a horizontal line develops out of it. By keen observation of light one can find that it is in the nature of light to form one perpendicular and one horizontal line. If it is the nature of the external light to form a cross it is also the nature of the inner light: the external light is the reflection of the inner light, and it is the nature of the inner light that is expressed in the outer light. So one can see that not only the inner light is manifest in the outer light, but that the outer light is the picture of the inner light.

We can also see by observing nature's forms – the form of a tree, of a plant, of a flower, the forms of the animals and birds, and in the end the most developed and finished form of the human being – that they all present a cross. One cross may be seen by observing the formation of man's head, the other cross can be seen by the whole form of mankind: it is ever a horizontal and a perpendicular line which suggest the symbol of the cross. There is no form that does not have a horizontal and a perpendicular line, and it is these two different aspects or directions which form the cross. In this way one can understand that in the mystery of form the cross is hidden.

Now coming to the first mystery mentioned above, namely that man's journey towards spiritual ideal can be pictured as a cross: in the first place man's ego, man's self is his enemy and stands as a hindrance to his progress. Feelings such as pride, conceit, selfishness, jealousy, envy and contempt are all feelings which hurt others and which destroy one's own life making it full of the misery which springs from that selfish personal feeling, that ego of man. The more egoistic, the more conceited he is, the more miserable a life he has in the world, the more he makes the lives of others miserable. It seems that this ego, which in Sufi terms is called *nafs*, is a natural development in man's life or heart. The more he knows of the world, the more egoistic he becomes; the more he understands and experiences the world, the more avaricious he becomes.

It is not that man brings his faults with him. He comes with innocence, with the innocent smiles of the infant, the friend of everyone who comes to him, ready to smile and ready to throw his loving glance on everybody, regardless of whether he is rich or poor, friend or foe; attracted by beauty in all forms. It is this in the infant which attracts every soul. This shows that the soul which comes with such purity of heart, purity of expression in the countenance, beauty in every movement it makes – that this same soul develops in his nature, as he grows up in the world, all that is hurtful and harmful to himself and others. This also shows that it is in the world that, growing up, he creates all this and this creation is called *nafs* or ego. Yet at the same time in the depth of the heart there is that goodness which is the divine goodness, that righteousness which man has inherited from the Father in heaven.

A longing for joy and rest and peace is in him, and this shows that in man there are two natures: one which is in the depth of his heart, another which has developed from his coming on earth. A conflict arises, a struggle between these two natures, when the nature which is in the depth begins to feel that it yearns for something, longs for something and feels it must have it: it must have goodness from other people, it must have peace in life. And when it cannot find these the inner conflict begins.

Man creates his own disharmony in his soul and then treats others in the same way; therefore he is not satisfied with his own life, nor is he satisfied with others because he feels that he has a complaint against others, although mostly it is caused by himself. What he gives he receives back, but he never sees that. He always thinks: what the depth of his being yearns for – love, goodness, righteousness, harmony and peace – everybody must give to him. But for him when it comes to giving he does not give because he lives in the other life he has created. This makes it plain that in every man a being is created; that being is called *nafs* and is the same as the conception of Satan which has always existed in the scriptures and traditions.

People have many times divided the world between two spirits: a small part of humanity for God and a great part of humanity for Satan, thus making the control of the Satan-spirit larger perhaps than the control of God. But if only one could understand the meaning of the idea of Satan, one would understand that it is this spirit of error which has collected and gathered in man after his coming on earth; it is *nafs* and stands as Satan, always guiding man astray and closing the eyes of his heart to the light of truth.

But when a revolution comes in the life of a man, as soon as he begins to see deeply into life, to acquire goodness – not only to get but to give – as soon as he begins to enjoy not only the sympathy of others but giving sympathy to others, then comes a period when he begins to see this Satan-spirit as apart from his real original being, standing before him constantly in conflict with his natural force, freedom and inclination. Then he sees that sometimes he can do what he desires, and that sometimes this spirit gets hold of him and does not allow him to do what he desires. Sometimes he finds himself weak in this struggle and sometimes he finds himself strong. His experience is that when he finds himself strong in this battle he is thankful and satisfied, and when he finds himself weak in it he repents, he is ashamed of himself and wishes to alter himself.

This is the period in which another epoch begins in man's life; from this time there is a constant conflict between himself and that spirit which is his ego. It is a conflict, it is a kind of hindrance to his natural attitude, to his natural inclination to do good and right. He constantly meets with that spirit because it was created in his own heart and has become part of his being. It is a very solid and substantial being, as real perhaps as he understands himself to be, and mostly more real: something real in the depth of his being, which is covered by it. This constant conflict between his real original self and that self which hinders his spiritual progress is pictured in the form of a cross.

This cross a man carries during his progress. It is the ugly passions, it is the love of comforts, and it is the satisfaction in anger and bitterness that he has to combat first. When he has conquered these, the next trouble he has to meet is that still more subtle enemy of himself in his mentality: the sensitiveness to what others say, to the opinion of others about himself. He is anxious to know what anybody holds as an opinion about him, what anybody says against him, or if in any way his dignity or position is hurt. Here again the same enemy, the *nafs*, takes another stand, and the crucifixion is when that thought of self, that *nafs*, is fought with – until there comes an understanding that there exists no self before the vision of God.

It is this which is the real crucifixion, but with this crucifixion there comes still another, which has always followed and which every soul has to experience; the perfection of every soul, the liberation of every soul lies in this crucifixion. It is that part of his being which he has created in himself, that false part of his being, which is crucified, not his real self, although on the way it always seems that he has crucified his own self.

This is not self-denial, it is the false self that is denied. The mystery of perfection lies in annihilation – not in annihilation of the real self, but of the false self, of the false conception which man has cherished in his heart and always has allowed to torture his life. Do we not see this with our friends and acquaintances? In those who attract us and whom we deeply love and admire there is only one quality which can really attract us: apart from our other interests in life it is man's personality alone which attracts us. It is not only that selflessness and the extent of that selflessness attract us, but what repels us in the life of others is nothing else than the grossness of their *nafs* – or one might call it the denseness and hardness of that spirit.

The teaching of Christ when he said, "Blessed are the poor in spirit", is little understood. He does not mean poor in divine spirit, but poor in this self-created spirit. Those who are poor in this self-created spirit are rich in divine spirit, and those who are rich in divine spirit are poor in this self-created spirit. The word which is used in the scriptures for *nafs* is that spirit of grossness – or spirit – but the better word is ego.

There have always been two tendencies: one of sincerity and the other of insincerity and falsehood. They have always worked together; the false and the true have always existed in life and in nature. Where there is real gold there is false; where there is a real diamond there is an imitation diamond; where there are sincere people there are insincere ones. In every aspect of life – in the life of spirituality, in the acquisition of learning, in the arts and sciences – we can see sincerity and insincerity. And the only way to recognize real spiritual development is to understand to what extent there is selflessness.

However much a person pretends to spirituality and wishes to be godly or pious or good, nothing can hide his true nature, for there is the constant tendency of that ego to leap out. It will leap out without man's control, and if he is insincere he cannot hide it. Just as the imitation diamond, however bright it may be, is dull compared with the real one and when tested and examined will prove to be an imitation, so real spiritual progress must be proved in the personality of a soul. It is the personality that should prove that he has touched that larger Self where self does not exist.

Now coming to the next and still greater mystery of the cross: this mystery can be seen in the life of the messengers, the prophets and holy beings. In the first place no one has entrance into the kingdom of God, into the abode of God, who has not been so crucified as I have said just now. There is a poem by the great Persian poet Iraqi in which he tells, "When I went to the gate of the divine Beloved and knocked at the door, a voice came and said – Who art thou?" When he had told, "I am so and so", the answer came, "There is no place for anyone else in this abode. Go back to whence thou hast come". He turned back and then, after a long time, after having gone through the process of the cross and of crucifixion, he again went there – with the spirit of selflessness. He knocked at the door; the word came, "Who art thou?", and he said, "Thyself alone, for no one else exists save Thee". And God said, "Enter into this abode for now it belongs to thee". It is such selflessness, to the extent that the thought of self is not there, it is being dead to the self, which is the recognition of God.

One finds this spirit to a small extent in the ordinary lover and beloved, when a person loves another from the depth of his heart. He who says, "I love you but only so much, I love you and give you sixpence but I keep sixpence for myself, I love you but I stand at a distance and never come closer, we are separate beings" – his love is with his self. As long as that exists, love has not done its full work. Love accomplishes its work when it spreads its wings and veils man's self from his own eyes. That is the time when love is fulfilled, and so it is in the life of the holy ones who have not only loved God by professing or showing it, but who have loved God to the extent that they forgot themselves. It is that state of realization of being which can be termed a cross.

Then such souls have a cross everywhere; every move they make is a cross, a crucifixion. In the first place, living in the world, a world full of falsehood, full of treachery, deceit and selfishness, every move they make, every act they perform, all they say and think, prove that their eyes and hearts are open to something else than that at which the world is looking. It is a constant conflict. It is living in the world, living among people of the world and yet looking at a place different from that which the world sees. If they tried to speak they could not. Words cannot express the truth; language is too inadequate to give a real conception of the ultimate truth. As it is said in the Vedanta, and as it was said in ancient times, the world is *maya*. *Maya* means something unreal, and to these souls the world becomes most unreal as soon as they begin to see the real, and when they compare the world with this reality it seems even more unreal. No one in the world can imagine to what an extent this world manifests itself to their eyes.

Think of people who are good – yet not having arrived at spiritual perfection – who are sensitive, tender and kind, and see how the world treats them, how they are misunderstood. See how the best is taken by the selfish, how the generous one has to give more and more, how the one who serves has to serve more and more, and still the world is not satisfied. He who loves has to love more and more, and the world is not satisfied. How jarring life is to these! Then think of those who have arrived at such a stage of realization that there is a vast gulf between the real and the unreal. When they arrive at that realization their language is not understood; they are forced to speak in a language which is not their own and to say something different from what they are realizing. It is more than a cross. It is not that Jesus Christ alone had a cross, but every teacher who has a portion of the message has a cross.

But then you may say, "The masters of humanity who have come at all times and had such a cross to bear, why did they not go to the forests, to the caves, to the mountains, why did they stay in the world?" There is a beautiful picture that Rumi has made. He tells why the melody of the reed flute makes such an appeal to your heart. It is, he says in his poetry, because first it is cut away from its original stem, then in its heart holes are made and, since the holes have been made in the heart, the heart has been broken and it begins to cry. So it is with the spirit of the messenger, with the spirit of the teacher: by bearing and by carrying his cross his self becomes like a reed, hollow. There is scope for the Player to play his melody when it has become nothing; then the Player takes it to play his melody. If something was still there the Player could not use it.

God speaks to everyone, not only to the messengers and teachers. He speaks to the ears of every heart, but it is not every heart which hears it. His voice is louder than the thunder, and His light is clearer than the sun – if one could only see it, if one could only hear it. In order to see it and in order to hear it man should remove this wall, this barrier which he has made of the self. Then he becomes the flute upon which the divine Player may play the music of Orpheus which can charm even the hearts of stone; then he rises from the cross into the life everlasting.

CHAPTER XXIII

The Mystical Meaning of the Resurrection

1

WHAT IS exactly meant when the resurrection is spoken of in the Bible?

The resurrection is that moment after death when the soul becomes conscious of all its experience. As the soul is connected with everything in the universe, the individual resurrection is a universal resurrection.

Now I will explain two passages from the Bible.[11] In one of them it is said: "Now is Christ risen from the dead and gone unto the Father, and is become the first-fruits of them that slept, and whosoever believeth in him should not die but live". The dead are those who have not realized their immortality. from which he rises who realizes his immortality. "He is gone unto the Father", means that he has gone from the personal being, which was meant for his message to be delivered upon earth, to that unlimited existence. "He hath become the firstfruits of them that slept", means: he has become an example to those who sleep, to those who are unconscious of their divine being.

"Whosoever believeth in him" has been interpreted to mean: who believes in his limited personal being. It means: who has the knowledge of God, of immortality, shall never die, and those whom the world calls dead, but who have the belief in God, which is knowledge, are not dead.

In another passage it is said , "For since by man came death, by man came also the resurrection from the dead". Man alone understands what death is; beasts and birds feel the inactivity, the absence, but they do not realize what death is.

I have seen a bird, when its mate fell dead shot by hunters, settle beside it, feel it with its beak and, when it felt the stillness and lifelessness, before the hunter could approach, it dropped its head and its life was gone. I have also seen a dog die instantly, when its companion dog with whom it had spent its life was dead. But still, animals feel only the inactivity, the absence of the friend. They do not realize the true nature of death.

It is only man who has understood the real nature of death in its full extent. Therefore Sufis in the East often make their houses, their cottages in the jungle or else near cemeteries: that by seeing the dead they may realize that now is the time to awaken, to conquer death, to realize their immortality.

And it is again man, as the holy being, who awakens man to the knowledge of his immortality.

2

If the resurrection merely meant that Christ after his death rose again, it would be a story to be believed or disbelieved. If it were believed as a belief, how long would this last? Its lesson is much greater than that. It means the resurrection from this mortal life to immortality.

Christ said, "The children of this world marry and are given in marriage, but they who are accounted worthy to obtain the resurrection from the dead neither marry nor are given in marriage, neither can they die any more; they are the children of the resurrection, being the children of God."[11] Those who have arisen to that immortal One Being where there is no distinction of husband and wife, brother or sister, father, mother, or child – they are the sons of the resurrection.

The story is that, when Mary Magdalene and the other Mary went to the tomb where Christ had been laid, they found the stone that was before the tomb rolled away, and looking in they saw the clothes* lying there, the turban lying by itself. But the body of Christ was not there. The stone is the same stone that is spoken of in the Hindu myth. Krishna is called Giridhar, he who holds the stone, who lifts it up. Under this stone, the stone of the external self, every individual soul in the world is suppressed. When it is lifted

---

*i.e. the wrappings and the head-cloth.

up, then man rises to immortality. From what does he rise? He rises from the body and above the mind. The clothes and the head-cloth lying separately, symbolizing the body and the mind, show this.

Great poets, great musicians, great writers often rise above the body. They do not know where they are sitting or standing, they are lost in their imaginations, unconscious of the physical existence, but they do not rise above the mind. When the consciousness rises above the mind, above the thoughts, then it is free, it is active in its own element, and then this consciousness can give of itself to the mind.

The rising to that consciousness in which there is no distinction is the highest degree of resurrection. There are other degrees, just as in the lift one cannot arrive at the seventh floor without passing by the second, third, fourth and all other floors.

There is that resurrection in which there is the exact counterpart of the physical body which walks, sits down, and can do all that the physical body can do. This is called by Sufis *alm-e-mithal*. There are mystics who have mastered this so completely that they can act independently of the physical body; death is nothing to them for they remain alive after death. This is done by *amal*. Someone who had been studying this wrote to me the other day, "I have lost all fear of death, because death has tied a turban on me". There is no death when this is mastered.

If a poet is writing his poetry and his wife, his servant, a hundred people pass before him, he does not see them, he does not know whether anyone has been there. If a little love of poetry can do this, how much more can the love, the absorption in the life within draw the consciousness within!

It is told in the Gospel that Christ after his resurrection was seen by the disciples several times. It is the experience of every person who has practised concentration, who has meditated, that he sees that which he has held in his consciousness not only inwardly but outwardly before him. This is the first experience that every mystic has. The disciples were lost, absorbed in the thought of Christ – how should they not see him?

Christ's words are, "Handle me, and see that it is myself, for a spirit hath not flesh and bones as ye see me having". And he said unto them, "Children, have ye anything to eat?" And they gave him a piece of a broiled fish, and he took it and did eat before them. The word spirit is used in many different meanings. It is used for ghost, or for the soul, but really it means the essence which is the opposite pole to substance.

All that the eye has seen resurrects in the eye. If someone mentions a certain person – though you had forgotten the person altogether – he rises up in your eye: in that house, in that place where you had seen him. It is not in this physical eye, but in that eye which is beyond. The materialist may say, "It is all in the brain". How could the brain contain so many thousands and millions of things and beings!

Of course without training a person does not see the spirit, but I will say that in the dream you see yourself, you experience yourself, in different surroundings, in the company of different people. If you say, "It is a dream", I will answer: When do you call it a dream? You call it a dream when you wake up. When you see the contrast with your surroundings in waking condition, then you say, "It was a dream. If not, it would have remained with me, but everything is different". But if, while you are dreaming, someone comes to you and says, "It is a dream", you will never believe it.

The resurrection is the rising to that real life, that true Friend on whom alone we can lean – upon all other things and beings upon which we think we can lean, we cannot rely – that Friend who alone is always unchanged, who has always been with us and will always be with us.

CHAPTER XXIV

Spiritual Circulation through the Veins of the Universe

WHEN ONE observes keenly the nature of this life of variety, one finds that behind the world of variety there is one life, the source and goal of all things. It is that life which may be called the blood of the universe circulating through the veins of the universe. It is substance or spirit or life: something out of which all that is seen and all intelligence is moulded, kept alive and in working order. It is this life which is so to speak the veins of the universe and we know it as what we term intelligence.

No doubt we often confuse intelligence with intellect, but intelligence is something which is to be found even in the lower creation. It can be traced in plant life and sensed even in the heart of the rock. The difference between modern psychology and ancient thought is that according to the former the intellect is a development which manifests in the life of man as mind, but that animals have no mind, that mind is a development of matter, the work of the brain. The idea of the mystics of all times, of the prophets and all meditative souls is different. They say, "What was, is, and will be; if that is the same substance or life it is not subject to change, nor does it develop". Yet a different grade which we are capable of grasping gives us the feeling that it is a development rising from matter. The great ones, the meditative souls who sat in the wilderness and the forests and communicated with the life around them, realized this truth, and very often they experienced a greater harmony, peace and upliftment where there was no visible life. Life is intelligence, even in the rock, and the more one communicates with life, the more one feels that even the rock is not without life, that through it pulses the blood of the universe.

Someone said to a Brahmin, "O Brahmin, how absurd it is for you to worship a God made of stone, an idol! The true God is the formless one, the one above all things of the world". The Brahmin replied, "Do you know the phenomenon of faith? If you have faith in the God of rock, you will get your answer, but if you have no faith in your formless God even He will not communicate with you". Life seen from this point of view tells us that there is no place, no object which is not sacred, that even in a rock one sees the source and goal of all things in that particular form.

Many who are experienced in plant life know how responsive plants are to the sympathy of a man who loves nature and looks after them. I was much interested in meeting a scientist in California who devoted his life to research into plant life.[12] How true it is that through whatever channel one pursues truth one arrives at an experience which shows truth. I was especially interested when he said, "I regard plants as really living beings. I work with them always feeling that they are living creatures, that they have their own trend of mind. They show obstinacy, they feel your sympathy, and if you learn to understand them you can manage to derive a great deal of benefit from them. All through my life I have talked to plants as I would talk to men". Here again is the blood of the universe in circulation – in a higher grade than in the rock.

Another scientist, Professor Chandra Bose of Bengal, has devoted much time and thought to prove that plants breathe. If breath is to be found in plant life, certainly there is intelligence too. I once happened to see a stone whose owner called it a magic stone. In reality it was quite ordinary, but it often changed its colour; especially when in the hand of a particular person it showed a different colour and shade. So a stone can respond to a person's mind, and this teaches that there is a great deal to explore in the mineral kingdom. This is not a discovery of to-day; it was known to the people of ancient times. We read in the Persian poems of Jelal-ud-Din Rumi that God slept in the mineral, dreamed in the vegetable, became conscious in the animal, and realized Himself in the human being.

But this one life is to be seen more pronounced in human beings, in the intellect they show, in the work they do, in the magnetizing of the atmosphere, in the thought power they exercise, in the influence of healing. Although one person is separated from another, although there may be no outer connection, yet even from a distance the influence of thoughts and feelings is felt. There were many instances of this during the war, when mothers and wives of soldiers in times of sorrow, illness and death felt their trouble without any outer source of communication. How often when people are in close touch do they feel each other's condition, not only by thought waves but in the realm of feeling also. This shows that there is one body, and in that body is one life which continually circulates, as does the blood in the veins.

This gives a logical explanation of the law of cause and effect. A wrongdoer may escape earthly witness, but he cannot escape this one life in which he lives and moves and has his being. A person who has done good to another may never see that other again, yet good must return to him because there is one body and one life. Just as with the circulation in the physical body all we eat is absorbed as essence in the blood, so our every thought, word and action affects the one life.

Often people wonder about certain superstitions and ridicule them, saying, "How can past, present and future be read from cards?" This, the science of astrology and crystal-gazing may be explained by the understanding that there is one life in which the circulation is always pulsing, one music, one rhythm. A person only needs to be acquainted with the theme of the music – then he can read and understand. Not only by cards and crystal-gazing can he read the past, present and future, but by all means. If a person is able to communicate with even one vein of this one life he is in touch with the veins of all the universe. Some means are better, some are worse, but through any medium he can understand, thus proving that there is one life behind all.

Man may be taught to do good, to learn righteousness, but this is virtue forced upon him as the result of a certain teaching. Real virtue only comes by understanding the oneness of life, binding man to friend or enemy. Jesus Christ teaches, "Love your enemies". While it is often difficult to love our friends, we are not able to love our enemies, unless we realize the secret of the one life behind all – inspite of the world of variety which continually creates illusion.

If by religion, philosophy, or mysticism this realization is attained, then the secret of life is touched and without any wonder-working a mighty power is gained. This lesson is easy to learn intellectually, but that is not enough. This truth can be taken – like food – in a moment, but to digest it the whole of life is not sufficient, for truth is mixed with facts, and when truth becomes a fact it has no importance. Absorbed in the world of variety we are apt to forget truth, for we are always absorbed in facts. Therefore meditative people who spend much time in meditation try to think of the oneness of being, try to meditate on the ultimate truth of being. It works like the winding of a clock: it only takes a minute to wind and all day long it goes on. So in meditation the same thought goes on, and in everything one does or says one uses this same truth.

What effect is caused by the lack of understanding of this truth? All disasters such as wars, floods, earthquakes, famines, all the things that cannot be helped by man, come from disorder in the body: the only body that exists. When the blood is disordered all goes wrong, and although sometimes it seems that what is disadvantageous to one part is advantageous to another, yet in the long run one sees that all suffer; the after-effect is felt by the whole world as strain and pain and all kinds of suffering. The soul of the whole creation is one, the life behind all these ever-moving phantoms is one. Meditation on this and awakening to this truth will harmonize the condition of the world.

The prophets and great mystics have come to the world from time to time as the physician comes to help the patient whose health is in disorder. And each time the great ones have come they have brought to the world another life, a new life brought to the whole organism of the universe to help it to run smoothly. The Sufis who in all times have existed as mystics, whose lives have been devoted to meditation and spiritual practices – what have they learned from these meditations? They have learned the essence of all, the oneness or unity, and in unity – in thinking it, realizing it and living it – one fulfils the purpose of life.

CHAPTER XXV

The Divine Blood circulating through the Veins of the Universe

OFTEN MAN has vague ideas as to the meaning of the word divine. The divine has become his ideal, but this ideal is first to be made a reality. An ideal can only serve its proper purpose when it is made into reality and if it is not made into reality its purpose is not accomplished. In the first place we must inquire what it is that reminds us of the divine. What brings us a feeling of the existence of the divine Being? It is what may be called beauty: the beauty, delicacy, and colour in the flower, the brilliancy and life of the precious stone; for what is beautiful in all this is intelligence – even manifest through material objects.

The secret of fragrance, the secret of the brilliancy of the diamond, the beauty of the pearl, the secret beneath all that appeals to man and attracts him is intelligence. Only, the intelligence in all things is so to speak imprisoned, covered. In living beings it begins to manifest itself. In man is the greatest possibility for the manifestation of this intelligence. Therefore, either in things or in beings, if anywhere a trace of the divine is to be found, it is in intelligence.

As many degrees may be found in beautiful flowers – one more beautiful than the other – and many different degrees between pebbles and a diamond, a million more degrees may be found between man and man. At this present time when man disregards that beauty and value which are hidden in the human personality, he disregards that divine substance which is hidden in man. To-day there is no place, no recognition for human culture, whereas every other object is classified, its value fixed. There are different studies and practices, different degrees in the universities and colleges, there are ranks and divisions in all other parts of life, but there is no distinct place for the understanding, for the intelligence of man in its true aspect. There is no loss for the person who possesses this wealth; only before the world there is nothing to distinguish him from others, and not for everyone is there a chance to find out what is behind the veil. If one could explain the real meaning of education, of true education, it would be from the beginning to the end of man's life the realization of the circulation of the divine blood through the veins of the universe – for there is no limitation of time for the study and practice of this: it is endless!

The secret behind magnetism which has its different aspects is one and the same. No doubt personal magnetism is of several distinct kinds. There is a physical magnetism which comes with youth, with energy, with the healthiness of the body. The more healthy a person is, especially at the time of youth, the more he begins to show a certain energy in every action and in his every movement; by this he expresses magnetism.

Then there is a greater magnetism: the magnetism of mind. A person with a living mind is like a light, and as light attracts and its warmth comforts, so comfort comes out of this person as radiance. Besides this there is a magnetism of culture. When a person is well trained and has a certain culture, his action, word and thought all become rhythmic.

A fourth kind of magnetism is that of the soul, the soul that is living, which means that it is not closed or covered by a grave, but manifests outwardly as well as inwardly. It is that soul which has another, a still greater magnetism, the greatest of all other aspects of magnetism. Now the question rises: how can one attain to this highest magnetism which alone is endurable? It is by watching the divine essence, by noticing the divine essence in all things. When comparing two persons of different temperaments you will always find that one of them is appreciative of music, poetry and art, respondent, ready to admire all that is good and beautiful, while the other closes himself; he is not open to appreciate anything, nor ready to respond or willing to admire. When the door is closed to the divine manifestation which is in all things, then the continual source of attracting that new life and magnetism is closed and the soul dies of poverty.

As to the physical body, since it is limited, its sustenance is also limited. But as the soul is not limited, so its sustenance is not limited. The soul is not satisfied with one moment's meditation only, nor is the soul satisfied by one good action in the week, nor by attending one prayer in perhaps a week's time. The soul's hunger is greater than the hunger of body or mind. Its hunger is satisfied by beauty, beauty in all aspects, beauty of colour, beauty of thought and imagination. Therefore the soul of the artist, the poet, the musician, of a thinker naturally is always living. But at the same time the one who is fond of beauty and derives that nourishment from beauty also has only a limited food, for perfect satisfaction only comes when one knows all beauty to be one beauty, and that one beauty to be the divine beauty.

Very often man questions the idea of divine communication, but it is not impossible, it is the most desirable thing there is. But the person who thinks that divine communication can be made by going to heaven and leaving this earth may well wait for some time. We have no lack of examples in the world, if only we can see. For instance, to a true musician, a real musician music is not only an art, a symphony, it is something which speaks to him, with which he communicates. When a musician arrives at this stage he may strike one chord and the continual striking of this one chord will bring him to ecstasy. For another person it is only striking a chord, but for him it is speaking with the piano, conversing with it.

Besides all the great men I have seen in my country I have met the great pianist of the Western world Paderewski and I valued my privilege of hearing him at his house when there were not many people, while he was himself. When he began to play it seemed as if there was a question of his soul and an answer of the piano. The whole time it was a question of his soul and an answer of music and in the end it seemed as if the soul of the player and the music became one and perfect.

Now this is one example, but there are many others. In order to attain this perfection one need not be a musician. The whole life before us can speak to us from morning to evening if we are able to speak to it, if we establish a communication with life. When man is not open he is not even open to himself, he cannot communicate with life; then he is lonely. The man who is in communication with himself may be in the forest, in the wilderness, yet he is in the world, the whole universe is around him. How many souls are among our friends who living in the world of crowds are yet lonely, while it is so natural and possible that a man outside that world keeps in connection with the whole Being.

A scientist has discovered that by touching an electric current, or by attaching oneself to it, one can obtain more energy in a certain part of the body where there is less energy. If this material aspect of electricity can give a new life, a new vigour to the body then, if one could come in contact with that continual battery of life, could one not obtain from it all one desires? An energy which is everywhere and with which one can get in touch everywhere, if only one knew how to communicate with it; an energy which is not without intelligence, but the perfection of intelligence. Mind and soul can become more and more intelligent by coming into contact with it.

Now one might ask, "How can we attain to it?" As it is necessary in order to sing well to cultivate the voice and as it is necessary in order to get muscular strength to make physical exercises, so it is most necessary in order to get in touch with the divine life which is all around and about us, which is within and without us, to practise getting in touch with it and to keep in touch with it. We see this in all different occupations of life, whether they concern scientific inventions, industry or business: one must be absorbed in it in order to do something worthwhile! The same law applicable to material work can be applied to spiritual work. Concentration is the main thing and, when concentration is not attained, whatever a person will do will not bring about worthwhile results. In all different occupations the cause of failures in ninety-nine among a hundred cases is lack of concentration. When a student fails in his examination, when a businessman fails in making a real success, when an industrialist fails to bring about success, in all these cases it is lack of concentration which causes the failure.

Spiritual or religious attitude apart, even from a material and selfish point of view one cannot deny the great value of concentration in life. When we come to realize that there is one energy, an energy which is not only energy but intelligence itself, which is divine and all over, then we have come face to face with the object we are searching. Then all that remains is to know that intellectual knowledge does not satisfy our purpose. What remains is to try to find out how we can communicate, how we can come into touch with this all-pervading energy. The answer is that one has to mould oneself, one has to prepare oneself in order to become a fitting instrument, in order to fit in with this all-pervading energy. If one asks how we have to prepare ourselves, the answer is that every soul has been made to respond in this symphony of the whole universe as a certain note. When a person will not give that note he will not fulfil his life's purpose, and thereby he will always feel dissatisfied with himself and others.

How will he be able to attain that note or to tune himself to it? By ear training in symbolical expression; plainly speaking, by studying the law, the nature and the secret of harmony in life. And how will he fit in with the rhythm? All distress, all misunderstanding, all the tragedy one experiences is also the lack of keeping a certain rhythm which life asks of man. Does this not teach us that there are two important things to remember: developing the sense of harmony in our everyday life and developing the sense of rhythm in everything we do? If one has developed the sense of harmony and yet does not know the secret of rhythm, he still will have difficulties. If one knows the rhythm of the universe and how to fit in with it and yet has no sense of the nature and secret of harmony, he also will meet with failures. It teaches us that the whole of life is as music and in order to study life we must study it as music. It is not only study, it is also practice which makes man perfect.

If someone tells me that a certain person is miserable or wretched or distressed, my answer will be that he is out of tune. Distress, disappointment or failure is caused by falling short of answering one's own duty in playing one's part in the symphony. Often people ask, "Here is a good man – why must he suffer? Here is a very nice person, a religious person – why has he distress?" There are others who will answer with a thousand different reasons. They will say that in a former life the person perhaps has done something wrong and therefore has to pay his debts, or some people will say that goodness must always suffer. But coming to the practical side of the question the answer is simple: man-made goodness is not nature's goodness. Nature demands, life demands a certain standard of understanding, of thinking, of living, and this can be learned by learning the tune and the rhythm – not only learning it, but putting oneself to that tune and setting oneself to that particular rhythm which make the music of life. It is in this manner that happiness is attained – that happiness which is the seeking of every soul – and it is in this manner that one will progress continually until one touches the divine Spirit, the Spirit that pervades all and is everywhere.

1. The Nizam of Hyderabad, Mir Maheboob Ali Khan (1866–1926) was an esteemed poet and patron of poets. The Biography of Pir-o-Murshid Inayat Khan and other literature include accounts of the Murshid's meetings with Indian monarchs and representatives of the Moghul tradition of culture and civilisation. Eventually Hazrat Inayat Khan gave up his contacts with the court in order to concentrate fully on mystical life and the tuition of his own initiator.

2. Three sorts of mystics: Yogis, Buddhists and Sufis: i.e. respectively ascetics, monastics, and mystics living life in the world rather than renouncing it.

3. These words are part of Hazrat Inayat Khan's sermon of the Burial Ceremony.

4. Kismet is the usual Turkish transcription of the Arabic *qismet* – portion, share, destiny.

5. GAYAN, Alapa 1:
> When a glimpse of Our image is caught in man,
> when heaven and earth are sought in man,
> then what is there in the world that is not in man?
> If one only explores him there is a lot in man.

This is a most interesting version in English of the classical, originally Arabic verse-form *muwashsha* which has three lines in high literary rhetoric style and the final punch-line either in very popular speech, or even in another language. Thus several Arabic *muwashshahat* with a Spanish punch-line have been preserved of both Andalusian-Moorish and Sephardic provenance.

6. Lacunae in this lecture's shorthand MS have prevented a complete and entirely consistent rendition of the original wording.

For the sake of completeness: the original shorthand – in addition to the advice against subjective enthusiasm for wakening those who are still meant to sleep – contains the following paragraph:

'In this instance he is most busy in this work. If not he would have said, "Well, I experience it, I enjoy it, is that not enough? Why must I trouble with others who stand before me like stone walls?" Such people have toiled and toiled their whole life and they have been exiled, flayed, martyred and crucified, and when they have awakened to a certain sphere where they enjoy and experience harmony and peace, they wish that others also experience it, may enjoy it in the same way. It is not much different from one who drinks and wants the other to be as happy as he is in drinking. It is exactly the same.'

7. Two lacunae in the shorthand report of this paragraph have been completed by the editors. These concern the words: "and receive from these souls certain impressions to which it is attracted" and in the last sentence the word "impressions".

An explanation of the phenomenon of exchange is to be found in Hazrat Inayat Khan's "The Soul Whence and Whither" – Ed. Nekbakht Foundation, Suresnes, 1984 – Chapter 40:

'The soul on its return from the goal, while in the sphere of the djinns, has some riches which it collected during its life on earth in the form of merits, qualities, experiences, convictions, talents, attitude and a certain outlook on life, although on its passing it has returned the belongings of the earth to the earth. These riches the soul in the spirit world offers, allows them to be taken from it, and imparts them to the souls coming from their source who are on their way to the earth. The souls on their way to the earth, full of heavenly bliss but poor in earthly riches, purchase the current coin of the earth in the djinn plane. Guarantees, contracts, mortgages and all the accounts that the spirit had left unfinishied on the earth – these they undertake to pay or to receive when coming on the earth.'

8. Cupid – In "The Soul Whence and Whither" we read, 'What is Cupid? It is the soul which is being born. Before it appears on the physical plane it is pictured by the wise as Cupid, an angel'. Desiring to manifest on the earth, Cupid brings man and woman together. And Hazrat Inayat Khan continues, 'Duality in every aspect of life is creative and its issue is the purpose, the outcome of the dual aspect of nature'.

9. This Question-and-Answer is added here in order to introduce the next one. It is extracted from a lecture on "Conscience" published in Volume XIII of this series: Gatha *Metaphysics*, III, No. 6. The question as well as the answer are Hazrat Inayat Khan's own words.

10. The reasons for maintaining this personal recollection which already appeared in Chapter VIII of the present volume, "Spirituality, the Tuning of the Heart", have been explained in the preface to Sufi Teachings, Volume VIII revised, page X.

11. Hazrat Inayat Khan quoted these Bible texts from memory. They read:

— (1 Corinthians 15: 20) 'But now is Christ risen from the dead, and become the first-fruits of them that slept'.

Here Hazrat Inayat Khan adds two thoughts which are not part of this Bible text but very closely related to it:

"And gone unto the Father"
"And whosoever believeth in Him"

(See the explanation in the lecture)

— (Luke 20: 35) 'But they which shall be accounted worthy to obtain that world, and the resurrection from the dead, neither marry, nor are given in marriage, neither can they die anymore: for they are equal to the angels and are the children of God, being the children of the resurrection'.

12. Hazrat Inayat Khan refers to Luther Burbank, an American plant cultivator (1849–1926) whom he had met in Santa Rosa in 1923. He wrote in his autobiography, "I was most delighted to see that not only fine arts and spiritual culture, but even the work with the earth can elevate a man to that serenity and simplicity and love which this scientist's soul expressed. This was a proof added to many other proofs I had in my life of seeing glimpses of divine perfection in the souls who in some form or other have touched perfection in their life's vocation whatever it may be.

This notion to me was as a bridge between science and mysticism; at the same time it was a promise that science in its full rise will some day be completed by mysticism. He told me he was busy at the time trying to take away thorns from the cactus, and asked me what I was doing. I humbly answered – My work is not very different from yours, Sir, for I am occupied taking away thorns from hearts of men – Thus we came to realize how a real work, through matter or spirit, in the long run brings about the same result which is the purpose of life."
(Biography of Pir-o-Murshid Inayat Khan, East-West Publications, London, 1979).

LIST OF LECTURES AND ARTICLES
THAT ARE THE SOURCES OF VOLUME XIV

(Hazrat Inayat Khan lived in London during and immediately after World War I. Several of his addresses and lectures given between 1916 and 1921 were noted down without indication of place and date. These are referred to below as "manuscripts from the early London period.")

PART I: *The Smiling Forehead*

THE SMILING FOREHEAD – London, 18th June, 1922

THE HEART QUALITY 1 – Suresnes, France, 6th September, 1925

THE HEART QUALITY 2 – Suresnes, 22nd August, 1926

THE HEART, APHORISMS – those aphorisms which were not published in Volume XI of this series are taken from Hazrat Inayat Khan's personal notebooks and from a collection of one of his disciples; the last item is a "phrase to be repeated".*

THE PATH OF DEVOTION – a manuscript from the early London period

LOVE – IDEAS, STORIES, ANSWERS AND APHORISMS – taken from Hazrat Inayat Khan's personal notebooks, from reports by his disciples, from questions and answers exchanged in Suresnes, Summer 1923; the last two items are "phrases to be repeated".

THE DIFFERENCE BETWEEN WILL, WISH AND DESIRE – Suresnes, 27th June, 1926

DESTINY AND FREE WILL – New York, 19th January, 1926

FREE WILL AND DESTINY – Suresnes, 12 July, 1925

KISMET – England, 1st July, 1917

FREE WILL, APHORISMS – same documents as mentioned for "The Heart"

*Phrases to be repeated – See "The Value of Repetition and Reflection" in Volume II (2nd revised edition) of this series.

PART II: *The Deeper Side of Life*

Man, The Seed of God 2 – Brussels, 16th December, 1923

Sufi Philosophy 1 – Los Angeles, 22nd March, 1926

Sufi Philosophy 2 – San Francisco, 5th April, 1926

The Gift of Eloquence – London, probable date December 1916

Evolution of the World – a manuscript from the early London period

Every Man Has His Own Little World – manuscripts from the early London period

Marriage – Suresnes, 20th September, 1926

Spirituality, the Tuning of the Heart 1 – Oakland (Calif), 20th February, 1926

Spirituality, the Tuning of the Heart 2 – San Francisco, 9th April, 1926

Optimism and Pessimism – Suresnes, 6th August, 1922

Conscience – Questons and Answers – The first two items and the last one, Los Angeles, 25th March, 1926; the other items, Suresnes, 20th July, 1923

Justice and Forgiveness – Questions and Answers – Suresnes, Summer 1923

Pairs of Opposites used in Religious Terms – Paris, 14th November, 1925

    What do you mean by God has no opposite? – Suresnes, 17th July, 1923
    God is not kind only to a few – from early London period
    How could God allow bloodshed? – from early London period
    As evil cannot come out of good – Suresnes, September 1924
    Why do people who do evil succeed – Paris, 29th November, 1923

Insight – Suresnes, Summer 1922

The Law of Attraction – England, February 1917

The Liberal and Conservative Point of View – Suresnes, 30th July, 1922

The Attitude – Suresnes, December 1922

INDEX

INDEX OF TERMS IN ORIENTAL LANGUAGES